Religion in American Life

GOLDENTREE BIBLIOGRAPHIES IN AMERICAN HISTORY

under the series editorship of ARTHUR S. LINK

THE AMERICAN COLONIES IN THE SEVENTEENTH CENTURY •
Alden T. Vaughan
THE AMERICAN COLONIES IN THE EIGHTEENTH CENTURY, 1689-1763 •
Jack P. Greene
THE AMERICAN REVOLUTION • John Shy
THE CONFEDERATION AND THE CONSTITUTION, 1781-1801 •
E. James Ferguson
AMERICAN NATIONALISM AND SECTIONALISM, 1801-1841 •
Edwin A. Miles
MANIFEST DESTINY AND THE COMING OF THE CIVIL WAR, 1841-1860 •
Don E. Fehrenbacher
THE NATION IN CRISIS, 1861-1877 • David Donald
THE GILDED AGE, 1877-1896 • Vincent P. De Santis
THE PROGRESSIVE ERA AND THE GREAT WAR, 1896-1920 • Arthur S. Link
& William M. Leary, Jr.
THE TWENTIES AND THE NEW DEAL, 1920-1940 • Robert E. Burke
THE SECOND WORLD WAR AND THE ATOMIC AGE, 1940-1970 •
E. David Cronon

THE OLD SOUTH • Fletcher M. Green
THE NEW SOUTH • Paul M. Gaston
AFRO-AMERICAN HISTORY • John Hope Franklin
THE FRONTIER AND THE AMERICAN WEST • Rodman W. Paul
AMERICAN SOCIAL HISTORY BEFORE 1860 • Gerald N. Grob
AMERICAN SOCIAL HISTORY SINCE 1860 • Robert H. Bremner
AMERICAN DIPLOMATIC HISTORY BEFORE 1890 • Norman A. Graebner
AMERICAN DIPLOMATIC HISTORY SINCE 1890 • Gaddis Smith
& W. B. Fowler
AMERICAN ECONOMIC HISTORY BEFORE 1860 • George Rogers Taylor
AMERICAN ECONOMIC HISTORY SINCE 1860 • Edward C. Kirkland
AMERICAN URBAN DEVELOPMENT • Seymour J. Mandelbaum
AMERICAN CONSTITUTIONAL DEVELOPMENT • Alpheus T. Mason
RELIGION IN AMERICAN LIFE • Nelson R. Burr
THE HISTORY OF AMERICAN EDUCATION • Jurgen Herbst

Religion in American Life

compiled by

Nelson R. Burr

APPLETON–CENTURY–CROFTS

Educational Division

New York MEREDITH CORPORATION

016.2009
B27r
82767
Mar. 1973

7120-1

Library of Congress Card Number: 70–136219

PRINTED IN THE UNITED STATES OF AMERICA

cloth: 390-15608-6
paper: 390-15607-8

Editor's Foreword

GOLDENTREE BIBLIOGRAPHIES IN AMERICAN HISTORY are designed to provide students, teachers, and librarians with ready and reliable guides to the literature of American History in all its remarkable scope and variety. Volumes in the series cover comprehensively the major periods in American history, while additional volumes are devoted to all important subjects.

Goldentree Bibliographies attempt to steer a middle course between the brief list of references provided in the average textbook and the long bibliography in which significant items are often lost in the sheer number of titles listed. Each bibliography is, therefore, selective, with the sole criterion for choice being the significance—and not the age—of any particular work. The result is bibliographies of all works, including journal articles and doctoral dissertations, that are still useful, without bias in favor of any particular historiographical school.

Each compiler is a scholar long associated, both in research and teaching, with the period or subject of his volume. All compilers have not only striven to accomplish the objective of this series but have also cheerfully adhered to a general style and format. However, each compiler has been free to define his field, make his own selections, and work out internal organization as the unique demands of his period or subject have seemed to dictate.

The single great objective of *Goldentree Bibliographies in American History* will have been achieved if these volumes help researchers and students to find their way to the significant literature of American history.

Arthur S. Link

Preface

THE FOLLOWING BIBLIOGRAPHY is intended for the use of graduate and advanced undergraduate students in courses on religion in the United States: its history, and its relation to other phases of American civilization and life. It should serve as a convenient guide to scholarship in the field. Because the amount of writing on religion in American life is so vast, this list necessarily is very selective. It is intended, however, to provide ample coverage of important works and topics, with emphasis on research in the twentieth century, and upon the sociological aspects of religion.

Publication in the field is not largely confined, as it formerly was, to books and a limited number of periodicals devoted to theology and ecclesiastical history. Many significant writings appear in sociological, literary, and even scientific and economic journals. Others are academic dissertations, not printed or obtainable only in typewritten copies or on microfilm. For some topics, dissertations and articles provide much of the coverage.

This bibliography attempts to occupy a middle ground between the brief lists of references included in textbooks, and the long narrative and professional (and heavily annotated) bibliographies that require indexes of both authors and subjects. It aims to assist the student in surveying a topic, writing reports, term papers and book reviews, preparing for examinations, or doing independent reading. Attention is directed to certain features intended to increase its utility:

(1) Extra margin on each page permits listing of library call numbers of often-used items.

(2) Extra space at the bottom of every page permits inclusion of additional entries.

(3) An index by author follows the bibliography proper.

(4) The index and cross-reference numbers direct the reader to the page and position on the page of the desired entry. Thus,

in an entry such as STEWART, Randall, *American Literature and Christian Doctrine*, See 63.14, the number 63.14 indicates that the entry referred to is on page 63, and is the fourteenth item on that page. Both page and individual entry numbers are conspicuous in size and position so that the process of finding entries is fast and simple.

(5) In the case of unpublished doctoral dissertations on microfilm, the number of the microfilm and the location in *Dissertation Abstracts* are given.

A list of "Abbreviations of Periodicals and Serials Cited" in this bibliography follows this preface.

A dagger following an entry indicates the work is listed in *Paperbound Books in Print.* Cross references are given to other entries in which the work cited is included, or for related topics.

N. R. B.

NOTE: The publisher and compiler invite suggestions for additions to future editions of this bibliography.

Abbreviations of Periodicals
and Serials Cited

Admin Sci Q	*Administrative Science Quarterly*
Am Anthro	*American Anthropologist*
Am Archiv	*American Archivist*
Am Book Coll	*American Book Collector*
Am Cath Socio Rev	*American Catholic Sociological Review*
Am Ch Mo	*American Church Monthly*
Am Eccles Rev	*American Ecclesiastical Review*
Am Her	*American Heritage*
Am Hist Rev	*American Historical Review*
Am Jew Archiv	*American Jewish Archives*
Am Jew Hist Q	*American Jewish Historical Quarterly*
Am J Rel Psycho Educ	*American Journal of Religious Psychology and Education*
Am J Socio	*American Journal of Sociology*
Am J Theol	*American Journal of Theology*
Am Lit	*American Literature*
Am Mer	*American Mercury*
Am Pol Sci Rev	*American Political Science Review*
Am Q	*American Quarterly*
Am Sch	*American Scholar*
Am Socio Rev	*American Sociological Review*
Am Theol Rev	*American Theological Review*
Ann Am Acad Pol Soc Sci	*Annals, American Academy of Political and Social Science*
Ann Assoc Amer Geog	*Annals, Association of American Geographers*
Ann Rep Am Hist Assn	*Annual Report, American Historical Association*
Ariz Q	*Arizona Quarterly*
At Mo	*Atlantic Monthly*
Anthro Rec	*Anthropological Records*
Berk Pub Soc Inst	*Berkeley Publications on Social Institutions*

Bull Bibl	Bulletin of Bibliography
Bull Bost Gen Theol Lib	Bulletin, Boston General Theologica Library
Bull Har Univ Div Sch	Bulletin, Harvard University Divinity School
Bull John Ry Lib	Bulletin, John Rylands Library, Manchester, England
Bull Res Group Europ Mig Prob	Bulletin, Research Group in European Migration Problems
Bull Soc Sci Res Coun	Bulletin, Social Science Research Council
Bull Stet Univ	Bulletin, Stetson University
Cal Rev	Calcutta Review
Calif Univ Chron	California University Chronicle
Cath Hist Rev	Catholic Historical Review
Cath Wor	Catholic World
Chi Jew For	Chicago Jewish Forum
Ch Cent	Christian Century
Chr and Crisis	Christianity and Crisis
Ch Hist Soc Pub	Church Historical Society Publications
Church Hist	Church History
Church State	Church and State
Coll Ill State Hist Soc	Collections, Illinois State Historical Society
Comp Stud Soc Hist	Comparative Studies in Social History
Cor Law Q	Cornell Law Quarterly
Cur Hist	Current History
Diss Abs	Dissertation Abstracts
Ecum Rev	Ecumenical Review
Em Univ Q	Emory University Quarterly
Ger Q	German Quarterly
Har Mag	Harper's Magazine
Har Theol Rev	Harvard Theological Review
Hist Educ Q	History of Education Quarterly
Hist Mag P E Ch	Historical Magazine of the Protestant Episcopal Church
Hunt Lib Q	Huntington Library Quarterly
Ill Law Rev	Illinois Law Review
Int Rev Miss	International Review of Missions
Isl Rev	Islamic Review
Jew Hist Q	Jewish Historical Quarterly
Jew J Socio	Jewish Journal of Sociology

Jew Soc Serv Q	*Jewish Social Service Quarterly*
J H Univ Stud Hist Pol Sci	*John Hopkins University Studies in History and Political Science*
J Abnorm Soc Psycho	*Journal of Abnormal Social Psychology*
J Am Acad Rel	*Journal of the American Academy of Religion*
J Am Folk	*Journal of American Folklore*
J Am Hist	*Journal of American History*
J Am Stat Assn	*Journal of the American Statistical Association*
J Bib Rel	*Journal of the Bible and Religion*
J Educ Socio	*Journal of Educational Sociology*
J Hist Ideas	*Journal of the History of Ideas*
J Hum Rel	*Journal of Human Relations*
J Intergr Rel	*Journal of Intergroup Relations*
J Neg Hist	*Journal of Negro History*
J Presby Hist Soc	*Journal of the Presbyterian Historical Society*
J Psycho	*Journal of Psychology*
J Rel	*Journal of Religion*
J Rel Hist	*Journal of Religious History*
J Rel Psycho	*Journal of Religious Psychology*
J Sci Stud Rel	*Journal for the Scientific Study of Religion*
J Soc Issues	*Journal of Social Issues*
J Soc Psycho	*Journal of Social Psychology*
J Socio	*Journal of Sociology*
J S Hist	*Journal of Southern History*
Jour Q	*Journalism Quarterly*
Law G Rev	*Lawyers Guild Review*
Liv Age	*Living Age*
Luth Q	*Lutheran Quarterly*
Menn Q Rev	*Mennonite Quarterly Review*
Meth Q Rev	*Methodist Quarterly Review*
Minn Law Rev	*Minnesota Law Review*
Miss Val Hist Rev	*Mississippi Valley Historical Review*
Mon fur Deut Unter	*Monatshefte fur Deutschen Unterricht*
Mus Lib Assn Notes	*Music Library Association, Notes*
Mus Wor	*Muslim World*
Music Q	*Musical Quarterly*
Negro Hist	*Negro History*
N Eng Hist Genea Reg	*New England Historical and Genealogical Register*
N Eng Q	*New England Quarterly*
N Y Gen and Biog Rec	*New York Genealogical and Biographical Record*

N Y Times Mag	*New York Times Magazine*
N Am Rev	*North American Review*
Overland Mo	*Overland Monthly*
Pac Hist Rev	*Pacific Historical Review*
Pac Spec	*Pacific Spectator*
Pap Am Soc Ch Hist	*Papers, American Society of Church History*
Pap Hymn Soc Am	*Papers, Hymn Society of America*
Pap Mich Acad Sci, Arts, and Letters	*Papers, Michigan Academy of Science, Arts, and Letters*
Parl Aff	*Parliamentary Affairs*
Penn Mag Hist Biog	*Pennsylvania Magazine of History and Biography*
Philo and Phenom Res	*Philosophy and Phenomenological Research*
Philo Rev	*Philosophical Review*
Pol Sci Q	*Political Science Quarterly*
Pol Sci Rev	*Political Science Review*
Proc Am Ant Soc	*Proceedings, American Antiquarian Society*
Proc Penna Ger Soc	*Proceedings, Pennsylvania German Society*
P E Rev	*Protestant Episcopal Review*
Psycho Rev	*Psychoanalytic Review*
Pub Col Soc Mass	*Publications, Colonial Society of Massachusetts*
Pub Opin Q	*Public Opinion Quarterly*
Pub Tex Folk Soc	*Publications, Texas Folklore Society*
Pub W	*Publisher's Weekly*
Queen's Q	*Queen's Quarterly*
R M Rev	*Rocky Mountain Review*
Rec Am Cath Hist Soc	*Records, American Catholic Historical Society*
Rel Life	*Religion in Life*
Rev Pol	*Review of Politics*
Rev Rel Res	*Review of Religious Research*
St Vlad Sem Q	*Saint Vladimir's Seminary Quarterly*
Sat Rev Lit	*Saturday Review of Literature*
Sci Mon	*Scientific Monthly*
Sew Rev	*Sewanee Review*
Soc Act	*Social Action*
Soc Com	*Social Compass*
Soc Forces	*Social Forces*
Soc Res	*Social Research*

Socio Anal	*Sociological Analysis*
S W J Anthro	*Southwestern Journal of Anthropology*
S W J Theol	*Southwestern Journal of Theology*
Stud Hist Econ Pub Law	*Columbia University Studies in History, Economics and Public Law*
Theol To	*Theology Today*
Tran N Y Acad Sci	*Transactions, New York Academy of Science*
Trinity Coll Hist Soc Pap	*Trinity College Historical Society Papers*
Un Sem Q Rev	*Union Seminary Quarterly Review*
Univ Calif Chron	*University of California Chronicle*
Univ Calif Pub Am Arch Ethnol	*University of California Publications in American Archaeology and Ethnology*
Univ Col Stud	*University of Colorado Studies*
Univ Mic	*University Microfilms*
Univ Neb Stud Lang Lit Crit	*University of Nebraska Studies in Language, Literature, and Criticism*
Univ Obs	*University Observer*
Univ To Q	*University of Toronto Quarterly*
Va Law Rev	*Virginia Law Review*
Va Q Rev	*Virginia Quarterly Review*
W Pol Q	*Western Political Quarterly*
W Res Law Rev	*Western Reserve Law Review*
Wm Mary Q	*William and Mary Quarterly*
Yale Rev	*Yale Review*
Yivo Ann Jew Soc Sci	*Yivo Annual of Jewish Social Science*

Contents

I

I. Bibliographical Guides and Selected Reference Works

1. Bibliography

A. General Bibliographies

1 BARROW, John Graves. *A Bibliography of Bibliographies in Religion.* Austin, 1955. (Bibliographies, guides, indexes, directories, yearbooks, handbooks.)

2 BEERS, Henry Putney. *Bibliographies in American History, Guide to Materials for Research.* Paterson, N. J., 1959. (Chap. X, "Religious History," comprises general and denominational history, miscellaneous topics.)

3 BERKOWITZ, Morris I., and J. Edmund JOHNSON, eds. *Social Scientific Studies of Religion: A Bibliography.* Pittsburgh, 1967. (Classified. Books and articles from about 80 journals.)

4 BURR, Nelson R., ed. *A Critical Bibliography of Religion in America.* 2 vols. Princeton, 1961. Vol. 4, pts 1 and 2, of *Religion in American Life,* ed. by James Ward Smith and A. Leland Jamison.

5 CASE, Shirley Jackson, et al. *A Bibliographical Guide to the History of Christianity.* Rev. ed. New York, 1951. (Selective list with author index; large section on the U.S.)

6 DIEHL, Katharine Smith. *Religions, Mythologies, Folklores: An Annotated Bibliography.* 2nd ed. New York, 1962. (American titles numerous in general references and national histories.)

7 GAUSTAD, Edwin Scott. *American Religious History.* Am Hist Assn, Service Center for Teachers of History. Publication no. 65. Washington, 1966. (Basic bibliog.)

8 HASTINGS, James, and John A. SELBIE, et al., eds. *Encyclopaedia of Religion and Ethics.* 13 vols., incl. index, 1 vol. New York, 1908–1929. Repr. 1955, 13 vols. (Indispensable, containing many bibliogs. with authoritative articles.)

9 JACKSON, Samuel Macauley. "A Bibliography of American Church History, 1820–1893." Vol. XII (1894). *The American Church History Series.* New York, 1893–1897, pp. 441–513.

10 LATOURETTE, Kenneth Scott. *A History of the Expansion of Christianity.* 7 vols. New York, 1937–1945. (Bibliogs. in later vols., particularly 3, 4, and 7; many titles on the U.S.)

11 SCHAFF, Philip, ed. *New Schaff-Herzog Encyclopedia of Religious Knowledge.* 13 vols. Grand Rapids, 1949–1950. (Many articles and bibliogs. on America.)

1 U.S. Library of Congress, General Reference and Bibliography Division. *A Guide to the Study of the United States of America.* Ed. by Donald H. Mugridge and Blanche McCrum. Washington, 1960. (Valuable, annotated section on religion, pp. 752–784.)

B. *Doctoral Dissertation Guides*

2 American Theological Library Association. *A Bibliography of Postgraduate Masters' Theses in Religion Accepted by American Theological Seminaries.* Ed. by Niels H. Sonne. Chicago, 1951. (Nearly 2,700 works.)

3 Catholic University of America. *Dissertations in American Church History, 1889–1932.* Washington, 1933. (Alphabetically by authors, full notes, manuscript dissertations by subjects.)

4 Council on Graduate Studies in Religion. *Doctoral Dissertations in the Field of Religion, 1940–1952.* New York, 1954. (More than 400 titles, theses submitted in the U.S., with summaries.)

5 *Dissertation Abstracts; Abstracts of Dissertations and Monographs in Microfilm.* Ann Arbor, University Microfilms, 1938– . Title varies: vols. 1–11 (1938–1951) *Microfilm Abstracts.* (Indispensable. "Religion" incl. history. theology, biography.)

6 KUEHL, Warren F., ed. *Dissertations in History: An Index to Dissertations Completed in History Departments of United States and Canadian Universities, 1873–1960.* Lexington, Ky., 1965. (About 300 on the U.S.)

7 LITTLE, Lawrence Calvin. *Toward Understanding the Church and Clergy: Contributions of Selected Doctoral Dissertations.* Pittsburgh, 1963. (Summarizes 60 dissertations; church and clergy in society.)

C. *Periodical Indexes*

8 American Theological Library Association. *Index to Religious Periodical Literature.* Ed. by Fay Dickerson. Annual, 1949– . (Very comprehensive, with list of periodicals, index of book reviews.)

9 *Associated Church Press Directory,* 1956–1957. New York, 1957. (131 periodicals, with denominational affiliations.)

10 *Catholic Periodical Index; a Cumulative Author and Subject Index to a Selected List of Catholic Periodicals.* 1930– .

11 *Christian Periodical Index. A Subject Index to Selected Periodical Literature.* 1956– . (Annual.)

12 JUDAH, J. Stillson, and L. J. ZIEGLER. *Index to Religious Periodical Literature: An Author and Subject Index to Periodical Literature, 1949–1952.* Chicago, 1953. (See other issues.)

13 *Methodist Periodical Index.* Nashville, 1960– .

14 *Religious Press Directory.* New York, Joseph E. Wagner Inc., 1943– . (By denominations and titles, full information.)

1 RICHARDSON, Ernest Cushing, comp. and ed. *An Alphabetical Subject Index and Index Encyclopedia to Periodical Articles on Religion, 1890–1899.* New York, 1907–1911. (Indispensable; 58,000 articles.)

2 ZAJACZKOWSKI, W. et al., eds. *The Catholic Periodical Index . . . January, 1963–December, 1964.* Haverford, Pa., 1965. (Continuing.)

D. Source Documents

3 ALLISON, William Henry. *Inventory of Unpublished Material for American Religious History in Protestant Church Archives and Other Repositories.* Washington, 1910. (About 10,000 entries by states with general index.)

4 BINSFIELD, Edmund L. "Church Archives in the United States and Canada; a Bibliography." *Am Archiv,* XXI (1958), 311–332. (219 entries: general works, guides to archives of denominations.)

5 BURR, Nelson R. "Sources for the Study of American Church History in the Library of Congress." *Church Hist,* XXII (1953), 227–238. (Manuscripts, transcripts, sermons, pamphlets, early American imprints, architectural archives, music, periodicals, illustrative materials.)

6 KIRKHAM, E. Kay. *A Survey of American Church Records for the Period Before the Civil War East of the Mississippi River.* 2 vols. Salt Lake City, 1959–1960. (By denominations and states; general inventories, local records, denominational bibliogs.)

7 MODE, Peter George. *Source Book and Bibliographical Guide for American Church History.* Menasha, Wis., 1921. (Most significant documents, mostly from printed sources; extensive bibliogs. of books and articles.)

8 U.S. Library of Congress. Library of Congress Catalogs. *National Union Catalog of Manuscript Collections.* 8 vols. Washington, 1962–1969. (Comp. by Library of Congress from reports. Indexes. (Many collections for general religious and church history.)

9 SMITH, Hilrie Shelton, Robert T. HANDY, and Lefferts A. LOETSCHER. *American Christianity: An Historical Interpretation with Representative Documents.* 2 vols. New York, 1960–1963. (Comprehensive source book and survey of general history. Indispensable.)

10 SWEET, William Warren. "Church Archives in the United States." *Church Hist.,* VIII (1939), 43–53. (Reviews resources of larger and some smaller denominations, state historical societies.)

11 U.S. National Historical Publications Commission. *A Guide to Archives and Manuscripts in the United States.* Ed. by Philip M. Hamer. New Haven, 1961. (Incl. religious and church records.)

2. Biography

12 BURR, Nelson R. *A Critical Bibliography of Religion in America.* Princeton, 1961. (Pt 1, pp. 47–55, College and seminary directories and general catalogs. For graduates who entered the ministry, lay leaders.)

1 *Encyclopedia of Living Divines and Christian Workers of all Denominations in Europe and America; being a Supplement to Schaff-Herzog Encyclopedia of Religious Knowledge.* Ed. by Philip Schaff and Samuel Macauley Jackson. New York, 1887.

2 FOTHERGILL, Gerald. *A List of Emigrant Ministers to America, 1690–1811.* London, 1904. (Essential for late colonial and early national periods.)

3 FOWLER, Henry. *The American Pulpit: Sketches of Living American Preachers, and of the Religious Movements Which They Represent.* New York, 1856. (Portraits.)

4 GIDDINGS, Edward J., comp. *American Christian Rulers or Religion and Men of Government . . . Who have had Connection with the National and State Governments and the Judicial Departments.* New York, 1889, 1890. (195 prominent laymen, since colonial period; civil officers who also were ministers.)

5 HERRINGSHAW, Thomas William, ed. and comp. *American Clergyman and Theologian Blue Book, A Vocational Blue Book of Biography.* Chicago, 1923. (Over 500 brief sketches of clergymen, other religious leaders.)

6 *Makers of Christianity.* 3 vols. New York, 1934–1937. (Vol. III, by William Warren Sweet, has Americans, 1630–1920.)

7 SCHAFF, Philip. *New Schaff-Herzog Encyclopedia of Religious Knowledge.* 12 vols. and index. New York, 1908–1912. Repr., 13 vols. Grand Rapids, 1949–1950. (Articles on living religious leaders, predominantly clerical.)

8 SCHWARZ, Julius C., ed. *Who's Who in the Clergy.* Vol. I, 1935–1936. New York, 1936. Continuation, *Religious Leaders of America,* as vol. II, 1941–1942. New York, 1941. (First issue has sketches of over 7,000 leaders.)

9 SPRAGUE, William Buell. *Annals of the American Pulpit; or, Commemorative Notices of Distinguished American Clergymen of Various Denominations, from the Early Settlement of the Country to the Close of the Year Eighteen Hundred and Fifty-Five.* 9 vols. New York, 1857–1869. (Between 1,300 and 1,400 ministers, with citations of writings.)

10 WEIS, Frederick Lewis. *The Colonial Churches and the Colonial Clergy of the Middle and Southern Colonies, 1607–1776.* Lancaster, Mass., 1938. (Although containing inaccuracies and omissions, this and the three following volumes are essential.)

11 WEIS, Frederick Lewis. *The Colonial Clergy and the Colonial Churches of New England.* Lancaster, Mass., 1936.

12 WEIS, Frederick Lewis. *The Colonial Clergy of Maryland, Delaware, and Georgia.* Lancaster, Mass., 1950.

13 WEIS, Frederick Lewis. *The Colonial Clergy of Virginia, North Carolina, and South Carolina.* Boston, 1955.

14 *Who's Who in the Protestant Clergy.* Encino, Calif., 1957.

3. Miscellaneous Sources of Information

15 *The American Christian Record, Containing the History, Confession of Faith, and Statistics of Each Religious Denomination in the United States and Europe.* New York, 1860. (One of the most complete ecclesiastical compendiums ever issued.)

BIBLIOGRAPHICAL GUIDES AND REFERENCE WORKS 5

1 *The American Year Book; a Record of Events and Progress 1911–1943.* 28 vols. New York and London, 1911–1942. (Publication suspended 1920–1924 and 1939. "Religion and Religious Organizations," activities for each year.)

2 BELCHER, Joseph. *The Religious Denominations of the United States: Their History, Doctrine, Government and Statistics.* . . . Philadelphia, 1857. New rev. ed., Philadelphia, 1861. (Huge, impartial, reliable.)

3 BISHOP, Charles Cager. *Churches, 253, 762; Their Doctrines, History, Government* (Wellington? Tex., 1951.)

4 BRANAGAN, Thomas. *Concise View of the Principal Religious Denominations in the United States of America, Comprehending a General Account of Their Doctrines, Ceremonies, and Modes of Worship.* Philadelphia? 1811. (Apparently first American ecclesiastical compendium.)

5 DORCHESTER, Daniel. *Christianity in the United States from the First Settlement down to the Present Time.* New York and Cincinnati, 1888. Rev. ed., 1890, 1895. (Popular survey, mass of data, plates, maps, tables, diagrams, chart.)

6 DORCHESTER, Daniel. *The Problem of Religious Progress.* New York and Cincinnati, 1881, Rev. ed., 1895, 1900. (Statistics of growth; much sociological data.)

7 FRY, Charles Luther. *The U.S. Looks at Its Churches.* New York, 1930. (Factual; sociological conclusions; economic, geographical, financial statistics.)

8 GAUSTAD, Edwin Scott. *Historical Atlas of Religion in America.* New York, 1962. (Text on history of religion; maps showing distribution of denominations, statistics.)

9 GORRIE, Peter Douglas. *The Churches and Sects of the United States: Containing a Brief Account of the Origin, History, Doctrines, Church Government, Mode of Worship, Usages and Statistics.* New York, 1850. (47 white and Negro groups, list of refs.)

10 HAYWARD, John. *The Religious Creeds and Statistics of Every Christian Denomination in the United States and British Provinces.* Boston, 1836. (Religious creeds by groups; list of sources.)

11 LANDIS, Benson Young. *Religion in the United States.* New York, 1965. (53 denominations and groups; views on public issues; religious terms; statistics.)†

12 MAYER, Frederick Emanuel. *The Religious Bodies of America.* 3rd ed. St. Louis, 1958. 4th, rev. ed., St. Louis, 1961. (Very thorough, scholarly, critical; many footnotes and bibliogs.)

13 MEAD, Frank Spencer. *Handbook of Denominations in the United States.* New 4th ed. New York, 1965. (Pub. since 1951. Factual reference book on history, beliefs; statistics of about 250 groups.)

14 MUNRO, William Fraser. *A Brief Dictionary of the Denominations.* Nashville, 1964. (Brief, factual sketches of history and beliefs of important bodies in U.S.)

15 PAULLIN, Charles Oscar. *Atlas of the Historical Geography of the United States.* Ed. by John K. Wright. Washington and New York, 1932. (Distribution of churches, 1775–1890, with notes.)

1 PHELAN, Macum. *Handbook of All Denominations, Containing an Account of Their Origin and History; a Statement of Their Faith and Usages; Together with the Latest Statistics on Their Activities, Locations and Strength.* Nashville, 1916–1933. (6th and 7th eds. called *New Handbook.*)

2 *Look Magazine. Religions in America; a Completely Revised and Up-to-date Guide to Churches and Religious Groups in the United States.* Ed. by Leo Rosten. New York, 1963. (Doctrines, beliefs, facts, membership, clergy, education, relations of religion to society.)†

3 RUPP, Israel Daniel. *He Pasa Ekklesia, An Original History of the Religious Denominations at Present Existing in the United States, Containing Authentic Accounts of Their Rise, Progress, Statistics and Doctrines. . . .* Philadelphia, 1844. (An enormous mass of interesting but poorly arranged information. 2nd "improved" ed., with additional matter, somewhat better arranged, comp. by John A. Ebaugh, J. Forsyth, et al., as *History of all the Religious Denominations in the United States. . . .* Harrisburg, 1849. 3rd ed., Harrisburg, 1852. 50 groups.)

4 SCHEM, Alexander Jacob. *The American Ecclesiastical Year-book.* New York, 1860. (Huge mass of details, statistics, creeds, etc. See also his *American Ecclesiastical and Educational Almanac, for Ministers and Laymen.* New York, 1868–1869.)

5 SMALL, Charles Herbert. *Cornerstones of Faith; or, The Origin and Characteristics of the Christian Denominations of the United States.* New York, 1898. (Bibliogs. Minor groups, movements toward unity, chronology.)

6 WEIGEL, Gustave. *Churches in North America: an Introduction.* Baltimore, 1961. (Brief, factual sketches of American denominations for Roman Catholics.)†

7 *Yearbook of American Churches.* Lebanon, Pa., New York, etc., 1916– . (Irregular, 1916–1931, then biennial, now annual. Official information, wide coverage.)

8 *Year Book of the Church and Social Service in the United States.* 2 vols. New York and Chicago, 1914–1916. (With bibliogs. Valuable for social service movement.)

A. Censuses

9 CARROLL, Henry King. *The Religious Forces of the United States Enumerated, Classified, and Described on the Basis of the Government Census of 1890. With an Introduction on the Condition and Character of American Christianity.* New York, 1893. Vol. I in "American Church History Series." (New ed., New York, 1912, compares returns for 1900, 1906, and 1910 with 1890; extensive comments.)

10 CARROLL, Henry King. *Statistics of the Churches of the United States for 1914.* New York, 1915.

11 ERSKINE, Hazel Gaudet. "The Polls: Church Attendance." *Pub Opin Q,* XXVIII (1964), 671–679. (Summarizes statistics collected since 1936 by various polling organizations.)

12 LANDIS, Benson Young. "Trends in Church Membership in the United States." *Ann Am Acad Pol Soc Sci,* CCCXXXII (1960), 1–8. (Growing at more rapid rate than population, especially conservative groups.)

1 LINFIELD, Harry Sebee. *State Population Census by Faiths; Meaning, Reliability and Value.* New York, 1938. (Interesting commentary on census of 1936, with bibliog.)

2 National Council of the Churches of Christ in the U.S.A. Bureau of Research and Survey. *Churches and Church Membership in the United States; an Enumeration and Analysis by Counties, States and Regions.* New York, 1956– . (Ser. A and B, issued in numbers.)

3 United States Bureau of the Census. *Census of Religious Bodies* for 1890, 1906, 1916, 1926, and 1936. Washington, 1894; 1910, 2 pts; 1919, 2 vols.; 1930, 2 vols.; 1939–1940, bull. 1–78, 78 vols. (Most complete body of statistics of American religion; statistical and historical.)

4 ZELINSKY, W. "An Approach to the Religious Geography of the United States: Patterns of Church Membership in 1952." *Ann Assoc Amer Geog*, LI (1961), 139–193. (Very detailed statistical analysis, by groups and regions, many maps.)

II. American Church History

1. Historiography

5 AHLSTROM, Sydney E. "The Moral and Theological Revolution of the Sixties and Its Implications for American Religious Historiography." In Herbert Bass, ed., *The State of American History*, Chicago, 1970. (The post-war "revival" past, the nation moving toward an unprecedented "crisis of conscience.")

6 BOWDEN, Henry Warner. "Studies in American Church Historiography, 1876–1918." (Princeton), 1966. *Univ Mic* (1966), no. 66–13,291. *Diss Abs*, XXVII (1967), 2594A. (Review of philosophies.)

7 BRAUER, Jerald C., ed. *Reinterpretation in American Church History.* Chicago, 1968. (Essays by eight prominent church historians, noticing use of secular tools and break from isolation.)

8 CLEBSCH, William A. "A New Historiography of American Religion." *Hist Mag P E Ch*, XXXII (1963), 225–257. (Emergence of realism, concerned with religion in general experience.)

9 KRAUS, Michael. *A History of American History.* New ed. Norman, Okla., 1953. (Bibliog. Covers religious history, varying interpretations.)

10 LANKFORD, John Errett. "The Contemporary Revolution in Historiography and the History of the Episcopal Church: Observations and Reflections." *Hist Mag P E Ch*, XXXVI (1967), 11–34. (Effect of social and behavioral sciences on religious history.)

11 MAY, Henry F. "The Recovery of American Religious History." *Am Hist Rev*, LXX (1964), 79–92. (Revival has brought renewed dialogue between secular and religious thought.)

1 MEAD, Sidney Earl. "Church History Explained." *Church Hist*, XXXII (1963), 17–31. (Plea for broader philosophy of church history, free from denominationalism.)

2 RAMSEY, Paul, ed. *Religion*. Englewood Cliffs, N.J., 1965. (Critical appraisal of works in history of American Christianity, pp. 195–217.)

3 TRINTERUD, Leonard John. "The Task of the American Church Historian." *Church Hist*, XXV (1956), 3–15. (American church historian must adjust himself to pluralistic culture.)

4 WILLIAMS, George Huntston. "Church History." In Arnold Samuel Nash, *Protestant Thought in the Twentieth Century: Whence and Whither?* New York, 1951. (Notes on U.S.; bibliogs. Discusses writings since 1888.)

2. General Histories

5 BENNETT, John Coleman, et al. *The Church Through Half a Century; Essays in Honor of William Adams Brown*. New York, 1936. (Liberal survey of religious thought and action, 1886–1936.)

6 BOORSTIN, Daniel J. *The Americans: The Colonial Experience*. New York, 1958. (Much perceptive comment on religious institutions.)†

7 CAIRNS, Earle Edwin. *Christianity in the United States*. Chicago, 1964. (Informative and interpretive, stressing setting and development, with bibliogs. and diagrams.)†

8 CLEBSCH, William A. *From Sacred to Profane America: The Role of Religion in American History*. New York, 1968. (Religion aspired to unify secular society, became such a society; now criticizes secularism.)

9 CURRAN, Francis X. *Major Trends in American Church History*. New York, 1946. (Bibliog. Survey of Protestantism, Negro problem, Catholicism as missionary minority.)

10 DIMAN, J. Lewis. "Religion in America, 1776–1876." *N Am Rev*, CXXII (1876), 1–47. (Condensed, scholarly, readable; reviewing preeminent features.)

11 EDWARDS, Martha L. "Religious Forces in the United States, 1815–1830." *Miss Val Hist Rev*, V (1919), 434–449. (Evolution of "American religion" under religious liberty.)

12 GARRISON, Winfred Ernest. *The March of Faith; the Story of Religion in America Since 1865*. New York and London, 1933. (Bibliog. Heavily accents social aspects.)

13 GAUSTAD, Edwin Scott. *A Religious History of America*. New York, 1966. (Comprehensive; last third on involvement of Americans in religious experience.)

14 GAUSTAD, Edwin Scott, comp. *Religious issues in American History*. New York, 1968. (Selected readings from documents on leading issues; general introduction; notes.)†

15 HEIMERT, Alan E. *Religion and the American Mind, from the Great Awakening to the Revolution*. Cambridge, Mass., 1966. (Detailed, scholarly reivew of liberal and evangelical religious literature.)

1 HUDSON, Winthrop Still. *Religion in America.* New York, 1965. (Interpretive of religious life as related to other experiences, stress on period since 1865.)†

2 MANWELL, Reginald Dickinson, and Sophia Lyon FAHS. *The Church Across the Street; an Introduction to the Ways and Beliefs of Fifteen Different Faiths.* Rev. ed. Boston, 1962. (Histories of denominations, dramatized by centering around pioneers; notes on present beliefs and activities.)

3 McLOUGHLIN, William Gerald, and Robert N. BELLAH, eds. *Religion in America.* Boston, 1968. (Articles analyzing and evaluating *contemporary* religion.)†

4 MEAD, Sidney Earl. *The Lively Experiment: the Shaping of Christianity in America.* New York, 1963. (Stresses uniqueness of American religion, influence of frontier, denominationalism, "Americanism," democracy.)

5 OLMSTEAD, Clifton E. *Religion in America, Past and Present.* Englewood Cliffs, N.J., 1961. (Lively, brief but amazingly comprehensive, with excellent selected bibliog., perhaps most ambitious and readable of all general histories.)†

6 SCHAFF, Philip, et al. *The American Church History Series.* 13 vols. New York, 1893–1897. (Vol. XII, pp. 441–513, Samuel Macauley Jackson, "A Bibliography of American Church History, 1820–1893," about 1,400 unclassified titles.)

7 SCHLESINGER, Arthur M., and Dixon Ryan FOX, eds. *A History of American Life.* 13 vols. New York, 1930–1948. (Religion considered from sociological viewpoint. Religion in bibliogs., vols. 1–8, 11–13.)

8 SCHNEIDER, Herbert Wallace. *Religion in 20th Century America.* Rev. ed. New York, 1964. (Changes in religion *itself*, background of "revival.")†

9 SMITH, James Ward, and A. Leland JAMISON, eds. *Religion in American Life.* 4 vols. Princeton, N.J., 1961. (Vols. I and II, essays on themes and relationships rather than institutions and creeds.)

10 SMITH, Timothy Lawrence. "Historic Waves of Religious Interest in America." *Ann Am Acad Pol Soc Sci*, CCCXXXII (1960), 9–19. (Four decades, 1790's–1850's, Christianity adjusting to new social conditions.)

11 SWEET, William Warren. *Religion in Colonial America.* New York, 1965 (Stresses neglected part of religion in popular life, democratization, emergence of religious freedom and "unchurched liberals." Large bibliog.)

12 SWEET, William Warren. *The Story of Religion in America.* 2nd rev. ed. New York, 1950. (Standard text, encyclopedic but readable. Extensive bibliog., religious census.)

13 WRIGHT, Louis Booker. *The Cultural Life of the American Colonies, 1607–1763.* New York, 1957. (Religion as a molder of cultural institutions.)†

10

3. *The Great Depression, 1929–1945*

1 ALMEN, Louis Theodore. "Work and Vocation in the Period of the Great Depression—1929–1941." (St Univ of Iowa), 1963. *Univ Mic* (1963), no. 63–7986. *Diss Abs*, XXIV (1963), 2583. (New ethic relevant to mass-production.)

2 HANDY, Robert T. "The American Religious Depression, 1925–1935." *Church Hist*, XXIX (1960), 3–16. (Depression drove weakened Protestantism to rethinking position and mission.)

3 KINCHELOE, Samuel C. "Research Memorandum on Religion in the Depression." *Bull Soc Sci Res Coun*, XXXIII (1937). (Considers many aspects, effects upon local church.)

4 LANDIS, Benson Young. "Organized Religion, 1933." *Am J Socio*, XXXVIII (1933), 905–912. (Situation, activities, radical rethinking of mission.)

5 LATOURETTE, Kenneth Scott. "The Condition of Religion in the United States." *Rel Life*, VII (1938), 335–345. (Optimistic, stresses interpenetration of secular life and religion.)

6 SPERRY, Willard Learoyd, ed. *Religion in the Post-war World.* 4 vols. Cambridge, Mass., 1945. (Symposium by Protestants, Catholics, Jews; decline of attachment to revelation and reason.)

7 WECTER, Dixon. *The Age of the Great Depression, 1929–1941.* New York, 1948. (Chap. X, "Age in Quest of Security," social idealism of churches, rise of cultism.)

4. *"Religious Revival," 1945–* .

8 AHLSTROM, Sydney E. "The Levels of Religious Revival." *Confluence*, IV 1955), 32–43. (Analyzes movement from popular literature to deep concern with theology and sacraments.)

9 BELL, Bernard Iddings. *Crowd Culture; an Examination of the American Way of Life.* New York, 1952, 1956. (Criticizes popular "revival of religion" as prop to secular ideals.)†

10 BERGER, Peter L. *The Noise of Solemn Assemblies: Christian Commitment and the Religious Establishment in America.* Garden City, N.Y., 1968. (Rigorous criticism of religious "revival" in the 1950's from a sociological viewpoint.)†

11 CAVERT, Samuel McCrea. "A Look at the American Churches." *Rel Life*, XVIII (1949), 323–331. (Cheerful view of "revival;" stresses Social Gospel and ecumenicity.)

12 ECKARDT, A. Roy. *The Surge of Piety in America.* New York, 1958. (Admits sincerity, but criticizes "revival" as "culture religion.")

13 ELSON, Edward L. R. *America's Spiritual Recovery.* Westwood, N.J., 1954. (Confident affirmation of religious reawakening.)

1 GREELEY, Andrew M., et al. *What Do We Believe? The Stance of Religion in America.* New York, 1968. (Surveys prove that most adults still hold to early religious convictions.)

2 GUSTAFSON, James M., ed. "The Sixties: Radical Change in American Religion." *Ann Am Acad Pol Soc Sci,* 387 (Jan., 1970), 1–140. (14 articles by distinguished authorities, on major topics.)

3 HERBERG, Will. "There is a Religious Revival!" *Rev Rel Res,* I (1959), 45–50. (Stresses general, secularized religion.)

4 HASELDEN, Kyle, and Martin E. MARTY, eds. *What's Ahead for the Churches?* New York, 1964.

5 LAMBERT, Richard D. "Current Trends in Religion: A Summary." *Ann Amer Acad Polit Soc Sci,* CCCXXXII (1960), 146–155. (Decline reversed, bland popular piety, interest of intellectuals, enhanced lay importance, business organization, mergers, growth of sects and cults.)

6 LIPSET, Seymour Martin. "Religion in America: What Religious Revival?" *Rev Rel Res,* I (1959), 17–24. (Doubts great "revival", stresses basic continuities, secularizing.)

7 MARTY, Martin E. *The New Shape of American Religion.* New York, 1959. (Revival of "Religion-in-General," erosion of classical Protestantism, approach to urbanism.)

8 MESERVE, Harry C. "The New Piety." In Joseph Henry Satin, *The 1950's; America's Placid Decade.* Boston, 1960. (An assessment, reprinted from *Atl Mo,* June, 1955.)†

9 NIEBUHR, Reinhold. "Is There a Revival of Religion?" *N Y Times Mag,* Nov. 19, 1950, pp. 13, 60, 62, 63. (Evidences not conclusive; real is taking place of rational quasi-religion.)

10 ORR, James Edwin. *Good News in Bad Times; Signs of Revival.* Grand Rapids, 1953. (Confident declaration of religious upswing.)

11 ROWLAND, Stanley J. *Land in Search of God.* New York, 1958. (Americans seeking fuller self-understanding through religion.)

12 SCHNEIDER, Louis, and Sanford M. DORNBUSCH. *Popular Religion. Inspirational Books in America.* Chicago, 1958. (Two sociologists thoroughly and objectively survey an aspect of mass religious culture.)

13 TAYLOR, Rachel Jean. "The 'Return to Religion' in America after the Second World War: A Study of Religion in American Culture 1945–1955." (Minn), 1961. *Univ. Mic* (1963), no. 63–1254. *Diss Abs,* XXIII(1963),3005–3006. (Genuine theological renaissance; religion more respectable among intellectuals; rediscovery of religious values.)

5. Foreign Observers

14 BERGER, Max. *The British Traveller in America, 1836–1860.* New York, 1943. New ed., 1964. (Large critical bibliog. Chap. VI on religion; footnotes on nearly all who mentioned it.)

15 BRAUER, Jerald C. *Images of Religion in America.* Philadelphia, 1967. (Writers critically reviewed; saw Christian and democratic faith combined in "American way.")†

1 BROOKS, John Graham. *As Others See Us, A Study of Progress in the United States*. New York, 1908. (Comments on authors note references to religion.)

2 BUCK, Solon J. "Travel and Description, 1765–1865." *Coll Ill State Hist Soc*, IX (1914). (Some foreign titles with refs. to religion in Illinois and Middle West.)

3 CHAMBERS, Samuel Tinsley. "Observations and Opinions of French Travellers in the United States from 1790 to 1835 together with: Some Comparisons with Observations and Opinions by British Travellers in the Same Period." Master's thesis (Georgetown), 1949. (Copies at Georgetown and Library of Congress. Chap. IV, observations on religion.)

4 COULTER, Ellis Merton, comp. *Travels in the Confederate States; a Bibliography*. Norman, Okla., 1948. (Remarks by foreigners on religion in the South, with bibliog., 1862–1945.)

5 DE ONIS, José. *The United States as Seen by Spanish American Writers, 1776–1890*. New York, 1952. (Bibliog.; some comment on religion.)

6 HANDLIN, Oscar. *This Was America . . . as Recorded by European Travelers . . . in the Eighteenth, Nineteenth, and Twentieth Centuries*. Cambridge, Mass., 1949. (Annotated selections from forty authors; observations on many religious topics.)

7 MESICK, Jane Louise. *The English Traveller in America, 1785–1835*. New York, 1922. (Bibliog.; chap. on religion, with refs. to observations on religion in books.)

8 MONAGHAN, Frank. *French Travelers in the United States, 1765–1932; a Bibliography*. New York, 1933. (Index includes refs. to religion.)

9 POWELL, Milton Bryan, comp. *The Voluntary Church: American Religious Life, 1740–1865, Seen Through the Eyes of European Visitors*. New York, 1967. (Excerpts; views by 18 individuals on voluntary support; contrast to European state churches.)

10 RYAN, Lee W. *French Travellers in the Southeastern United States, 1775–1800*. Bloomington, Ind., 1939. (Bibliog. of travel books and refs. to religion.)

11 SHERRILL, Charles H. *French Memoirs of Eighteenth-Century America*. New York, 1915. (Chap. on "Religious Observances.")

12 THWAITES, Reuben Gold, ed. *Early Western Travels, 1748–1846*. 32 vols. Cleveland, 1904–1907. (Numerous narratives with comments on religion, by travelers, missionaries, explorers.)

13 TUCKERMAN, Henry T. *America and Her Commentators, with a Critical Sketch of Travel in the United States*. New York, 1864. (Comments on European travelers and critics, with refs. to observations on religion.)

III. The Classic Denominational Pattern

1. Protestant Denominations. General Works

1 BALTZELL, Edward Digby. *The Protestant Establishment; Aristocracy & Caste in America.* New York, 1964. (Social and economic dominance of white Anglo-Saxon Protestants.)†

2 BRAUER, Jerald C. *Protestantism in America; a Narrative History.* Rev. ed. Philadelphia, 1965. (General rather than denominational; similarities rather than peculiarities.)

3 CARTER, Paul Allen. "Recent Historiography of the Protestant Churches in America." *Church Hist*, XXXVII (1968), 95–107. (Survey and estimate, with bibliog).

4 DOUGLASS, Harlan Paul. *The Protestant Church as a Social Institution.* New York and London, 1935. (Summarizes many research projects on common characteristics and enterprises.)

5 FERM, Vergilius Ture Anselm, ed. *The American Church of the Protestant Heritage.* New York, 1953. (Essays by various authors on 21 Protestant denominations; brief bibliogs.)

6 HANDY, Robert T. *The Protestant Quest for a Christian America, 1830–1930.* Philadelphia, 1967. (Protestant churches, in effort to Christianize America, became secularized in a pluralistic society.)†

7 HARDON, John A. *The Protestant Churches of America.* Rev. ed. Westminster, Md., 1958. (Explains Protestant denominationalism to Roman Catholics.)†

8 HARDON, John A., ed. *The Spirit and Origins of American Protestantism: A Source Book in Its Creeds.* Dayton, Ohio, 1968. (Anthology of significant statements of faith; historical introduction, confessional index.)

9 HUDSON, Winthrop Still. *American Protestantism.* Chicago, 1961. (Readable and concise history, and exposition of the contemporary crisis of Protestantism.)†

10 MARTY, Martin E. *Second Chance for American Protestants.* New York, 1963. ("Christendom" has vanished, Christians are dispersed in secular culture to realize ideal of a promised land.)

11 MIYAKAWA, Tetsuo Scott. *Protestants and Pioneers. Individualism and Conformity on the American Frontier.* Chicago, 1964. (Sociological analysis of frontier religion as molded by regional influences.)

12 SMITH, Timothy Lawrence. "Congregation, State and Denomination: The Forming of the American Religious Structure." *Wm Mary Q*, 25, 3rd ser, 2 (Apr., 1968), 155–176. (Sociological, economic, psychological study of the 17th century, failure of state control, turn to denominationalism.)

1 WAMBLE, G. Hugh. *The Shape of Faith*. Nashville, 1962. (Attempts to present for average layman an objective, fair survey of history and distinguishing features of seven evangelical denominations.)†

2 WHALEN, William Joseph. *Separated Brethren; a Survey of Non Catholic Christian Denominations in the United States*. 2nd rev. ed. Milwaukee, 1966. (Comprehensive, including non-Christian groups; for intelligent Roman Catholics.)†

2. Anglicans

3 ADDISON, James Thayer. *The Episcopal Church in the United States, 1789–1931*. New York, 1951. Reissued, 1969. (Bibliog. Popular, with social background.)

4 ALBRIGHT, Raymond Wolf. *A History of the Protestant Episcopal Church*. New York, 1964. (Scholarly, heavily stressing period to close of Civil War.)

5 BOSCHER, Robert S., comp. "The Episcopal Church and American Christianity: A Bibliography." *Hist Mag P E Ch*, XIX (1950), 369–384.

5a BRIDENBAUGH, Carl. *Mitre and Sceptre; Transatlantic Faiths, Ideas, Personalities, and Politics, 1689–1775*. New York, 1962. (Episcopate controversy as part of struggle for independence, religious freedom.)†

6 BRYDON, G. MacLaren. *Virginia's Mother Church and the Conditions under Which It Grew*. 2 vols. Richmond, 1947–1952. (Evolution of typical Anglican establishment.)

7 CHESHIRE, Joseph Blount. *The Church in the Confederate States; a History of the Protestant Episcopal Church in the Confederate States*. New York, 1914. (Little-known phase of American Anglicanism.)

8 CHORLEY, Edward Clowes. *Men and Movements in the American Episcopal Church*. Hamden, Conn., 1961. (Impartial account of leaders, parties, controversies.)

9 CROSS, Arthur Lyon. *The Anglican Episcopate and the American Colonies*. Hamden, Conn., 1964. (Authoritative account of effort to secure a colonial bishop, and opposition.)

10 DAWLEY, Powel Mills. *The Episcopal Church and its Work*. Greenwich, Conn., 1955. (Bibliog.)

11 DE MILLE, George Edmed. *The Catholic Movement in the American Episcopal Church*. 2nd ed. rev. and enl. Philadelphia, 1950. (Bibliog. Most complete account.)

12 KLINGBERG, Frank Joseph. "Contributions of the S. P. G. to the American Way of Life." *Hist Mag P E Ch*, XII (1943), 215–244. (First organized colonial effort to elevate laboring and dependent classes.)

13 KLINGBERG, Frank Joseph. "The Expansion of the Anglican Church in the Eighteenth Century." *Hist Mag P E Ch*, XVI (1947), 292–301. (Church as promoter of humane culture in America.)

1 LOVELAND, Clara O. *The Critical Years; the Reconstitution of the Anglican Church in the United States of America: 1780–1789.* Greenwich, Conn., 1956. (Bibliog. From establishment to independence.)

2 McCULLOCH, Samuel Clyde. "The Foundation and Early Work of the Society for Promoting Christian Knowledge." *Hist Mag P E Ch*, XVIII (1949), 3–22. (Civilizing influence through disseminating literature.)

3 McCULLOCH, Samuel Clyde. "The Foundation and Early Work of the Society for the Propagation of the Gospel in Foreign Parts." *Hist Mag P E Ch*, XX (1951), 121–135. (Education of the Negro; stimulation of intellectual and spiritual life.)

4 MANROSS, William Wilson. "Catalog of Articles in the 'Historical Magazine.' " *Hist Mag P E Ch*, XXIII (1954), 367–420. (Most complete guide to special writings, articles, book reviews.)

5 MANROSS, William Wilson. *A History of the American Episcopal Church.* 2nd ed. rev. and enl. New York, 1950. (Valuable bibliog. Scholarly; the church as living institution.)

6 PITTENGER, W. Norman. *The Episcopalian Way of Life.* Englewood Cliffs, N.J., 1957. (Popular exposition of piety and works.)

7 SONNE, Niels Henry. "Bibliographical Materials on the Episcopal Church." *Rel. Life*, XXV (1956), 442–451. (Some comments. Incl. major archives.)

3. Baptists

8 ARMSTRONG, O. K. and Marjorie M. *The Indomitable Baptists: a Narrative of Their Role in Shaping American History.* Garden City, N.Y., 1967. (Influence in attaining religious liberty and individual expression.)

9 BAKER, Robert Andrew. *A Baptist Source Book, with Particular Reference to Southern Baptists.* Nashville, 1966. (Select documents by periods; introductory notes, incl. some on Negro and Northern Baptists.)

10 *Baptist Advance; the Achievements of the Baptists of North America for a Century and a Half.* Nashville, 1964. (Encyclopedic; on history, conventions, contributions to religious and secular life.)

11 BARNES, William Wright. *History of the Southern Baptist Convention, 1845–1953.* Nashville, 1954. (Wide divergence from liberalism in Northern churches.)

12 BAXTER, Norman Allen. *History of the Freewill Baptists: A Study in New England Separatism.* Rochester, N.Y., 1957. (Bibliog. Revolt against Calvinism; social welfare work.)

13 CHILDERS, James Saxon, ed. *A Way Home; the Baptists Tell Their Story.* Atlanta, 1964. (Very readable essays on history, beliefs, religious and social services.)

1 CRISMON, Leo T. "The Literature of the Baptists." *Rel Life*, XXV (1955–1956), 128–131. (Fairly complete listing of major American works.)

2 *Encyclopedia of Southern Baptists.* 2 vols. Nashville, 1958. (Use with William Wright Barnes. See 15:11.)

3 HAYS, Brooks, and John E. STEELY. *The Baptist Way of Life.* Englewood Cliffs, N.J., 1963. (Popular, sometimes humorous, emphasizing frontier heritage of individualism.)

4 HILL, Samuel S., Jr., and Robert G. TORBET. *Baptists: North and South.* Valley Forge, Pa., 1964. (Candid, interpretive analysis of differences since schism of 1845.)†

5 STARR, Edward Caryl. *A Baptist Bibliography.* 6 vols. Philadelphia, 1947–1958. (Most extensive; continuing.)

6 SWEET, William Warren, ed. *The Baptists, a Collection of Source Material.* New York, 1964. (1785–1825; illustrating frontier religion, missions, preaching, anti-slavery movements, revivals.)

4. Congregationalists

7 ATKINS, Gaius Glenn, and Frederick Louis FAGLEY. *History of American Congregationalism.* Boston and Chicago, 1942. (Bibliog. Orderly, accurate account of growth, thought, work.)

8 BURTON, Malcolm King. *Destiny for Congregationalism.* Oklahoma City, 1953. (Merger of Congregational Christian and Evangelical and Reformed Church.)

9 FAGLEY, Frederick Louis. *Story of the Congregational Christian Churches.* Boston and Chicago, 1941. (Bibliog. Typical union of two liberal churches.)

10 HORTON, Douglas. *The United Church of Christ: Its Origins, Organization, and Role in the World Today.* New York, 1962. (Based upon analysis of constitution; typical product of ecumenicity.)

11 LOBINGIER, John Leslie. *Pilgrims and Pioneers in the Congregational Christian Tradition.* Philadelphia, 1965. (Heritage of the United Church of Christ in popular biographical sketches.)†

12 STARKEY, Marion Lena. *The Congregational Way; the Role of the Pilgrims and Their Heirs in Shaping America.* Garden City, N.Y., 1966. (Popular, fluent. Stressing Western missions, education, democratic idealism, social reform, ecumenicity.)

13 SWEET, William Warren, ed. *The Congregationalists, a Collection of Source Materials.* New York, 1964. (1790's–1840's, illustrating expansion of home and Indian missions, with maps and large bibliog.)

5. *The Puritan Theocracy and Culture*

1 ANDREWS, Charles McLean. *The Rise and Fall of the New Haven Colony.* New Haven, 1936. (Quintessence of the Puritan "Holy Commonwealth.")

2 BAINTON, Roland Herbert. *Christian Unity and Religion in New England.* Boston, 1964. (Essays 15–19, scholarly and readable insights into Puritan religion and culture.)

3 BUFFINTON, Arthur H. "The Massachusetts Experiment of 1630." *Pub Col Soc Mass,* XXXII (1935), 308–320. (Puritan theocracy derived from Hebrew commonwealth and medieval church-state.)

4 JAMES, Sydney V., ed. *The New England Puritans. Interpretations of American History.* New York, 1968. (Selections from six significant contributions to understanding the movement; introduction on recent historiography.)†

5 MILLER, Perry. "Declension in a Bible Commonwealth." *Proc Am Ant Soc,* LI (1941), 37–94. (Bibliog. Puritan ideal of thrift encouraged materialism, which destroyed theocracy.)

6 MORGAN, Edmund Sears. *The Puritan Family.* . . . Boston, 1944. (Family and theocracy, religious beliefs and domestic relations.)†

7 MORISON, Samuel Eliot. *Builders of the Bay Colony.* Boston, 1930. (Bibliog. Appreciation of Puritan way of life, reaction from "debunking.")†

8 MORISON, Samuel Eliot. *The Puritan Pronaos, Studies in the Intellectual Life of New England in the Seventeenth Century.* New York, 1936. (Puritans as transmitters of culture to America.)

9 OBERHOLZER, Emil, Jr. *Delinquent Saints.* . . . New York, 1956. (Bibliog. Puritan control of morality, seen in church records.)

10 PERRY, Ralph Barton. *Puritanism and Democracy.* New York, 1944. (Theocracy to charter of 1691; appraisal of Puritanism and its critics.)

11 SCHNEIDER, Herbert Wallace. *The Puritan Mind.* Ann Arbor, 1958. (Surveys New England intellectual history and "Holy Commonwealth" ideal.)†

12 SHIPTON, Clifford K. "A Plea for Puritanism." *Am Hist Rev,* XL (1935), 460–467. (Criticizes theory of an unpopular theocracy.)

13 SIMPSON, Alan. *Puritanism in Old and New England.* Chicago, 1955. (Covenanted church as foundation of New England theocracy.)†

14 SMITH, Chard Powers. *Yankees and God.* New York, 1954. (Puritan theocratic replaced by Yankee commercial New England.)

15 STEPHENSON, George Malcolm. *The Puritan Heritage.* New York, 1952. (Bibliog. Puritan worship of God as foundation of civil liberties.)

1 WALLER, George M. *Puritanism in Early America*. Boston, 1950. (Bibliog. Readings. Introduction discusses modern literature on Puritanism.)†

2 WINSLOW, Ola Elizabeth. *Meeting-house Hill, 1630–1783*. New York, 1952. (The house as focus of community life shaped by divine intent.)

6. *Disciples and Christians*

3 ABBOTT, Byrdine Akers. *The Disciples; an Interpretation*. St. Louis, 1964. (Brief history, general description of doctrines, practices, practical activities.)

4 BANOWSKY, William Slater. *The Mirror of a Movement; Churches of Christ As Seen Through the Abilene Christian College Lectureship*. Dallas, 1965. (Historical and theological interpretation of conservative wing of indigenous American church.)

5 GARRISON, Winfred Ernest, and Alfred Thomas DeGROOT. *The Disciples of Christ: A History*. St. Louis, 1948. (Standard, basic account.)

6 HARRELL, David Edwin. *A Social History of the Disciples of Christ*. Nashville, 1966– . (Stresses humanitarianism, accomplishments in meeting social problems. Vol. I, to 1866; vol. II will cover 1866–1900.)

7 MURCH, James DeForest. *Christians Only, a History of the Restoration Movement*. Cincinnati, 1962. (Comprehensive history, stressing supernatural and providential causation.)

8 PIERSON, Roscoe M. "The Literature of the Disciples of Christ and Closely Related Groups." *Rel Life*, XXVI (1957), 274–288. (Evaluative discussion.)

9 SHORT, Howard E. *Doctrine and Thought of the Disciples of Christ*. St. Louis, 1951. (Popular and definitive; typical American liberalism.)

10 SPENCER, Claude Elbert. *An Author Catalog of Disciples of Christ and Related Religious Groups*. Canton, Mo., 1946. (Most scholarly and extensive bibliog.)

7. *Lutherans*

11 ARDEN, Gothard Everett. *Augustana Heritage; a History of the Augustana Lutheran Church*. Rock Island, Ill., 1963. (Comprehensive history of Swedish Lutheranism, 1638–1962.)

12 ARDEN, Gothard Everett. *Meet the Lutherans; Introducing the Lutheran Church in North America*. Rock Island, Ill., 1962. (Popular, outlining denomination's history, beliefs, worship, organization, activities.)

13 JENSEN, John Martin. *The United Evangelical Lutheran Church, an Interpretation*. Minneapolis, 1964. (Realistic story of poor immigrant church that merged with Lutheran Church in America.)

1 KEINATH, Herman Ottomar Alfred. *Documents Illustrating the History of the Lutheran Church in America, with Special Emphasis on the Missouri Synod.* River Forest, Ill., 1947.

2 MEUSER, Fred W. *The Formation of the American Lutheran Church: A Case Study in Lutheran Unity.* Columbus, Ohio, 1958. (Traces movement in detail from early 19th century; large bibliog.)

3 MEYER, Carl Stamm, ed. *Moving Frontiers; Readings in the History of the Lutheran Church—Missouri Synod.* St. Louis, 1964. (Excellent documentary collection, with explanatory notes, large select bibliog.)

4 MORTENSEN, Enok. *The Danish Lutheran Church in America; the History and Heritage of the American Evangelical Lutheran Church.* Philadelphia, 1967. (Maintained contact with motherland, had impressive record of humanitarian service.)

5 NELSON, E. Clifford, and Eugene L. FEVOLD. *The Lutheran Church Among Norwegian Americans, A History of the Evangelical Lutheran Church.* 2 vols. Minneapolis, 1960. (Emphasizes trend toward unity.)

6 QUALBEN, Lars Pederson. *The Lutheran Church in Colonial America.* New York, 1940. (Selected bibliog.)

7 SCHMIDT, Herbert H. "The Literature of the Lutherans in America." *Rel Life,* XXVII (1958), 583–603. (Very comprehensive.)

8 STAUDERMAN, Albert P. *Our New Church.* Philadelphia, 1962. (Merger of four churches to form Lutheran Church in America; description of organization, work, teaching of new body.)

9 WENTZ, Abdel Ross. *A Basic History of Lutheranism in America.* Rev. ed. Philadelphia, 1964. (Environment of American civilization, social and cultural history of Lutheran people.)

10 WOLF, Richard Charles, ed. *Documents of Lutheran Unity in America.* Philadelphia, 1966. (From colonial period to formation of American Lutheran Church in 1962, with historical notes.)

8. Methodists

11 COLEMAN, Robert Emerson. "Factors in the Expansion of the Methodist Episcopal Church from 1784 to 1812." (St Univ Iowa), 1954. *Univ Mic* (1954), no. 10–201; *Diss Abs* (1954), XIV, 2419–2420. (Identification of Methodism with common people.)

12 FARISH, Hunter Dickinson. *The Circuit Rider Dismounts, A Social History of Southern Methodism, 1865–1900.* Richmond, 1938. (Adjustment to Reconstruction, becoming conservative denomination.)

13 FORTNEY, Edward L. "The Literature of the History of Methodism." *Rel Life,* XXIV (1955), 443–451. (Incl. American Methodism.)

14 *History of American Methodism.* Emory Stevens Bucke, general editor, et al. 3 vols. New York, 1964. (Comprehensive; stressing Methodism's contributions to American life as "an experiment in secular Christianity.")

1 JENNINGS, Henry C. *The Methodist Book Concern; a Romance of History.* New York and Cincinnati, 1924. (Effect upon American culture.)

2 KENNEDY, Gerald H. *The Methodist Way of Life.* Englewood Cliffs, N.J., 1958. (Popular history and description, stressing social outreach.)

3 MASER, Frederick E. *The Dramatic Story of Early American Methodism.* New York, 1965. (Brief, popular history to organization of Methodist Episcopal Church, 1784.)

4 Methodist Church (United States) Dept. of Research and Survey. *The Methodist Church in Urban America, a Fact Book.* Philadelphia, 1962. (Study of trends of Methodist Church membership, 1950–1960, showing social trends affecting church.)

5 MORROW, Ralph Ernest. *Northern Methodism and Reconstruction.* East Lansing, Mich., 1956. (Bibliog. Estrangement between Northern and Southern churches.)

6 PILKINGTON, James Penn. *The Methodist Publishing House, a History: Beginnings to 1870.* Nashville, 1968. (Vol. 1 of 2 projected volumes. Valuable insights into its religious and cultural influences.)

7 SCHOFIELD, Charles Edwin. *The Methodist Church; a Study of the Organization and Work.* Rev. ed. New York, 1949. (Bibliog. Stresses practical social activity.)

8 SWEET, William Warren. *Methodism in American History.* Rev. ed. New York, 1954. (Considered in relation to history of the people.)

9 SWEET, William Warren, ed. *The Methodists, a Collection of Source Materials.* New York, 1964. (Mostly journals and letters of circuit riders who evangelized Trans-Allegheny region; introductory history to 1850.)

9. Polish National Catholic Church

10 FOX, Paul. *The Polish National Catholic Church.* Scranton, 1961? (History and character of ethnic and independent Catholic church.)

11 JANOWSKI, Robert William. *The Growth of a Church; a Historical Documentary.* Scranton, 1965. (Collection of newspaper articles, historical sketch, illus. On origins.)

12 Polish National Catholic Church of America. *Album . . . 1897–1957.* Scranton, 1957? (Attractive history and photographic album, in English and Polish.)

10. Presbyterians

13 ANDERSON, Charles A. *The Presbyterian Enterprise; Sources of American Presbyterian History.* Philadelphia, 1956. (Bibliog. Brief explanatory notes.)

1 FUNK, Henry D. "The Influence of the Presbyterian Church in Early American History." *J Presby Hist Soc*, XII (1924–1926), 26–63, 152–189, 281–316. (Educational and moral influences.)

2 Presbyterian Church in the U.S.A. *Records of the Presbyterian Church, 1706–1788.* Philadelphia, 1904. (Minutes of synods and original presbytery.)

3 SLOSSER, Gaius Jackson, ed. *They Seek a Country: The American Presbyterians, Some Aspects.* New York, 1955. (Essays by various authors, covering especially services to the nation.)

4 SPENCE, Thomas H., Jr. "A Brief Bibliography of Presbyterian History." *Rel Life*, XXV (1956), 603–612. (Many titles on American Presbyterianism.)

5 SPENCE, Thomas H., Jr. *The Historical Foundation and Its Treasures.* Montreat, N.C., 1956. (Full account of American Presbyterian archives.)

6 SWEET, William Warren. *The Presbyterians, a Collection of Source Materials.* New York, 1964. (Expansion in Trans-Allegheny region, 1785–1840, illustrated by minutes, letters, autobiographies.)

7 THOMPSON, Ernest Trice. *The Changing South and the Presbyterian Church in the United States.* Richmond, 1950. (Bibliog. refs. A study of conservative sectionalism.)

8 THOMPSON, Ernest Trice. *Presbyterians in the South.* Richmond, 1963– . (Comprehensive history of conservative wing of American Presbyterianism since early 17th century. Bibliog. Vol. 1, 1607–1861.)

9 TRINTERUD, Leonard John. *The Forming of an American Tradition: A Re-examination of Colonial Presbyterianism.* Philadelphia, 1949. (Its composition from various national elements, with bibliog.)

10 TRINTERUD, Leonard John, comp. *A Bibliography of American Presbyterianism during the Colonial Period.* Philadelphia, 1968. (About 1,100 printed sources for 12 bodies, including the Revolutionary period.)

11. Reformed Churches

11 BAIRD, George Washington. *History of the Huguenot Emigration to America.* 2 vols. New York, 1885. (Refs. to French Reformed churches.)

12 BARTHOLOMEW, Alfred Clinton. "An Interpretation of the Evangelical and Reformed Church." (Drew), 1950. (The response of the Reformed tradition to changes in American life.)

13 CORWIN, Charles E. *A Manual of the Reformed Church in America, 1628–1922.* 5th ed. New York, 1922. (Bibliog. Reviews history as an established church.)

14 *Ecclesiastical Records, State of New York.* Vol. I. Albany, 1901. (Documents on established Reformed Dutch Church of New Netherland.)

1 FOOTE, William Henry. *The Huguenots; or, Reformed French Church.* Richmond, 1870. (Pt 3, "The Huguenot at Home in America," colonial settlements and churches and later history.)

2 HOEKSEMA, Herman. *The Protestant Reformed Churches in America, Their Origin, Early History, and Doctrine.* Grand Rapids, 1936. (Secession from the Christian [Dutch] Reformed Church, 1924–1925, typical creation of a denomination.)

3 HORSTMANN, Julius Herman Edward, and Herbert H. WERNECKE. *Through Four Centuries; the Story of the Beginnings of the Evangelical and Reformed Church.* St. Louis, 1938. (Reviews the German Reformed tradition.)

4 KALASSAY, Louis A. "The Educational and Religious History of the Hungarian Reformed Church in the United States." (Pitts), 1940. (Most complete account.)

5 KROMMINGA, Diedrich Hinrich. *The Christian Reformed Tradition from the Reformation till the Present.* Grand Rapids, 1943. (Orthodox Calvinist church in Western States.)

6 KROMMINGA, John Henry. *The Christian Reformed Church, a Study in Orthodoxy.* Grand Rapids, 1949. (Bibliog. Scholarly; theological conservatism.)

7 Reformed Church in America, Tercentenary Committee on Research and Publication. *Tercentenary Studies, 1928, Reformed Church in America; a Record of Beginnings.* New York, 1928. (Bibliogs. Scholarly historical essays.)

8 SCHNEIDER, Carl E. "The Genius of the Reformed Church in the United States." *J Rel,* XV (1935), 26–41. (Traces history leading to formation of Evangelical and Reformed Church, 1934.)

9 ZWIERLEIN, Frederick James. *Religion in New Netherland 1623–1664.* Rochester, N.Y., 1910. (Select bibliog. Reformed Church as legal, tax-supported institution.)

IV. Roman Catholic Church

1. Bibliography and Historiography

10 BROWNE, Henry Joseph. "American Catholic History: A Progress Report on Research and Study." *Church Hist,* XXVI (1957), 372–380. (General critical survey, 1946–1956, with refs.)

11 CADDEN, John Paul. *The Historiography of the American Catholic Church: 1785–1943.* Washington, 1944.

12 Catholic University of America. *Studies in American Church History.* 40 vols. Washington, 1922–1953.

13 CLARK, Aubert J. "Seventy-Five Years of American Church History." *Am Eccles Rev,* CLI (1964), 73–96. (Detailed survey with bibliog. in notes.)

14 CODE, Joseph Bernard. *Dictionary of the American Hierarchy.* New York, 1940. (Incl. lives of over 500 bishops; very complete, reliable.)

1 ELLIS, John Tracy. *A Guide to American Catholic History.* Milwaukee, 1959. (Very comprehensive; incl. manuscripts, books, periodicals, historical societies.)

2 ELLIS, John Tracy, ed. *Documents of American Catholic History.* Rev. ed. Chicago, 1967. 2 vols. (Chronological, 1493–1961, with introductory notes and complete index.)

3 O'BRIEN, David Joseph. "American Catholic Historiography: A Post-Conciliar Evaluation." *Church Hist,* XXXVII (1968), 80–94. (Survey and estimate of recent writings, with bibliog. in footnotes.)

4 Saint Mary's College, Notre Dame, Ind. *The Church in the World: A Bibliography.* Ed. by Sister Maria Assunta. Cincinnati, 1963. (Selections on general topics; more than 150 titles on history and character of R. C. Church in the U.S.)

5 SHEARER, Donald C. *Pontificia Americana: A Documentary History of the Catholic Church in the United States, 1784–1884.* Washington, 1933. (Original languages, comments, summaries in English.)

6 VOLLMAR, Edward R. *The Catholic Church in America: An Historical Bibliography.* New Brunswick, N.J., 1956. 2nd ed., New York, 1963. (Writing since colonial period; topical index.)

2. General Histories

7 *American Catholic Horizons.* Ed. by Eugene K. Culhane. Garden City, N.Y., 1966. (Articles from *America* discuss contemporary conditions, problems, attitudes, history that explains them.)

8 BIANCHI, Eugene C. "John XXIII, Vatican II, and American Catholicism." In *Ann Am Acad Pol Soc Sci,* 387 (Jan., 1970), 30–40. (Growing breach between conservatives and progressives, posing question of schism or a new kind of unity.)

9 ELLIS, John Tracy. *American Catholicism.* Chicago, 1956. 2nd ed., rev. (Considered to be the best succinct history yet to appear.)†

10 ELLIS, John Tracy. *Catholics in Colonial America.* Baltimore, 1965. (From early Spanish missions to Bishop John Carroll of Baltimore, 1790.)

11 ELLIS, John Tracy. "Contemporary American Catholicism in the Light of History." *Critic,* XXIV (1966), 8–19. (Candid assessment of strengths and weaknesses; the Negro and intellectual life.)

12 EBERHARDT, Newman C. *A Survey of American Church History.* St. Louis, 1964. (Mostly sober factual account in the U.S., with political and social background; reading list.)†

13 GUILDAY, Peter Keenan. *A History of the Councils of Baltimore, 1791–1884.* New York, 1932. (Councils that enacted formative legislation.)

14 HAMILTON, Raphael N. "The Significance of the Frontier to the Historian of the Catholic Church." *Cath Hist Rev,* XXV (1939), 160–178. (Approach to the immigrant and the native.)

1 HANDLIN, Oscar. *The Uprooted.* Boston, 1951. (Chap. V, "Religion as a Way of Life," for the bewildered Catholic immigrant.)†

2 HERR, Dan, and Joel WELLS, eds. *Through Other Eyes; Some Impressions of American Catholicism by Foreign Visitors from 1777 to the Present.* Westminster, Md., 1965. (Selections from 29 writers of several nationalities, mostly since 1865.)

3 LANDIS, Benson Young. *The Roman Catholic Church in the United States; a Guide to Recent Developments.* New York, 1966. (Eminent Protestant layman discusses general character and "updating" movements, particularly decentralizing and laicizing.)

4 McAVOY, Thomas Timothy. *The Americanist Heresy in Roman Catholicism, 1895–1900.* Notre Dame, Ind., 1963. (Controversy about authoritarian and democratic views of religion, adaptation to American environment.)†

5 McAVOY, Thomas Timothy. "The Catholic Church in the United States Between Two Wars." *Rev Pol,* IV (1942), 409–431. (Emphasizes action for social reconstruction and education.)

6 McGUIRE, Constantine E., ed. *Catholic Builders of the Nation, A Symposium of the Catholic Contribution to the Civilization of the United States.* 5 vols. New York, 1935. (Popular rather than scholarly.)

7 MAYNARD, Theodore. *The Story of American Catholicism.* New York, 1949. (Extensive bibliog. Emphasizes American characteristics, social and political matters.)

8 SHEA, John Dawson Gilmary. *A History of the Catholic Church Within the Limits of the United States.* 4 vols. New York, 1886–1892. (First complete history, still valuable.)

9 WAKIN, Edward, and Joseph F. SCHEUER. *The De-Romanization of the American Catholic Church.* New York, 1966. (A collection of addresses.)

10 WITTE, Raymond. *Twenty-five Years of Crusading; a History of the National Catholic Rural Life Conference.* Des Moines, 1948. (Effort to colonize and evangelize rural America.)

3. *Anti-Catholicism*

11 BARRY, Colman J. "Some Roots of American Nativism." *Cath Hist Rev,* XLIV (1958), 137–146. (Motives basically religious.)

12 BILLINGTON, Ray Allen. *The Protestant Crusade, 1800–1860.* New York, 1938. (Charge of Catholicism as incompatible with American patriotism.)†

13 BILLINGTON, Ray Allen. "Tentative Bibliography of Anti-Catholic Propaganda in the United States, 1800–1860." *Cath Hist Rev,* new ser., XII (1933), 492–513.

14 HIGHAM, John. *Strangers in the Land: Patterns of American Nativism, 1860–1925.* New Brunswick, N.J., 1955. (Largely on American Protective Association and Ku Klux Klan.)†

15 KANE, John Joseph. *Catholic-Protestant Conflicts in America.* Chicago, 1955. (Bibliogs. Extensive analysis of American Catholics in social, economic, political life.)

1 KINZER, Donald Louis. *An Episode in Anti-Catholicism: the American Protective Association.* Seattle, 1964. (Recurring intimate connection between anti-Catholicism, politics, and the "patriotic" press.)

2 KNUTH, Helen. "The Climax of American Anglo-Saxonism, 1898–1905." (N W Univ.), 1958. *Univ Mic* (1958), no. 58–5763; *Diss Abs*, XIX (1958), 1355–1356. (Chap. V discusses anti-Catholic phase.)

3 SEWRY, Charles. "The Alleged 'Un-Americanism' of the Church as a Factor in Anti-Catholicism in the United States, 1860–1914." (Minn), 1955. *Univ Mic*, no. 13–793; *Diss Abs* (1956), XVI, 111. (Decline due to gradual Americanizing of Catholics.)

V. Eastern Orthodox Churches

1. General Histories

4 ATTWATER, Donald. *The Christian Churches of the East.* 2 vols. Milwaukee, 1947–1948. (Chap. VII in vol. II, "The Orthodox in America.")

5 BOGOLEPOV, Aleksandr Aleksandrovich. *Toward an American Orthodox Church; the Establishment of an Autocephalous Orthodox Church.* New York, 1963. (Development of branches of Orthodoxy in the U.S. in 20th century. Bibliog.)

6 DOROSH, John T., comp. *The Eastern Church; a Bibliography of Publications in the Roman Alphabet with Indication of Location.* Washington. Library of Congress, 1946. Typ., and microfilm no. 52,361. (Large section on the U.S.)

7 EMHARDT, William Chauncey. *The Eastern Church in the Western World.* Milwaukee and London, 1928. (American missions, history, divisions, beginning of adaptation.)

8 GRIGORIEFF, Dimitry. "The Historical Background of Orthodoxy in America," *St. Vlad Sem Q*, V, no. 1–2 (1961), 3–113. (Reviews history of Orthodoxy in America, and unity of the church. Valuable bibliog. footnotes.)

9 ROMANIDES, John. "The Orthodox: Arrival and Dialogue." In Kyle Haselden and Martin E. Marty, eds., *What's Ahead for the Churches?* New York, 1964, 156–169. (Stress on the absolute value of doctrine and tradition impedes renewal and growth.)

10 ROMANIDES, John. "Orthodoxy in America." Ed. by George Mantzarides. *Essays in Honor of Panagiotes K. Chrestou.* Thessalonike, Greece, 1967, pp. 501–516. (Indicates a change of attitude concerning the future of Orthodoxy.)

11 SCHMEMANN, A. "Problems of Orthodoxy in America: The Canonical Problem." *St. Vlad Sem Q*, 8 (1964), 67–85. (Major question of existence of many overlapping and confusing ecclesiastical jurisdictions.)

1 SCHMEMANN, A. "Problems of Orthodoxy in America: The Liturgical Problem." *St. Vlad Sem Q*, 8 (1964), 164–185. (Discussion of call for English in worship, involving its structure and vitality of symbolism.)

2 SCHMEMANN, A. "Problems of Orthodoxy in America: The Spiritual Problem." *St. Vlad Sem Q*, 9 (1965), 171–193. (Critical examination of inroads of secularism into orthodox parishes.)

3 SCHMEMANN, A. "The Task of Orthodox Theology in America Today." *St. Vlad Sem Q*, 10 (1966), 184. (Ecumenical commitment generally conceived as a mission to convert other churches to Orthodoxy.)

4 SCHNEIRLA, William S. "The Future of American Orthodoxy." *St. Vlad Sem Q*, V, no. 4 (1961), 24–42. (Reviews proposals for unity, relations with other Christians and with Orthodox churches abroad, etc.)

5 SHAW, Plato Ernest. *American Contacts with the Eastern Churches, 1820–1870*. Chicago, 1937. (Bibliog. Difficulties of Eastern churches in the U.S.; contacts with Anglicans.)

6 STYLIANOPOULOS, Theodore G. "The Orthodox Church in America." *Ann Am Acad Pol Soc Sci*, 387 (Jan., 1970), 41–48. (Gradual consolidation, fuller adaptation to environment, need for unity and liturgical renewal, sense of unique mission, internal tension about ecumenicity.)

7 TINCKOM-FERNANDEZ, W. G. "Eastern Orthodox Peoples and Churches in the United States." *Christendom*, IV (1939), 423–436. (Growing adaptation and unity in America.)

8 UPSON, Stephen H. R. *Orthodox Church History*. 2nd ed. Brooklyn, N.Y., 1954. (Section on national churches in North America.)

9 Work Projects Administration, Historical Records Survey, New York City. *Inventory of the Church Archives in New York City, Eastern Orthodox Churches and the Armenian Church in America*. New York, 1940. (History, organization, records, directory, chronology of churches, bibliog.)

2. National Churches

10 American Carpatho-Russian Youth Organization. *The Dawn of a New Day*. Johnstown, Pa., 1954. (General account of Carpatho-Russian Orthodox Church.) See also: *What Is the Orthodox Greek Catholic Church?* Johnstown, Pa., 1954; *American Carpatho-Russian Youth Annual*, vol. IX (1957).

11 BASANOFF, V. "Archives of the Russian Church in Alaska in the Library of Congress." *Pac Hist Rev*, II (1933), 79–84. (Since 1762, mostly 19th century.)

12 BENSIN, Basil M. *History of the Russian Orthodox Greek Catholic Church of North America*. New York, 1941. (Bibliog. Since 1794. Russian Orthodoxy in American social and cultural development.)

13 BILON, Peter. *Ukrainians and Their Church*. Johnstown, Pa., 1953. (Brief general history.)

1 BOLSHAKOFF, Serge. *The Foreign Missions of the Russian Orthodox Church*. London and New York, 1943. (Bibliog. Chap. IV has history in Western Hemisphere.)

2 HARDY, Edward Rochie, Jr. "The Russian Orthodox Church at Home and Abroad." *Christendom*, XI (1946), 153–164. (Growing autonomy of American churches since 1934.)

3 INKERSLEY, Arthur. "The Greek [i.e., Russian] Church on the Pacific." *Overland Mo*, XXVI (1895), 469–482. (Alaska and Pacific Coast since 1759.)

4 KALOUSTIAN, Shnork Vartabad. *An Outline of the History of the Armenian Church*. New York, 1953. (Section on the U.S.)

5 St. Sava Serbian Orthodox Monastery. *Spomenica of the Thirtieth Anniversary . . . and the Sixtieth Anniversary of the Serbian Orthodox Church in the United States and Canada*. Libertyville, Ill., 1953. (General and parish history.)

6 SALOUTOS, Theodore. *The Greeks in the United States*. Cambridge, Mass., 1964. (Large bibliog.; origin and history of Greek Orthodox Church.)

7 SCHRANK, Marvin Leonard James. "Problems of Orthodoxy in America: The Russian Church." *St. Vlad Sem Q*, VI, no. 4 (1962), 185–205. (Reviews historical background, problems caused by relations with church in Russia.)

VI. Sects and Cults

1. General Works

8 BACH, Marcus L. *Faith and My Friends*. Indianapolis, 1951. (By-paths of American cult religion.)

9 BRADEN, Charles Samuel. *These Also Believe; A Study of Modern American Cults and Minority Religious Movements*. New York, 1949. (Careful, scholarly; annotated bibliog.)

10 CLARK, Elmer Talmage. *The Small Sects in America*. Rev. and enl. ed. New York, 1949. (First study of numerous little-known bodies; bibliog.)†

11 DAVIES, Horton. *Christian Deviations: the Challenge of the New Spiritual Movements*. Philadelphia, 1965. (2nd rev. of his *Christian Deviations* (1954), rev. in 1961 as *The Challenge of the Sects*.)†

12 EDDY, C. Norman. "Store-Front Religion." *Rel Life*, XXVIII (1958–1959), 68–85. (Clear explanation of humble sectarian religion in socially disorganized areas of big cities.)

13 JAMISON, A. Leland. "Religions on the Christian Perimeter." *The Shaping of American Religion*. Ed. by James Ward Smith and A. Leland Jamison. ("Religion in American Life." Vol. I, pp. 162–231.)

1   KELLETT, Arnold. *Isms and Ologies; a Guide to Unorthodox and Non-Christian Beliefs.* New York, 1965. (Good especially for Jehovah's Witnesses, Mormons, Christian Science; brief directory, good bibliog.)

2   MARTIN, Walter Ralston. *The Kingdom of the Cults; an Analysis of the Major Cult Systems in the Present Christian Era.* London, Edinburgh, 1967. (Unfavorable, orthodox viewpoint, much valuable detail on history of cult religions.)

3   MATHISON, Richard R. *Faiths, Cults and Sects of America from Atheism to Zen.* Indianapolis, New York, 1960. (Interesting and useful comments. (Rev., with title *God Is a Millionaire*.)†

4   ROBERTSON, Archie. *The Old Time Religion.* Boston, 1950. (Journalistic account of sect and cult religion.)

5   TANIS, Edward J. *What the Sects Teach; Jehovah's Witnesses, Seventh-Day Adventists, Christian Science* [and] *Spiritism.* Grand Rapids, 1958. (Origins and beliefs.)†

6   TYLER, Alice Felt. *Freedom's Ferment; Phases of American Social History to 1860.* Minneapolis, 1944. (Insight into basic causes of sectarianism.)†

7   WHALEN, William Joseph. *Faiths for the Few; a Study of Minority Religions.* Milwaukee, 1963. (An astounding variety of proselyting faiths reveals unreality of considering the United States as a three-faith country. Valuable bibliog.)

8   YINGER, J. Milton. "Religion and Social Change: Functions and Dysfunctions of Sects and Cults among the Disprivileged." *Rev Rel Res,* IV (1963), 65–84, 129–148. (Cults in anomie of the disprivileged; standard religion adjusting privileged to pluralism and ecumenicity.)

2. Adventists

9   *Seventh-Day Adventist Encyclopedia.* Washington, 1966. (First alphabetical dictionary about beliefs, philosophies, organization, work, methods.)

10 SPALDING, Arthur Whitefield. *Origin and History of Seventh-Day Adventists.* Washington, 1961– . (Popular, illus. chronicle and explanation of significant events.)

11 UTT, Richard H. *A Century of Miracles.* Mountain View, Calif., 1963. (Growth and good works of dynamic, worldwide missionary movement.)

3. Christian Scientists

12 BEASLEY, Norman. *The Cross and the Crown: the History of Christian Science.* New York, 1952. (Non-Scientist depicts typically American religious movement.)

1 BRADEN, Charles Samuel. *Christian Science Today: Power, Policy, Practice.* Dallas, 1958. (Objective, analytical, full-length history.)

2 JOHN, DeWitt, and Erwin D. CANHAM. *The Christian Science Way of Life; with a Christian Scientist's Life.* Englewood Cliffs, N.J., 1962. (Defense, with constant references to life and thought of Mrs. Eddy.)

3 PEEL, Robert. *Christian Science: Its Encounter with American Culture.* Garden City, N.Y., 1965. (Philosophical influences impinging upon it, especially Transcendentalism.)

4 PFAUTZ, Harold W. "A Case Study of an Urban Religious Movement: Christian Science." *Contributions to Urban Sociology.* Ed. by Ernest W. Burgess and Donald J. Bogue. Chicago, 1964, pp. 284–303. (Role of social and mental unrest in cities as stimulant; development from cult to institution.)†

4. Holiness Groups

5 CHESHAM, Sallie. *Born to Battle; the Salvation Army in America.* Chicago, 1965. (Detailed illus. narrative of the Army's work since 1879.)

6 CLEAR, Val. "The Church of God: A Study in Social Adaptation." *Rev Rel Res,* II (1961), 129–133. (Tendency of sect to conform to standard Protestant pattern.)

7 HOLT, John B. "Holiness Religion: Cultural Shock and Social Reorganiza-tion." *Am Socio Rev,* V (1940), 740–747. (Southern sects trying to recapture social security by revivalism and reform.)

8 PETERS, John Leland. *Christian Perfection and American Methodism.* New York, 1956. (Emergence of Holiness movement from Wesleyan doctrine of perfection.)

9 SMITH, Timothy Lawrence. *Called unto Holiness; the Story of the Nazarenes: The Formative Years.* Kansas City, Mo., 1962. (Documented, stressing derivation from John Wesley's ideal of Christian perfection.)

5. Jehovah's Witnesses

10 BRAM, Joseph. "Jehovah's Witnesses and the Values of American Culture." *Tran N Y Acad Sci,* XIX (1956), 47–54. (The movement as "nativist" protest against strangeness and complexity.)

11 COHN, Werner. "Jehovah's Witnesses as a Proletarian Movement." *Am Sch,* XXIV (1955), 281–289. (Explores social sources.)

12 COLE, Marley. *Triumphant Kingdom.* New York, 1957. (Sympathetic effort to defend.)

13 MARTIN, Walter Ralston, and Norman H. KLANN. *Jehovah of the Watchtower; a Thorough Exposé of the Important Anti-Biblical Teachings of Jehovah's Witnesses.* Rev. and enl. ed. Grand Rapids, 1956. (Typical hostile criticism, with bibliog.)

1 STROUP, Herbert Hewitt. *The Jehovah's Witnesses.* New York, 1967. (Reviews history, organization, relations with American society.)

2 WHALEN, William Joseph. *Armageddon Around the Corner; a Report on Jehovah's Witnesses.* New York, 1962. (Roman Catholic layman's objective analysis, suggesting transformation into a Protestant denomination.)

3 WHITE, Timothy. *A People for His Name: A History of Jehovah's Witnesses and an Evaluation.* New York, 1968. (By a member, scholarly, based on sources; development in terms of leaders, schismatic groups.)

6. Mormons

4 ANDERSON, Nels. *Desert Saints: the Mormon Frontier in Utah.* Chicago, 1966. (Mormon's sociological analysis of a cooperative religious community.)†

5 ARRINGTON, Leonard J. *Great Basin Kingdom. An Economic History of the Latter-Day Saints, 1830–1900.* Cambridge, Mass., 1958. (Concern of church leaders for material welfare and economic development.)†

6 BACKMAN, Milton Vaughn. *American Religions and the Rise of Mormonism.* Salt Lake City, 1965. (General review of history and beliefs, with many refs. and good bibliog.)

7 DePILLIS, Mario S. "The Quest for Religious Authority and the Rise of Mormonism." *Dialogue: a Journal of Mormon Thought,* I (1966), 68–88. (Roman Catholic appreciation of effort to overcome socially divisive sectarianism.)

8 DePILLIS, Mario S. "The Social Sources of Mormonism." *Church Hist,* XXXVII (1968), 50–79. (Attributes origin to disorientation of values associated with migration to frontier areas.)

9 ERICKSEN, Ephraim E. *The Psychological and Ethical Aspects of Mormon Group Life.* Chicago, 1922. (Classic account.)

10 FIFE, Austin E., and Alta FIFE. *Saints of Sage & Saddle; Folklore Among the Mormons.* Bloomington, Ind., 1956. (Derived largely from hundreds of interviews, including words and melodies of songs.)

11 HILL, Marvin S. "The Historiography of Mormonism." *Church Hist,* XXVIII (1959), 418–426. (Critical review, deplores too little interpretation.)

12 HOWELLS, Rulon Stanley. *The Mormon Story; a Pictorial Account of Mormonism.* 11th ed. Salt Lake City, 1963. (Heavy stress upon contemporary religious and social activities.)

13 MUELDER, William. *Homeward to Zion.* Minneapolis, 1957. (Mormon immigration from Scandinavia, and Americanization.)

14 MUELDER, William. *The Mormons in American History.* Salt Lake City, 1957. (Mormonism "a dynamic reworking of the diverse elements of American culture.")

1 NELSON, Lowry. *The Mormon Village: A Pattern and Technique of Land Settlement.* Salt Lake City, 1952. (Intense religious motivation as cause of success in farm village. Bibliog.)

2 ROBERTS, Brigham H. *A Comprehensive History of the Church of Jesus Christ of Latter-Day Saints.* 6 vols. Salt Lake City, 1930. ("Official" account, rich in detail from archives.)

3 TURNER, Wallace. *The Mormon Establishment.* Boston, 1966. (Strains caused by pressures of modernity, doctrine of Negro inferiority, political prestige, relations to "rightist" movements.)

4 VETTERLI, Richard. *Mormonism, Americanism, and Politics.* Salt Lake City, 1961. (Defensive, emphasizing economic and political reasons for mob persecution, religious basis of Mormon social policy.)

5 WHALEN, William Joseph. *The Latter-Day Saints in the Modern Day World; an Account of Contemporary Mormonism.* New York, 1964. (Appraisal of the faith's prospects of survival under modern conditions.)†

7. Moral Rearmament

6 CLARK, Walter H. *The Oxford Group, Its History and Significance.* New York, 1951. (Thorough analysis.)

7 EISTER, Allan W. *Drawing-Room Conversion: A Sociological Account of the Oxford Group Movement.* Durham, N.C., 1950. (Analysis of basic motives, of character as sect and cult.)

8 HOWARD, Peter. *Frank Buchman's Secret.* London, 1961. (Appreciation of controversial American leader, technique for meliorating world by morally changing people.)

9 LUNN, Sir Arnold. *Enigma: A Study of Moral Rearmament.* London, 1957. (Thorough.)

10 WILLIAMSON, Geoffrey. *Inside Buchmanism.* New York, 1954. (One of the best accounts, from personal experience.)

8. Penitentes

11 HENDERSON, Alice (Corbin). *Brothers of Light; the Penitentes of the Southwest.* Chicago, 1962. (Colorfully written, illus. description of primitive flagellants.)

12 TATE, Bill. *The Penitentes of the Sangre de Cristos: An American Tragedy.* 2nd ed. Truchas, N.M., 1967. (Artist and writer describes Spanish-American group who re-enact Christ's passion.)

9. Pentecostal Churches

13 BRUMBACK, Carl. *Suddenly . . . From Heaven; a History of the Assemblies of God.* Springfield, Mo., 1961. (American Pentecostal movement, revolt against formality.)

1 CONN, Charles W. *Like a Mighty Army Moves the Church of God.* Cleveland, Tenn., 1955. (Best history and defense.)

2 GROMACKI, Robert Glenn. *The Modern Tongues Movement.* Philadelphia, 1967. (Unfavorably critical, with notes on origins, rise and progress of Pentecostalism in the U.S.)

3 HORTON, Wade H., ed. *The Glossolalia Phenomenon.* Cleveland, Tenn., 1966. (Notes on rise and history of movement in the U.S. since 1800; favorable essays, large bibliog.)

4 KELSEY, Morton T. *Tongue Speaking. An Experiment in Spiritual Experience.* Garden City, N.Y., 1964. (Penetration of "mainline" churches; impartial, effort to explain, with large bibliog.)†

5 KENDRICK, Klaude. "The History of the Modern Pentecostal Movement." (Tex), 1959. *Univ Mic* (1959), no. 59–6,715. *Diss Abs,* XX (1960), 2776. (Detailed account of American churches from origin in 1901; growing importance.)

6 NICHOL, John Thomas. "Pentecostalism: A Descriptive History of the Origin, Growth, and Message of a Twentieth Century Religious Movement." (Bos), 1965. *Univ Mic* (1965), no. 65–11,223. *Diss Abs,* XXVI (1965), 2713–2714. (American origin emphasized, exhaustive bibliog.; growing importance.)

7 SHERRILL, John L. *They Speak With Other Tongues.* New York, 1964. (Mostly a vivid narrative of personal experience in the "Pentecostal revolution.")†

8 WINEHOUSE, Irwin. *The Assemblies of God, A Popular Survey.* New York, 1959. (First authentic and comprehensive account of largest Pentecostal group.)

9 WOOD, William W. *Culture and Personality Aspects of the Pentecostal Holiness Religion.* The Hague, 1965. (Analysis of communities in the South, to determine what kind of people are Pentecostals and why.)

10. Quakers

10 BRONNER, Edwin B., ed. *American Quakers Today.* Philadelphia, 1966. (Essayists review historical divisions, trends toward greater unity, contributions to social and religious life.)

11 DOHERTY, Robert W. *The Hicksite Separation; a Sociological Analysis of Religious Schism in Early Nineteenth Century America.* New Brunswick, N.J., 1967. (Quakerism as a social institution, tables showing social position of Orthodox and Hicksites.)

12 JACOB, Caroline N. *Builders of the Quaker Road.* Chicago, 1953. (Eminent American leaders.)

13 JAMES, Sydney V. *A People Among Peoples; Quaker Benevolence in Eighteenth-Century America.* Cambridge, 1963. (Conscience shatters sectarianism to meet social needs through cooperative action.)

1   JORNS, Auguste. *The Quakers as Pioneers in Social Work.* New York, 1931. (Practical application of ideals of Woolman and other social Quakers.)

2   TOLLES, Frederick B. *Meeting House and Counting House; The Quaker Merchants of Colonial Philadelphia.* Chapel Hill, N.C., 1963. (Studies secularizing of religious pattern.)†

3   TOLLES, Frederick B. *Quakers and the Atlantic Culture.* New York, 1960. (Relations of Quakerism to politics, economics, science, art, revivalism, culture of Pennsylvania.)

4   TRUEBLOOD, David Elton. *The People Called Quakers.* New Yorki 1966. (Philosophical account of the Quaker *way of life* as experiment in radical Christianity.)

5   WEST, Jessamyn, ed. *The Quaker Reader.* New York, 1962. (Anthology of writings by Quakers, including Americans, with chronology.)

6   WILLIAMS, Walter Rollin. *The Rich Heritage of Quakerism.* Grand Rapids, 1962. (Detailed general history, stressing biographies, many forms of social ministry.)

11. Shakers

7   ANDREWS, Edward Deming. *The People Called Shakers; a Search for the Perfect Society.* New enl. ed. New York, 1963. (Authoritative, on the longest-lived American experiment in religious socialism.)†

8   MELCHER, Marguerite Fellows. *The Shaker Adventure.* Princeton and London, 1941. (Comprehensive, with sources and list of societies.)†

12. Successful Living Cults

9   DILLETT, James. *The Story of Unity.* Lee's Summit, 1954. (General history.)

10   GORDON, Arthur. *Norman Vincent Peale; Minister to Millions, a Biography.* Englewood Cliffs, N.J., 1958. (Serious study of appeal and influence.)

11   GRISWOLD, Alfred Whitney. "New Thought: A Cult of Success." *Am J Socio,* XL (1934), 309–318. (Metropolitan religion, flourishing especially in 1890–1915; bibliog.)

12   MEYER, Donald B. *The Positive Thinkers, a Study of the American Quest for Health, Wealth and Personal Power from Mary Baker Eddy to Norman Vincent Peale.* Garden City, N.Y., 1965. (Skeptical review of religiously-oriented "success cults.")

13   OATES, Wayne E. "The Cult of Reassurance." *Rel Life,* XXIV (1954–1955), 72–82. (Criticism of "Pealeism" as making religion only a "useful" means to an end.)

1 TEENER, James Woodruff. *Unity School tf Christianity.* Chicago, 1942. (Lithoprinted summary, with bibliog. footnotes. is Htory and discussion of theology.)

VII. German Sects

2 AURAND, A. Monroe, Jr. *Historical Account of the Ephrata Cloister and the Seventh Day Baptist Society.* Harrisburg, Pa., 1940. (Illus. ed.)

3 EISENBACH, George John. *Pietism and the Russian Germans in the United States.* Berne, Ind., 1948. (Typical expression of German sectarian religiosity. Bibliog.)

4 SACHSE, Julius Friedrich. *The German Pietists of Provincial Pennsylvania, 1694–1708.* Philadelphia, 1895. (Mystical groups.)

5 SACHSE, Julius Friedrich. *The German Sectarians of Pennsylvania, 1708–1742, A Critical and Legendary History of the Ephrata Cloister and the Dunkers.* Philadelphia, 1899.

1. Brethren

6 BRUMBAUGH, Martin Grove. *A History of the German Baptist Brethren in Europe and America.* North Manchester, Ind., 1961. (Small church, from its origins in German Pietism.)

7 DURNBAUGH, Donald F., and L. W. SHULTZ. *A Brethren Bibliography, 1713–1963: Two Hundred Fifty Years of Brethren Literature.* Elgin, Ill., 1964.

8 DURNBAUGH, Donald F., comp. *The Brethren in Colonial America. A Source Book on the Transplantation and Development of the Church of the Brethren in the Eighteenth Century.* Elgin, Ill., 1967. (Original sources, mostly translated from German, a picture of sectarian spirituality.)

2. Hutterites

9 GROSS, Paul S. *The Hutterite Way: The Inside Story of the Life, Customs, Religion, and Traditions of the Hutterites.* Saskatoon, Can., 1965. (Including the U.S. A communal Christian group of German origin.)

10 HOSTETLER, John Andrew, and Gertrude Enders HUNTINGTON. *The Hutterites in North America.* New York, 1967. Bibliog.)

3. *Mennonites*

1 BENDER, Harold Stauffer. *Two Centuries of American Mennonite Literature . . . 1727–1928.* Goshen, Ind., 1929. (Classified, critical notes, index.)

2 DYCK, Cornelius J., ed. *An Introduction to Mennonite History; a Popular History of the Anabaptists and the Mennonites.* Scottdale, Pa., 1967. (History and doctrinal development since the 16th century, with much on the U.S.)

3 HOSTETLER, John Andrew. *Amish Society.* Baltimore, 1963. Rev. ed. 1968. (Intensive study of exclusive sect under pressure of modern technological and cultural changes.)

4 HOSTETLER, John Andrew. *Annotated Bibliography on the Amish. . . .* Scottdale, Pa., 1951. (Books, pamphlets, theses, articles, unpublished sources.)

5 KAUFFMAN, J. Howard. "Report on Mennonite Sociological Research." *Menn Q Rev,* XXXVII (1963), 126–131. (Valuable brief criticism, bibliog. of 37 doctoral theses, 1940's–1960's.)

6 *The Mennonite Encyclopedia, a Comprehensive Reference Work on the Anabaptist-Mennonite Movement.* 5 vols. Hillsboro, Kan., 1955–1959. (First such reference work in English.)

7 SCHREIBER, William Ildephonse. *Our Amish Neighbors.* Chicago, 1962. (Scholarly, personal report on way of life, without idealizing; drawings by Sybil Gould.)

8 SMITH, Charles Henry. *The Story of the Mennonites.* 4th ed. Newton, Kan., 1957. (Rev. and enl. by Cornelius Krahn. Much on the U.S. Bibliog.)

9 STORMS, Everek Richard. *History of the United Missionary Church.* Elkhart, Ind., 1958. (Detailed history of a Mennonite branch. Bibliog.)

10 WENGER, John Christian. *The Mennonite Church in America. Sometimes Called Old Mennonites.* Scottdale, Pa., 1966. (General sketch of origins and growth, with illus. Discussion of theology.)

4. *Moravians*

11 GOLLIN, Gillian Lindt. *Moravians in Two Worlds; a Study of Changing Communities.* New York, 1967. (Incl. detailed sociological study of a German Pietest community at Bethlehem, Pa.)

12 HAMILTON, John Taylor and Kenneth G. *History of the Moravian Church; the Renewed Unitas Fratrum, 1722–1957.* Bethlehem, Pa., 1967. (Updating of edition of 1900, very comprehensive and authoritative.)

VIII. Southern Religion

1 BAILEY, Kenneth Kyle. *Southern White Protestantism in the Twentieth Century*. New York, 1964. Bibliog. essay.)

2 BLACKWELL, Gordon W., et al. *Church and Community in the South*. Richmond, 1949. (Very complete survey of social and economic factors, digests of studies, large bibliog.)

3 EATON, Clement. *Freedom of Thought Struggle in the Old South*. Durham, N. C., 1940. (Decline of Jeffersonian religious liberalism, rise of conservative creed to bolster social system.)†

4 HILL, Samuel S., Jr. *Southern Churches in Crisis*. New York, 1967. (How traditional evangelical Protestantism can adapt to social and cultural changes.)

5 HIX, Clarence Eugene, Jr. "The Conflict Between Presbyterianism and Free Thought in the South, 1776–1838." (Chi), 1937. Abs. lithoprinted [Chicago] 1940. (Growing conservatism in politically and socially influential group.)

6 LA BARRE, Weston. *They Shall Take up Serpents; the Psychology of the Southern Snake-Handling Cult*. Minneapolis, 1961. (Elaborate inquiry into origins and meaning, religious characteristics of Southern "poor whites.")

7 POSEY, Walter Brownlow. *Religious Strife on the Southern Frontier*. Baton Rouge, 1965. (Competition for allegiance of new settlers, stress upon dissimilarities, lack of ecumenical feeling.)

8 PREECE, Harold, and Celia KRAFT. *Dew on Jordan*. New York, 1946. (Varieties of folk cults in Southern hill country.)

9 SONNE, Niels Henry. *Liberal Kentucky, 1780–1828*. Lexington, Ky., 1968. (Bibliog. Religious liberalism of Upper South, derived from Enlightenment and Jefferson.)

10 WEATHERFORD, Willis Duke, and Earl D. C. BREWER. *Life and Religion in Southern Appalachia*. New York, 1962. (Excellent survey of religious history, conditions, practices, attitudes, pp. 66–163.)†

11 WEAVER, R. M. "The Older Religiousness in the South." *Sew Rev*, LI (1953), 237–249. (Religion as conserving force, bulwark in a changing world.)

IX. Liberal Religion

12 CAUTHEN, Kenneth. *The Impact of American Religious Liberalism*. New York, 1962. (Closely examines general character and eight individual expressions of very varied movement.)

1 GILES, Charles Burke. "Benjamin Coleman: A Study of the Movement toward Reasonable Religion in the 17th Century." (Calif Los Ang), 1963. *Univ Mic* (1964), no. 64–4772. *Diss Abs*, XXIV (1964), 5356–5357. (Decline of dogmatic and rise of liberal, socially-oriented religion.)

2 HOWLETT, Duncan. *The Fourth American Faith.* New York, 1964. Rev. ed., 1968. (Explains a rational, inquiring religion, rooted in American liberalism.)†

3 KOCH, G. Adolf. *Republican Religion: The American Revolution and the Cult of Reason.* New York, 1964. (Period 1775–1810; first comprehensive treatment.)

1. Deism

4 ALDRIDGE, Alfred Owen. *Benjamin Franklin and Nature's God.* Durham, 1967. (A humanitarian rather than a theological Deist, exponent of 18th-century Enlightenment religion.)

5 CHRISTENSON, Merton A. "Deism in Joel Barlow's Early Work." *Am Lit*, XXVII (1956), 509–520. (His free religion, a gospel of "Progress" for the U.S.)

6 CLARK, Harry Hayden. "An Historical Interpretation of Thomas Paine's Religion." *Univ Calif Chron*, XXXV (1933), 56–87; and "Toward a Reinterpretation of Thomas Paine." *Am Lit*, V (1933), 133–145. (Influence of scientific Deism upon his social, economic, political thought.)

7 CLARK, Harry Hayden, ed. *Poems of Freneau.* New York, 1929. (Introduction has notes on his Deism and its influence in American verse.)†

8 HORNBERGER, Theodore. "Samuel Johnson (1696–1772) of Yale and King's College; a Note on the Relation of Science and Religion in Provincial America." *N Eng Q*, VIII (1935), 378–397. (On his Berkeleyan idealism and anti-Deism; no religion-science conflict.)

9 MORAIS, Herbert Montfort. *Deism in Eighteenth Century America.* New York and London, 1934. (Complete, scholarly study, 1713–1835, with sources.)

10 SCHANTZ, Bradford Torrey. "Ethan Allen's Religious Ideas." *J Rel*, XVIII (1938), 183–217. (Kinship with scientific Deists.)

11 SCHNEIDER, Herbert Wallace. "The Significance of Benjamin Franklin's Moral Philosophy." Vol. II of *Studies in the History of Ideas.* New York, 1935, pp. 291–312. (Reference to his Deistic ideas.)

2. Ethical Culture

12 *The Fiftieth Anniversary of the Ethical Movement, 1876–1926.* New York and London, 1926. (Founding, development, interpretation of American phase.)

1   JACOBS, Leo. *Three Types of Practical Ethical Movements of the Past Half Century*. New York, 1922. (Bibliog. Surveys of history.)

2   MEYERHARDT, M. W. "The Movement for Ethical Culture at Home and Abroad." *Am J Rel Psycho Educ*, III (1908), 71–153. (Surveys founding and first 30 years, social and school work.)

3   NEUMANN, Henry. *Spokesmen for Ethical Religion*. Boston, 1951. (Best recent account, for 75th anniversary of New York society.)

3. Free Thought

4   Free Religious Association. *Free Religion. Report of Addresses at a Meeting . . . to Consider the Conditions, Wants, and Prospects of Free Religion in America*. Boston, 1867. (Comprehensive gathering, illustrating various liberal forces.)

5   Free Religious Periodicals. *The Index, A Weekly Paper Devoted to Free Religion*. Toledo, Ohio, 1870–1886. (Varying titles.) *Radical Religion*, 1936–1940, became *Christianity and Society*, 1940–1956. New York, 1936–1956. (Pub. by the Fellowship of Socialist Christians.)

6   MacDONALD, George E. H. *Fifty Years of Free-Thought; Being the Story of the Truth Seeker*. 2 vols. New York, 1929–1931. (Story of a magazine, 1875–1925.)

7   MARTY, Martin E. *The Infidel: Freethought and American Religion*. Cleveland and New York, 1961. (Protestantism has become so secularized that the "infidel" no longer has a cause.)†

8   PERSONS, Stow. *Free Religion, an American Faith*. New Haven, 1947. (Stresses influence for socially-aware religion.)†

9   POST, Albert. *Popular Freethought in America, 1825–1850*. New York, 1943. (Concentrates on religious aspect, faith in reason.)

10   RILEY, Isaac Woodbridge. *Early Free-thinking Societies in America*. Repr. from *Har Theol Rev*, XI (1918). (Revolution to about 1830, battle between liberalism and orthodoxy.)

11   WARREN, Sidney. *American Freethought, 1860–1914*. New York, 1966. (Phases of attack upon dogmatic religion and religious counter-attack.)

4. Jefferson's Liberalism

12   FOOTE, Henry Wilder. *The Religion of Thomas Jefferson*. Boston, 1960. (Emphasizes part of his liberalism in securing religious freedom.)†

13   GOULD, W. D. "The Religious Opinions of Thomas Jefferson." *Miss Val Hist Rev*, XX (1933), 191–209. (General agreement with the Unitarians.)

14   KNOLE, George Harmon. "The Religious Ideas of Thomas Jefferson." *Miss Val Hist Rev*, XXX (1943), 187–204. (Belief in rational religion, near Deist position.)

1 KOCH, Adrienne. *The Philosophy of Thomas Jefferson.* New York, 1943. (Most thorough and equitable analysis of his religious opinions. Large bibliog.)†

5. Transcendentalism

2 CAMERON, Kenneth Walter. *Emerson the Essayist . . . and Selected Documents of New England Transcendentalism.* 2 vols. Raleigh, 1945. (Essential annotated bibliog. and source book.)

3 CHRISTY, Arthur Edward. *The Orient in American Transcendentalism; a Study of Emerson, Thoreau and Alcott.* New York, 1932. (Use of Oriental spirituality to refute rationalistic materialism.)

4 FROTHINGHAM, Octavius Brooks. *Transcendentalism in New England; a History.* New York, 1886. (First comprehensive history; religious and social gospel.)

5 GOHDES, Clarence Louis Frank. *The Periodicals of American Transcendentalism.* Durham, N. C., 1931. (Incl. 11, 1835–1886, with historical review.)

6 HOCHFIELD, George, ed. *Selected Writings of the American Transcendentalists.* New York, 1966. (Bibliog.)†

7 HUTCHISON, William R. *The Transcendentalist Ministers: Church Reform in the New England Renaissance.* New Haven, 1959. (Essentially a religious movement, important in literature, philosophy, social reform.)†

8 KRISHNAMACHARI, V. "Transcendentalism in America." *Cal Rev,* CXVI (1950), 10–27. (Discussion of the Hindu strain.)

9 LADU, Arthur J. "Channing and Transcendentalism." *Am Lit,* XI (1939), 129–137. (Discusses scholarly interpretations of his religion.)

10 LEIGHTON, Walter Leatherbee. *French Philosophers and New England Transcendentalism.* Charlottesville, Va., 1908. (Influence of French idealism, particularly Victor Cousin. Bibliog.)

11 MILLER, F. De Wolfe. *Christopher Pearse Cranch and his Caricatures of New England Transcendentalism.* Cambridge, Mass., 1951. (Rather eccentric character and behavior of adherents.)

12 MILLER, Perry, ed. *The Transcendentalists.* Cambridge, Mass., 1950. (Introductory remarks on Henry David Thoreau's association with Transcendentalism.)

13 POCHMANN, Henry August. *New England Transcendentalism and St. Louis Hegelianism; Phases in the History of American Idealism.* Philadelphia, 1948. (Both groups opposed to naturalism and materialism.)

14 QUINN, Patrick F. "Emerson and Mysticism." *Am Lit,* XXI (1950), 397–414. (His "practical" mysticism, a religion of daily life and conduct.)

15 SHEPARD, Odell. *Pedlar's Progress. The Life of Bronson Alcott.* Boston, 1937. (Transcendentalism as religion and philosophy of social reform.)

1 SMITH, Hilrie Shelton. "Was Theodore Parker a Transcendentalist?" *N Eng Q*, XXIII (1950), 351–364.

2 VOGEL, Stanley Morton. *German Literary Influences on the American Transcendentalists*. New Haven, 1955. (Bibliogs. Infiltration of German philosophical and religious idealism.)

3 WARREN, Austin. "The Concord School of Philosophy." *N Eng Q*, II (1929), 199–233. (Brief bright history of symposium of two schools of idealism.)

4 WELLEK, René. "The Minor Transcendentalists and German Philosophy," and "Emerson and German Philosophy." *N Eng Q*, XV (1942), 652–680; XVI (1943), 41–62. (Confirmation of non-materialist views already rooted in their American thought.)

5 WELLS, Ronald Vale. *Three Christian Transcendentalists: James Marsh, Caleb Sprague Henry, Frederic Henry Hedge*. New York, 1943. (Bibliog. incl. letters. Defense of "reasonable" and personal religion.)

6 WHICHER, George Frisbie, ed. *The Transcendentalist Revolt Against Materialism*. Rev. by Gail Kennedy. Lexington, Mass., 1968. (Emphasizes religious background and concern for "regenerated humanity.")†

6. Unitarians and Universalists (now merged)

7 ADAMS, John Coleman. *Hosea Ballou and the Gospel Renaissance of the Nineteenth Century*. Boston and Chicago, 1903. (Universalist influence upon American 19th-century religious thought.)

8 AKERS, Charles W. *Called unto Liberty; a Life of Jonathan Mayhew, 1720–1766*. Cambridge, Mass., 1964. (Colonial pioneer of Unitarianism, gave religious sanction to ideals of political liberty.)

9 BROWN, Arthur W. *William Ellery Channing*. New York, 1962. (Considers him as central figure in 19th-century crusades for liberty and human rights.)†

10 CHEETHAM, Henry H. *Unitarianism and Universalism: an Illustrated History*. Boston, 1962. (Brief review of history, principles, accomplishments of two movements and their union.)

11 COLE, Alfred Storer. *Our Liberal Heritage*. Boston, 1951. (Humanistic orientation of modern Universalism.)

12 COMMAGER, Henry Steele. *Theodore Parker: Yankee Crusader*. Boston, 1947. (Promoter of liberalized and socialized American religion. Large bibliog.)†

13 CROMPTON, Arnold. *Unitarianism on the Pacific Coast: The First Sixty Years*. Boston, 1957. (Mostly from original records.)

14 EDDY, Richard. *Universalism in America, A History*. 2 vols. Boston, 1884–1886. (Only really adequate, complete account. Exhaustive bibliog.)

15 ELIOT, Samuel Atkins, ed. *Heralds of a Liberal Faith. . . .* 4 vols. Boston, 1910–1952. (Lives of over 500 ministers since about 1750; bibliogs. of writings.)

1 FROTHINGHAM, Octavius Brooks. *Boston Unitarianism, 1820–1850; a Study of the Life and Work of Nathaniel Langdon Frothingham.* New York, 1890. (Charming picture of "religion of unadorned good sense.")

2 LYTTLE, Charles H. *Freedom Moves West: a History of the Western Unitarian Conference, 1852–1952.* Boston, 1952. (Emergence of more radical views, incl. religious humanism. Bibliog.)

3 SCOTT, Clinton Lee. *These Live Tomorrow: Twenty Unitarian Universalist Biographies.* Boston, 1964. (Popular lives of leaders of American liberal Christianity since the 18th century.)

4 SKINNER, Clarence Russell, and Alfred Storer COLE. *Hell's Ramparts Fell, the Life of John Murray.* Boston, 1941. (Appreciation of America's apostle of universal salvation. Bibliog.)

5 WILBUR, Earl Morse. *A History of Unitarianism in Transylvania, England, and America.* Cambridge, Mass., 1952. (Massively documented, much bibliog. in notes.)

6 WRIGHT, Conrad. *The Beginnings of Unitarianism in America.* Boston, 1955. (Period 1735–1805, with biog. appendix and bibliog. note.)†

X. Judaism

1. Bibliography and Sources

7 BLAU, Joseph Leon, and Salo W. BARON, eds. *The Jews of the United States, 1790–1840.* 3 vols. New York and Philadelphia, 1963. (Collection of public and private papers.)

8 BLOCH, Joshua. *Of Making Many Books; an Annotated List of the Books Issued by the Jewish Publication Society of America, 1890–1952.* Philadelphia, 1954.

9 Hebrew Union College, Jewish Institute of Religion, Library. *Jewish Americana . . . a Supplement to A. S. M. Rosenbach, An American Jewish Bibliography.* Cincinnati, 1954.

10 KAGANOFF, Nathan M. "Judaica Americana." *Am Jew Hist Q.* LII (1962), 58–66. (Annotated bibliog. of literature since 1960, received in library of the Am Jew Hist Soc.)

11 KRESH, Paul, comp. *The American Judaism Reader; Essays, Fiction, and Poetry from the Pages of American Judaism.* London, New York, 1967. (Illustrates rich diversity of Jewish life; incl. reflections on contemporary religion, sometimes very critical.)

12 MARCUS, Jacob Rader, ed. *American Jewry Documents: Eighteenth Century.* Cincinnati and New York, 1959. (Religious life, participation in American community.)

13 RISCHIN, Moses. *An Inventory of American Jewish History.* Cambridge, Mass., 1954. (Bibliog. manual stressing Jewish contributions to cultural life.)†

1 ROSENBACH, Abraham Simon Wolf. *An American Jewish Bibliography.* . . . Baltimore, 1926. (Publications by or about Jews printed in the U.S. until 1850.)

2 SCHAPPES, Morris Urman. *A Documentary History of the Jews in the United States, 1654–1875.* New York, 1950. (159 documents, some on religious life, with comments and notations.)

2. General Histories

3 BOROWITZ, Eugene B. "Jewish Theology Faces the 1970's." *Ann Am Acad Pol Soc Sci,* 387 (Jan., 1970), 22–29. (New theology not theoretical, interested in finding meaningful forms of *living* Judaism.)

4 DRESNER, Samuel H. *The Jew in American Life.* New York, 1963. (Jews in a "Christian" world, tending to be religious "by proxy.")

5 EDIDIN, Ben M. *Jewish Community Life in America.* New York, 1947. (Trend toward the "community" religious and secular center.)

6 FONER, Philip S. *The Jews in American History, 1654–1865.* New York, 1946. (Services of Jews to American causes; select bibliog.)

7 FRIEDMAN, Theodore, and Robert GORDIS, eds. *Jewish Life in America.* New York, 1956. (Essays on religious and secular movements, culture, interfaith relations, Zionism.)

8 GLAZER, Nathan. *American Judaism.* Chicago, 1957. (Concise, readable history from 1654, sociological and objective.)†

9 GOLDBERG, Israel. *The Jews in America, a History.* Cleveland, 1954. (Rise of conservative tendencies, Judaism as a religious culture.)

10 GORDIS, Robert, et al. "Special Tercentenary Issue—September, 1954." *Judaism,* III (1954), 293–510. (Critical appraisal of Judaism in American life over 300 years.)

11 HANDLIN, Oscar. *Adventure in Freedom: Three Hundred Years of Jewish Life in America.* New York, 1954. (Interprets main lines of development, reordering of communal life since 1920.)

12 HERTZ, Richard C. *The American Jew in Search of Himself; a Preface to Jewish Commitment.* New York, 1962. (Suggested answer to the often painful question: how can one be a real Jew in 20th-century America?)

13 JANOWSKY, Oscar Isaiah. *The American Jew, a Composite Portrait.* New York and London, 1942. (New type of community life in religious-secular centers; return to tradition. Bibliog.)

14 KAPLAN, Mordecai Menahem. *The Greater Judaism in the Making; a Study of the Modern Evolution of Judaism.* New York, 1960. (Creation of new American types of Judaism.)†

15 LEBESON, Anita Libman. *Pilgrim People.* New York, 1950. (Excellent. Highly varied bibliog. on many phases of American Judaism.)

1 LEVENTMAN, Seymour, and Judith R. KRAMER. *Children of the Gilded Ghetto: Conflict Resolutions of Three Generations of American Jews.* New Haven, 1961. (Analysis of "third generation," its Jewishness religiously rather than socially defined. Bibliog.)

2 LEVINGER, A. *Jewish Adventures in America: The Story of 300 Years of Jewish Life in the United States.* New York, 1955.

3 LIPTZIN, Solomon. *Generation of Decision; Jewish Rejuvenation in America.* New York, 1958. (Most recent developments with relation to American life.)

4 LURIE, Harry L. *A Heritage Affirmed: The Jewish Federation Movement in America.* Philadelphia, 1961. (Organization and participation in the community of religiously inspired philanthropy.)

5 MARCUS, Jacob Rader, ed. *Memoirs of American Jews, 1775–1865.* 3 vols. Philadelphia, 1955–1956. (New settlements; early efforts to organize.)

6 MENKUS, Belden, ed., assisted by Arthur Gilbert. *Meet the American Jew.* Nashville, 1963. (Jewish essayists explain American Jewish community to questioning Christians.)

7 PODHORETZ, N., et al. "Jewishness and the Younger Intellectuals: A Symposium." *Commentary,* XXXI (1961), 306–359. (Relation of Judaism to American life, assimilation or involvement in Jewish community, religious "revival.")

8 VOGEL, Manfred. "Some Reflections on the Jewish-Christian Dialogue in the Light of the Six-Day War." *Ann Am Acad Pol Soc Sci,* 387 (Jan., 1970), 96–108. (Lack of Christian understanding of Jews as political entity, no concept of Jewish religious nationhood.)

9 WAXMAN, Meyer. *American Judaism in the Light of History; Three Hundred Years.* Chicago, 1955. (Notes on degrees of assimilation. Judaism as a religious and cultural force.)

3. *Divisions*

A. *Conservative*

10 DAVIS, Moshe. *The Emergence of Conservative Judaism; the Historical School in 19th Century America.* Philadelphia, 1963. (Very complete story of a type trying to be loyal to tradition and adapted to American life.)

11 SKLARE, Marshall. *Conservative Judaism; an American Religious Movement.* Glencoe, Ill., 1955. (First complete study of a peculiarly American interpretation.)

12 WAXMAN, Mordecai, ed. *Tradition and Change; the Development of Conservative Judaism.* New York, 1958. (An American Jewish "middle way.")

B. *Orthodoxy*

1 BELKIN, Samuel. *Essays in Traditional Jewish Thought*. New York and Philadelphia, 1956. (Several chapters on preservation of Orthodoxy.)

2 NUSSENBAUM, Max Samuel. "Champion of Orthodox Judaism: A Biography of the Reverend Sabato Morais, LL.D." (Yeshiva), 1964. *Univ Mic* (1964), no. 64–9395. *Diss Abs*, XXV (1964), 1879. (Includes much history of American Orthodox Judaism.)

3 POLL, Solomon. *The Hasidic Community of Williamsburg*. New York, 1962. (Sociological study of an ultra-conservative Jewish community in New York City.)

4 TCHERIKOWER, Elias. "Jewish Immigrants to the United States, 1881–1900." *Yivo Ann Jew Soc Sci*, VI (1951), 157–176. (Problems in adapting East European Orthodoxy to American life.)

C. *Reconstruction*

5 KAPLAN, Mordecai Menaham. *The Future of the American Jew*. New York, 1948. (Social and psychological problem of living in two cultures.)

6 KAPLAN, Mordecai Menaham. *The Greater Judaism in the Making; a Study of the Modern Evolution of Judaism*. New York, 1960. (Reviews emergence of new American types.)

7 KAPLAN, Mordecai Menaham. *Judaism as a Civilization; Toward a Reconstruction of American-Jewish Life*. New York, 1967. (First published, 1934, inspired Reconstructionism; much on history and character of American Judaism.)†

D. *Reform*

8 GOLDBERG, Martin Lloyd. "Fluctuations Between Traditionalism and Liberalism in American Reform Judaism from 1855 to 1937." (Pitts), 1955. *Univ Mic* (1955), no. 13–866. *Diss Abs*, XV (1955), 1920–1921. (Explains various causes.)

9 HELLER, James Gutheim. *Isaac M. Wise: His Life, Work, and Thought*. New York, 1965. (Special emphasis upon his effort to adapt Judaism to life in the U.S.)

10 PHILIPSON, David. *The Reform Movement in Judaism*. New and rev. ed. New York, 1967. (The most authoritative work; long chapter on rise and accomplishments in U.S.)

11 RYBACK, Martin B. "The East-West Conflict in American Reform Judaism." *Am Jew Archiv*, IV (1952), 3–25. (Struggle between sectarian and liberalizing viewpoints.)

E. *Zionism*

12 MARCUS, Jacob Rader. "Zionism and the American Jew." *Am Sch*, II (1933), 279–292. (Various Jewish reactions to the movement.)

1 MEYER, Isadore S. *Early History of Zionism in America*. . . . New York, 1958. (Collection of essays, history to 1921, with bibliog. in notes.)

XI. Oriental Religions

2 BARROWS, John Henry, ed. *The World's Parliament of Religions*. 2 vols. Chicago, 1893. (Impact of representatives of Oriental faiths upon Americans.)

3 CHRISTY, Arthur Edward, ed. *The Asian Legacy and American Life*. New York, 1945. (Essays on cultural exchanges, rise of Eastern cults.)

4 JUDAH, J. Stillson. *The History and Philosophy of the Metaphysical Movements in America*. Philadelphia, 1967. (Rooted in anti-creedal, humanistic, pragmatic, optimistic and individualist features of native American liberal religion.)

5 KING, Winston L. "Eastern Religions: A New Interest and Influence." *Ann Am Acad Pol Soc Sci*, 387 (Jan., 1970), 66–76. (Interest mostly among scholars, most Americans find them too exotic to be relevant.)

6 "The Mission to America." *Rel Life*, XXVIII (1959), 323–364. (Reviews Asiatic religious penetration.)

1. Buddhism

7 AMES, Van Meter. *Zen and American Thought*. Honolulu, 1962. (Effort to find affinities to Zen Buddhism in American philosophers.)

8 KIRTHISINGHE, Buddhadasa P. "Buddhism in the United States." *Maha Bodhi*, LXXI (1963), 4–6. (History since 1905, rapid growth, appeal to Caucasians, wide influence of Shin sect and Zen, propaganda organs.)

9 KUBOSE, G. M. "American Buddhism." *Golden Lotus*, XX (1963), 225–227. (Non-sectarian adaptation to America.)

10 MURANO, Senchu. "Buddhism in the United States." *Golden Lotus*, XX (1963), 55–56. (Suggested emergence of new type of American Buddhism.)

11 ROGER, John. "Founders of American Buddhism." *Golden Lotus*, XVIII (1961), 127–128–XXIII (1966), 63–66. (Series of articles with various subtitles. 49 short essays, comprising history of Buddhism in the U.S., leaders, writings, sects, organizations, periodicals, work in colleges and universities.)

12 RUST, William C. "The Shin Sect of Buddhism in America: Its Antecedents, Beliefs, and Present Condition." (S Calif), 1951. (Illus.)

2. Hindu Cults

1 DEVAMATA, Sister. *Swami Paramananda and His Work*. La Crescenta, Calif., 1926. (American travels, founding of Ananda Ashrama.)

2 GOODSPEED, George Stephen. *The World's First Parliament of Religions*. Chicago, 1895. (Vedanta's friendly American hearing.)

3 GRISWOLD, Hervey DeWitt. *Insights into Modern Hinduism*. New York, 1934. (Hindu influence upon American Christian leaders.)

4 JACKSON, Carl Thomas. "The Swami in America: A History of the Ramakrishna Movement in the United States, 1893–1960." (Calif, Los Ang), 1964. *Univ Mic* (1964), no. 64–12,194. *Diss Abs*, XXV (1964), 3524–3525. (Influential beyond its numbers, affected indigenous American groups.)

5 PITT, Malcolm. *Introducing Hinduism*. New York, 1955. (Ramakrishna Mission and Vedanta in America; reading list.)†

6 SWAMI NIKHILANANDA. *Vivekananda, a Biography*. New York, 1953. (Stresses his role as Vedanta's American founder.)

7 THOMAS, Wendell Marshal. *Hinduism Invades America*. New York, 1930. (First thorough study of impact of Hindu philosophy and culture.)

8 Vedanta Society. *Hinduism Comes to America*. Chicago, 1933. (Forerunners, swamis, centers and leaders, progress.)

9 *With the Swamis in America*. By "A Western Disciple." Almora, India, 1938. (Acceptance of Vedanta as Christianized American version of Hindu thought.)

3. Islam (including Baha'i movement)

10 BACH, Marcus L. *They Have Found a Faith*. Indianapolis and New York, 1946. (Chap. VII, history of Baha'i movement in America from 1893.)

11 Baha'i Publishing Committee. *The Baha'i Community; a Summary of Its Foundation and Organization*. Wilmette, Ill., 1947.

12 BRADEN, Charles Samuel. "Islam in America." *Int Rev Miss*, XLVIII (1959), 309–317. (Ahmaddiya missionary movement since about 1925; Black Muslims, description of movement and publications.)

13 ELKHOLY, Abdo A. *The Arab Moslems in the United States; Religion and Assimilation*. New Haven, 1966. (History and analysis of communities in Detroit and Toledo. Bibliog.)

14 HITTI, Philip K. "America and the Arab Heritage," in N. A. Faris, ed. *The Arab Heritage*. Princeton, 1946. (Rise of Islamic settlement and studies in the U.S.)

15 NADIM AL-MAQDISSI. "The Muslims of America, 80,000 Muslims and 12 Mosques in the United States and Canada." *Isl Rev*, XLIII (1955), 28–31. (Outline history of American Islam from its origins.)

1 National Spiritual Assembly of the Baha'is of the United States and Canada. *The Baha'i Centenary*, 1844–1944. Wilmette, Ill., 1944. (Most comprehensive account of American movement.)

2 WEBB, [Muhammad] Alexander Russell. *Islam in America, a Brief Statement of Mohammedanism and an Outline of the American Islamic Propaganda.* New York, 1893. (American mission, organizations, publications by supposed first native convert.)

3 WOLF, C. Umhau. "Muslims in the American Mid-West." *Mus Wor*, L (1960), 39–48. (Lutheran pastor reviews Islam in the U.S. since start of immigration in 1860's.)

4. Theosophy and Spiritualism

4 BLAVATSKY, Helene Petrovna (Hahn-Hahn). *Personal Memoirs.* Comp. by Mary K. Neff. Wheaton, Ill., 1967. (Has material on history of spiritualism and theosophy in the U.S.)

5 BRITTEN, Emma Hardinge. *Modern American Spiritualism.* 4th ed. New York, 1870. (Most thorough early account partly from personal experience.)

6 DOYLE, Sir Arthur Conan. *The History of Spiritualism.* 2 vols. New York, 1926. (Extensive survey of the American movement.)

7 OLCOTT, Henry Steel. *Old Diary Leaves, the True Story of the Theosophical Society.* New York and London, 1895. ("Inside" story and defense of American movement.)

8 PODMORE, Frank. *Modern Spiritualism: A History and a Criticism.* 2 vols. London and New York, 1902. (Large section, "American Spiritualism," Vol. I, Book 2.)

9 SARMA, Dittakavi S. *Studies in the Renaissance of Hinduism in the Nineteenth and Twentieth Centuries.* Benares, 1944. (Excellent bibliog. on theosophy in the U.S.)

10 Theosophical Society. *The Theosophical Society, Its Nature and Objectives.* Point Loma, Calif., 1940. (Probably best account of modern American theosophy.)

11 United Lodge of Theosophists, New York. *The Theosophical Movement, 1875–1925, a History and a Survey.* New York, 1925. (Comprehensive. Controversies, divisions. Continued by *The Theosophical Movement, 1875–1950.* Los Angeles, 1951. Bibliog.)

XII. Indian Religion

1. Native Religion

12 ALEXANDER, Hartley Burr. "North American Mythology." Vol. 10 of *The Mythology of All Races.* Ed. by Louis Herbert Gray and George Foot Moore. New York, 1964. (By regions, much on religion; illus., large bibliog.)

1 BAILEY, Paul. *Wovoka, The Indian Messiah.* Los Angeles, 1957. (Paiute leader of messianic religious cult, doctrine, ghost dance. Illus., bibliog., notes.)

2 BURLAND, Cottie Arthur. *North American Indian Mythology.* London, 1966. (Popular. On beliefs and ceremonies. List of gods and spirits, bibliog., illus.)

3 EMERSON, Ellen Russell. *Indian Myths; or Legends, Traditions, and Symbols of the Aborigines of America.* Minneapolis, 1965. (Thorough on beliefs and rituals; many illus., large bibliog.)

4 LaBARRE, Weston. *The Peyote Cult.* New, enl. ed. Hamden, Conn., 1964. (Definitive study, with large bibliog. and comments on Peyote studies.)

5 MILLER, David Humphreys. *Ghost Dance.* New York, 1959. (Scholarly, from interviews and research; a last protest of nativism in religion. Bibliog.)

6 PARK, Willard Zerbe. *Shamanism in Western North America: A Study in Cultural Relationships.* Evanston and Chicago, 1938. (Sociological study of various tribes, religious healing. Bibliog.)

7 PARSONS, Elsie W. C. *Pueblo Indian Religion.* 2 vols. Chicago, 1939. (Religion controlling and regulating all of life—"instrumental." Illus., bibliog.)

8 SETON, Ernest Thompson, and Julia M. SETON, comps. *The Gospel of the Redman: A Way of Life.* Santa Fe, 1963. (Includes religion and spiritual life, prayers, myths, ethics.)

9 SLOTKIN, James S. *The Peyote Religion: A Study in Indian-White Relations.* Glencoe, Ill., 1956. (Documented exposition by a member, with large bibliog.; authoritative.)

2. Missions Among Indians

10 BEAVER, Robert Pierce. *Church, State, and the American Indians; Two and a Half Centuries of Partnership in Missions Between Protestant Churches and Government.* Saint Louis, 1966. (Very detailed, from 1640's to 1890's, showing joint efforts of government and missionaries to "civilize.")

11 BEAVER, Robert Pierce, ed. *Pioneers in Mission. The Early Missionary Ordination Sermons, Charges, and Instructions. A Source Book on the Rise of American Missions to the Heathen.* Grand Rapids, 1966. (Introd. and notes give much data on early Indian work; very large bibliog.)

12 BELVIN, Benjamin Franklin. *The Status of the American Indian Ministry.* Shawnee, Okla., 1949. (Protestant missions; selected bibliog.)

13 BERKHOFER, Robert Frederick, Jr. *Salvation and the Savage: An Analysis of Protestant Missions and American Indian Response, 1787–1862.* Lexington, Ky., 1965. (Ultimate failure due to white racism and persistence of aboriginal culture; bibliog. essay.)

14 FORREST, Earle R. *Missions and Pueblos of the Old Southwest.* 2 vols. Chicago, 1962. (Myths, legends, fiestas, ceremonies, dances; Penitentes; many illus.)

1   GRAY, Elma E., and Leslie ROBB. *Wilderness Christians: The Moravian Mission to the Delaware Indians.* Ithaca, 1956. (Scholarly, based on archives; Pennsylvania, Ohio, Michigan.)

2   HINMAN, George W. *The American Indian and Christian Missions.* New York, 1933. (Exhaustive discussion of policy and activity.)

3   HUMPHREYS, Mary Gay, ed. *Missionary Explorers Among the American Indians.* New York, 1913. (Lone Protestant pioneers, 18th and 19th centuries.)

4   JOHNSON, Margery Ruth. "The Mayhew Mission to the Indians, 1643–1806." (Clark), 1966. *Univ Mic* (1966), no. 66–11,757. *Diss Abs*, XXVII (1967), 2480A. (Successful effort to accommodate Indians to American and Christian life.)

5   KELLAWAY, William. *The New England Company, 1649–1776. Missionary Society to the American Indians.* New York, 1962. (First major organized effort for conversion; based on MSS.)

6   LINDQUIST, Gustavus E. E. *Indians in Transition; a Study of Protestant Missions to Indians in the United States.* New York, 1951. (Assessment of achievement and value.)

7   LOTH, John H. *Catholicism on the March: The California Missions.* New York, 1961. (Brief history to the 1830's, with bibliog. notes, bibliog., maps.)

8   MOFFETT, Thomas C. *The American Indian on the New Trail.* New York 1914. (Beginning of more "social" concept of missions.)

9   WEBER, Francis J. *A Historiographical Sketch of Pioneer Catholicism in the Californias: Missions and Missionaries.* Van Nuys, Calif., 1961. (Notes on missions to Indians, to 1840.)

XIII.   Negro Religion

1. General Histories

10   BRINK, W., and L. HARRIS. *The Negro Revolution in America.* New York, 1963. (Includes religious inspiration and aspects.)†

11   BURNHAM, Kenneth Edward. "Father Divine: A Case Study of Charismatic Leadership." (Penn), 1963. *Univ Mic* (1963), no. 63–7027. *Diss Abs*, XXIV (1963), 1737. (Insistence on racial equality and right and necessity to work.)

12   CAYTON, Horace R., and St. Clair DRAKE. *Black Metropolis: A Study of Negro Life in a Northern City.* New York, 1945. (Sociological study of religion, reference to classes.)†

13   FAUSET, Arthur Huff. *Black Gods of the Metropolis: Negro Religious Cults of the Urban North.* Philadelphia and London, 1944. (Satisfaction of emotional and social longings.)

14   Fisk University. *God Struck Me Dead, Religious Conversion Experiences and Autobiographies of Negro Ex-Slaves.* Nashville, 1945. (Integrating power of religious ecstasy.)

1 FRAZIER, Edward Franklin. *The Negro Church in America.* New York, 1964. (Traces evolution of religion in terms of social disorganization.)†

2 HARDING, Vincent. "The Religion of Black Power." *The Religious Situation: 1968.* Ed. by Donald R. Cutler. Boston, 1968, pp. 3–38. (With refs.)

3 HARRIS, Sara, and Harriet CRITTENDEN. *Father Divine: Holy Husband.* New York, 1953. (Analysis of motives for membership in the cult.)

4 HAYNES, Leonard L. *The Negro Community Within American Protestantism, 1619–1844.* Boston, 1953. (Best comprehensive review, with extensive bibliog.)

5 JOHNSTON, Ruby Funchess. *The Religion of Negro Protestants, Changing Religious Attitudes and Practices.* New York, 1956. (Considers factors in decline of traditional religion, rise of sects and cults, and need of more relation to life.)

6 JONES, Raymond J. *A Comparative Study of Religious Cult Behavior among Negroes.* Washington, 1939. (Sociological, with directory of cults and bibliog.)

7 LOESCHER, Frank S. *The Protestant Church and the Negro.* Philadelphia, 1948. (Acceptance of segregation, hopeful for more liberalism.)

8 MAYS, Benjamin, and Joseph NICHOLSON. *The Negro's Church.* New York, 1933. (First comprehensive contemporary study, considers forces that made the Negro church.)

9 MILLER, Robert Moats. "The Attitudes of American Protestantism Toward the Negro, 1919–1939." *J Neg Hist,* XLI (1956), 215–240. (Reviews policies of various denominations.)

10 MYRDAL, Gunnar. *An American Dilemma; the Negro Problem and Modern Democracy.* 2 vols. New York, 1944. Rev. ed., 1962. (Chap. XL, "The Negro Church." Analysis of religious life, class structure and religious organization.)†

11 PERKINS, Haven P. "Religion for Slaves: Difficulties and Methods." *Church Hist,* X (1941), 228–245. (Documented, mostly 1830–1850, religion as social control.)

12 PIPES, William H. *Say Amen, Brother! Old-Time Negro Preaching: A Study in American Frustration.* New York, 1951. (Relation of church and minister to democratic social ideals; annotated bibliog.)

13 RICHARDSON, Harry Van Buren. *Dark Glory, A Picture of the Church among Negroes in the Rural South.* New York, 1947. (First such study, depressing but with bright exceptions; bibliog.)

14 WASHINGTON, Joseph R., Jr. *Black Religion; the Negro and Christianity in the United States.* Boston, 1964. (Bibliog. in notes.)†

15 WEATHERFORD, Willis Duke. *American Churches and the Negro, an Historical Study from Early Slave Days to the Present.* Boston, 1957. (Documented study of white churches' evangelization.)

16 WILSON, Gold Refined: "The Religion of the American Negro Slave: His Attitude Toward Life and Death." *J Neg Hist,* VIII (1923), 41–71. (The Negro as a new type of primitive Christian.)

1 WOODSON, Carter G. *The History of the Negro Church.* 2nd ed. Washington, 1945. (First important work; incl. recent trends and cult leaders.)

2. Black Muslims. Religious Nationalism

2 BALDWIN, James. *The Fire Next Time.* New York, 1963. (Incl. Black Muslim movement.)†

3 BROTZ, Howard. *The Black Jews of Harlem.* London, 1964. (Association of Negro Judaism and Black Muslims with Negro nationalism; relation with white Jews.)

4 CONE, James H. "Black Consciousness and the Black Church: A Historical-Theological Interpretation." *Ann Am Acad Pol Soc Sci,* 387 (Jan., 1970), 49–55. ("Black Power" stresses liberation as a manifestation of God's work; blacks cannot accept a Christ not related to civil freedom.)

5 CONE, James H. *Black Theology and Black Power.* New York, 1969. (Such theology redefines all religious forms in the light of liberation of an oppressed people.)†

6 EHRMAN, Albert. "The Commandment Keepers: A Negro 'Jewish' Cult in America Today." *Judaism,* VIII (1959), 266–270. (Documented study of origins, growth, activities.)

7 ESSIEN-UDOM, E. U. *Black Nationalism.* Chicago, 1962. (Nigerian sees American Negro seeking identity in a national-religious movement.)†

8 LINCOLN, C. Eric. *The Black Muslims in America.* Boston, 1961. (Protest against discrimination, essentially of lower-class origin.)†

9 LOMAX, Louis E. *When the Word is Given; a Report on Elijah Muhammad, Malcolm X, and the Black Muslim World.* New York, 1964. (Depth study of anti-Christian religious protest against American Negro's lot.)†

10 PARENTI, Michael. "The Black Muslims: From Revolution to Institution." *Soc Res,* XXXI (1964), 175–194. (Millenarian, messianic and racist religious cult slowly adopts Puritan, middleclass American ethic.)

XIV. Ecumenical Movements

1. General Histories

11 BURKHART, Roy Abram. *How the Church Grows.* New York, 1947. (Recent aspects of community church movement.)

12 CAVERT, Samuel McCrea. *The American Churches in the Ecumenical Movement, 1900–1968.* New York, 1968. (Written by a leader, showing growth of coordination and leadership.)

1   CATE, William B. *The Ecumenical Scandal on Main Street.* New York, 1965. (Factors hindering religious unity in increasing urban culture; need for new ministry witnessing for justice.)

2   CROW, Paul A., Jr. *The Ecumenical Movement in Bibliographical Outline.* New York, 1965. (Many refs. to the U.S.)

3   DOUGLASS, Harlan Paul. *United Local Churches; an Interpretation Illustrated by Case Studies.* New York, 194 –   ? (With bibliog.)

4   FOSTER, Charles I. *An Errand of Mercy: The Evangelical United Front 1790–1837.* Chapel Hill, N.C., 1960. (Interdenominational cooperation in evangelism and philanthropy.)

5   GARRISON, Winfred Ernest. *Christian Unity and Disciples of Christ.* St. Louis, 1955. (Historical study; bibliog. of Disciples' books on unity.)

6   HUNT, George Laird, ed. *Where We Are in Church Union; a Report on the Present Accomplishments of the Consultation on Church Union.* New York, 1965. (Writers from several denominations review causes, history, motives, ideals, issues, problems of "C.O.C.U.")

7   Inter-Church Conference on Federation (New York, 1905). *Church Federation.* Ed. by Elias B. Sanford. New York and Chicago, 1906. (Surveys unity movement since 1867.)

8   KNAPP, Forrest Lamar. *Church Cooperation: Dead-end Street or Highway to Unity?* Garden City, N.Y., 1966. (Discusses progress and obstacles, attitudes, relation of councils of churches to ecumenicity and unity.)

9   LEE, Robert. *The Social Sources of Church Unity.* Nashville, 1960.

10 LOETSCHER, Lefferts A. "The Problem of Christian Unity in Early Nineteenth Century America." *Church Hist,* XXXII (1963), 3–16. (The "Evangelical Empire" of cooperation for missions and benevolence, counter to denominationalism.)

11 MODE, Peter George. "Aims and Methods of Contemporary Church-Union Movements in America." *Am J Theol,* XXIV (1920), 224–251. (Reviews unity and cooperative movements since 1801.)

12 National Council of Community Churches. *"That They All May Be One,"* A *Handbook of the Community Church Movement, Its Organization and Its Program.* Columbus, Ohio, 1948? (Recent development.)

13 National Council of the Churches of Christ in the U.S.A. *Christian Faith in Action, Commemorative Volume.* New York, 1951. (Outlines founding of the organization.)

14 OSBORN, Ronald E. *The Spirit of American Christianity.* New York, 1958. (Emphasizes similarities of denominations, trend towards unity.)†

15 SANDERSON, Ross W. *Church Cooperation in the U.S.: The Nationwide Backgrounds and Ecumenical Significance of State and Local Councils of Churches in Their Historical Perspectives.* New York, 1961.

1 SILLS, Horace S., ed. *Grassroots Ecumenicity; Case Studies in Local Church Consolidation.* Philadelphia, 1967. (Instances of unity in town and country churches across denominational lines.)†

2 WEINLICK, John Rudolf. *Count Zinzendorf.* Nashville, 1956. (An early Moravian promoter of ecumenicity in the U.S.)

3 WEST, William Garrett. *Barton Warren Stone: Early American Advocate of Christian Unity.* Nashville, 1954. (A founder of the Disciples, ardent advocate of sect-transcending faith.)

2. *Intergroup Relations*

4 BAKER, Newton Diehl; Carlton J. H. HAYES; and Roger Williams STRAUS, eds. *The American Way; a Study of Human Relations among Protestants, Catholics, and Jews.* Chicago and New York, 1936. (Tendency toward evolution of a general religious ethos.)

5 BISHOP, L. K. "Catholic-Protestant Relations in the United States." *J Hum Rel*, IX (1960), 29–47. (Evolution from hostility to purging of guilt in creative cooperation.)

6 CLINCHY, Everett Ross. *The Growth of Good Will: A Sketch of Protestant-Catholic-Jewish Relations.* New York, 1953.

7 ERSKINE, Hazel Gaudet. "The Polls: Religious Prejudice, Part I." *Pub Opin Q*, XXIX (1965), 486–496. (Period 1930's to 1960's; generalities, anti-Catholicism.)

8 GORDON, Albert I. *Intermarriage: Interfaith, Interracial, Interethnic.* Boston, 1964. (Interfaith marriages growing in pluralistic society; personal and official church attitudes.)†

9 HAGER, D. J. et al., eds. "Religious Conflict in the United States." *J Soc Issues*, XII, (1956), 1–66. (Social and psychological principles, value orientations.)

10 HERTZBERG, Arthur; Martin E. MARTY; and Joseph N. MOODY. *The Outbursts That Await Us, Three Essays on Religion and Culture in the United States.* New York, 1963. (Aims to increase mutual understanding between Protestants, Catholics, and Jews in religio-cultural areas.)

11 RAAB, Earl, ed. *Religious Conflict in America: Studies of the Problems Beyond Bigotry.* Garden City, N.Y., 1964. (Essays on tensions among four socio-religious groups.)†

12 SILCOX, Clarence Edwin. *Catholics, Jews and Protestants: A Study of Relationships in the United States and Canada.* New York and London, 1934. (Explores contrary forces making for isolation or cooperation.)

13 SMYLIE, James Hutchinson. "Phases in Protestant-Roman Catholic Relations in the United States." *Rel Life*, XXXIV (1965), 258–269. (History from colonial times, review of debates, present ecumenical dialogue.)

14 STARK, Rodney. "Through a Stained Glass Darkly: Reciprocal Protestant-Catholic Images in America." *Socio Anal*, XXV (1964), 159–166. (Data from church members on the West Coast, 25 points of variance, persistence of distrust.)

XV. Religion and Politics

1. General Histories

1 BARNES, Roswell P. *Under Orders: The Churches and Public Affairs.* Garden City, N.Y., 1961.

2 BELLAH, Robert N. "Civil Religion in America." *The Religious Situation, 1968.* Ed. by Donald R. Cutler. Boston, 1968, pp. 331–355. (Statement that "the relation between religion and politics in America has been singularly smooth.")

3 BODO, John R. *The Protestant Clergy and Public Issues, 1812–1848.* Princeton, 1954. (Activity regarding social and political questions.)

4 DERRIG, James Raymond. "The Political Thought of the Catholic Press, 1880 to 1920." (St. Louis), 1960. *Univ Mic* (1961), no. 61–746. *Diss Abs,* XXI (1961), 3504. (Social and political reform, satisfaction with church-state relations.)

5 EBERSOLE, Luke E. *Church Lobbying in the Nation's Capital.* New York, 1951. (Describes methods in politics.)

6 FARNHAM, Wallace D. "The 'Religious Issue' in American Politics: An Historical Commentary." *Queen's Q,* LXVIII (1961), 47–65. (Explanation of 1960 presidential election in terms of religion-politics question.)

7 FREEMAN, Donald McKinley. "Religion and Southern Politics: The Political Behavior of Southern White Protestants." (NC), 1964. *Univ Mic* (1965), no. 65–86. *Diss Abs,* XXV (1965), 5362–5363). (Sects less liberal than socially select churches. Baptists and sects more favorable to welfare state policies.)

8 FUCHS, Lawrence H. "The Religious Vote: When, Why and How Much." *Cath Wor,* CC (1965), 285–293. (Shifting and inconsistent pattern in presidential elections since mid-19th century.)

9 HADDEN, Jeffrey K. "Clergy Involvement in Civil Rights." *Ann Am Acad Pol Soc Sci,* 387 (Jan., 1970), 118–127. (Schism in churches due to confrontation between social justice clergy and resistant laity.)

10 HIGH, Stanley. *The Church in Politics.* New York and London, 1930. (Lobbying in the national capital, by an observer.)

11 JOHNSON, Benton. "Ascetic Protestantism and Political Preference." *Pub Opin Q,* XXVI (1962), 35–46. (Liberal and Fundamentalist groups have different political orientations; conviction often overcomes class.)

12 LaNOUE, George R. *Bibliography of Doctoral Dissertations Undertaken in American and Canadian Universities, 1940–1962, on Religion and Politics.* New York, 1963.

1 MARQUIS, Lucian C. "Religious Diffusion and Political Consensus in the United States." *Parl Aff*, XVII (1964), 200–206. (Political consensus based upon identity of religious and secular creeds.)

2 MEYER, Donald B. *Protestant Search for Political Realism, 1919–1941.* Berkeley and Los Angeles, 1960.

3 NASH, James Allen. "Church Lobbying in the Federal Government: A Comparative Study of Four Church Agencies in Washington." (Bos), 1967. *Univ Mic* (1967), no. 67–13,320. *Diss Abs*, XXVIII (1967), 1891A–1892A. (How church can be influential without legal establishment.)

4 ODEGARD, Peter H. *Pressure Politics: The Story of the Anti-Saloon League.* New York, 1967. (Best source on activities of a church-supported lobby.)

5 POPE, Liston. "Organized Religion and Pressure Groups." Vol. V of *Conference on Science, Philosophy and Religion, a Symposium.* New York, 1945, pp. 444–449. (Necessity of pressure to deal with supra-individual forces.)

6 RAMSEY, Paul. *Who Speaks For the Church?* Nashville, 1967. (Criticism of "liberal Protestant curia," as excluding dissent from the higher councils of religion.)†

7 ROUCEK, Joseph S. "American Ethnic and Religious Minorities in American Politics." *Politico*, XXIV (1959), 84–100. (Catholics, Jews, Zionists, religious group leaders.)

8 ROUCEK, Joseph S. "The Role of Religion in American Politics." *J Hum Rel.* XI (1963), 350–362. ("Church lobby" in Washington; disappearance of real distinction between church and world of politics.)

9 STEDMAN, Murray Salisbury, Jr. *Religion and Politics in America.* New York, 1964. (Consideration throughout American history, especially since 1945; churches as "interest groups.")†

10 WARD, Harry Frederick. "Organized Religion, the State, and the Economic Order." *Ann Am Acad Pol Soc Sci*, CCLVI (1948), 120–131. (Details methods of influencing public opinion.)

2. Religion and Democracy

11 BATES, Ernest Sutherland. *American Faith; Its Religious, Political, and Economic Foundations.* New York, 1957. (Radical Reformation sectarianism of lower classes as inspiration of democracy.)

11a DAVIES, Arthur Powell. *America's Real Religion.* Boston, 1965. (Secular ideal of democracy supported by religion.)†

12 GABRIEL, Ralph Henry. *The Course of American Democratic Thought, an Intellectual History Since 1815.* 2nd ed. New York, 1956. (Ties between democratic thought and democratic church elements.)

13 HANLEY, Thomas O'Brien. "Colonial Protestantism and the Rise of Democracy." *Am Eccles Rev*, CXLI (1959), 24–32. (Stress on ideological influence of Quakers, Baptists, Deism, Unitarians, revivalism.)

1   LERNER, Max. "Christian Culture and American Democracy." *Am Q*, VI (1954), 126–136. (Protestant church leadership opposition to conformism.)

2   NICHOLS, Roy F. *Religion and American Democracy*. Baton Rouge, La., 1959. ("Intimate wedding" of politics and religious affairs; influence of beliefs on statesmen and education. Bibliog.)

3   NIEBUHR, H. Richard. "The Protestant Movement and Democracy in the United States." Vol. I of *The Shaping of American Religion*. Ed. by James Ward Smith and A. Leland Jamison. Princeton, 1961, pp. 20–71.

4   NIEBUHR, Reinhold. "Christianity as a Basis for Democracy." *Univ Obs*, I (1947), 90–95. (American democracy kept from secular utopian fanaticism by Christian culture.)

5   PERRY, Ralph Barton. *Puritanism and Democracy*. New York, 1944. (Contribution of religious tradition to political thought of Revolutionary leaders.)

6   ROSSITER, Clinton. *Seedtime of the Republic*. New York, 1953. (Analysis of relation of sectarian religion to democratic aspiration.)†

7   SHIPTON, Clifford K. "Puritanism and Modern Democracy." *N Eng His Genea Reg*, CI (1947), 181–198. (Puritanism as "the bridge between medieval society and modern American democracy.")

8   SWEET, William Warren. *American Culture and Religion; Six Essays*. Dallas, 1951. (Roots of democracy in popular Protestantism, trend toward ecumenism.)

3. Religion and Nationalism

9   BELLAH, Robert N. "Civil Religion in America." *The Religious Situation: 1968*. . . . Ed. by Donald R. Cutler. Boston, 1968, pp. 331–393. (Refs., and commentary by other writers.)

10   BRAUER, Jerald C. "The Rule of the Saints in American Politics." *Church Hist*, XXVII (1958), 240–255. (Transformation of Puritan theocratic ideals into "Manifest Destiny." Bibliog.)

11   DOHEN, Dorothy Marie. *Nationalism and American Catholicism*. New York, 1967. (Danger that Catholicism, eager to be American, may become merely a social and patriotic function.)

12   DOHEN, Dorothy Marie. "The Social Functions of Nationalism and Religion in a Pluralist Society." (Fordham), 1966. *Univ Mic* (1966), no. 66–13,501. *Diss Abs*, XXVII (1966), 1937A–1938A. (Historical review of fusion of religious with national symbols.)

13   DRUCKER, Peter F. "Organized Religion and the American Creed." *Rev Pol*, XVIII (1956), 296–304. (Contrasts European hostile and American friendly concept regarding religion and the secular state.)

14   HUMPHREY, Edward Frank. *Nationalism and Religion in America, 1774–1789*. Boston, 1924. (Biblical origin of American ideals of religious and political liberty. Bibliog.)

1 MARSH, Daniel L. *Unto the Generations.* New Canaan, Conn., 1969? (A former president of Boston University lists documents of American history linked to the Bible.)

2 MARTY, Martin E. *The New Shape of American Religion.* New York, 1959. (Supports and illustrates Herberg's view of pluralistic national religion.)

3 MEAD, Sidney Earl. "From Denominationalism to Americanism." *J Rel,* XXXVI (1956), 1–16. (Tendency to identify generalized religion with Americanism. Bibliog. in notes.)

4 MILLER, William Lee. "The 'Religious Revival' and American Politics." *Confluence,* IV (1955), 44–56. (Danger of confusing spiritual values with secular nationalist ideals.)

5 NIEBUHR, Reinhold. *Pious and Secular America.* New York, 1958. (Conflict between religious and secular ideals of nationalism.)

6 THOMPSON, J. Earl, Jr. "A Perilous Experiment: New England Clergymen and American Destiny 1796–1826." (Princeton). *Univ Mic* (1966), no. 66–9645. *Diss Abs,* XXVII (1966), 1106A. (460 politico-religious sermons, stressing divine national mission of the U.S.)

7 WEISS, Benjamin. *God in American History: A Documentation of America's Religious Heritage.* Grand Rapids, 1966. (Popular faith in God, revealed in anthology of constitutional documents, presidential pronouncements, inscriptions, patriotic songs.)

8 WILLIAMS, Ray S. "The American National Covenant: 1730–1800." (Fla St), 1965. *Univ Mic* (1966), no. 66–5461. *Diss Abs,* XXVI (1966), 7302. (God-people convenant· idea helped give sense of purpose to American nation.)

4. Religion and the Presidents

9 BARRET, Patricia. *Religious Liberty and the American Presidency: A Study in Church-State Relations.* New York, 1963. (Candid discussion of unsettled question. Bibliog. of campaign literature.)

10 BOLLER, Paul F. *George Washington and Religion.* Dallas, 1963. (Contribution to religious liberty; letters, and addresses to religious organizations; large bibliog.)

11 BURNS, James McGregor. *John Kennedy: a Political Profile.* New York, 1959. (His religio-political ideals.)†

12 HAMPTON, Vernon Boyce. *Religious Background of the White House.* Boston, 1932. (Bibliog.)

13 HAMPTON, William Judson. *The Religion of the Presidents.* Somerville, N.J., 1925. (Brief essays; special notes on religion of Calvin Coolidge.)

14 HUTCHINSON, Paul. "The President's Religious Faith." *Life,* XXXVI (1954), 151–170. (Pietism translated into a religion of decency and democracy.)

1   ISELY, Bliss. *The Presidents: Men of Faith*. Boston, 1953. (Bibliog.)

2   KELLEY, Robert. "Presbyterianism, Jacksonianism, and Grover Cleveland." *Am Q*, XVIII (1966), 615–636. (Cleveland's religious heritage as motivating factor in his public career.)

3   SPEEL, Charles J., II. "Theological Concepts of Magistracy: a Study of Constantinus, Henry VIII, and John F. Kennedy." *Church Hist*, XXXII (1963), 130–149. (Kennedy's relation to church-and-state question in light of U.S. Constitution and character of presidential office.)

4   STORER, James Wilson. *These Historic Scriptures; Meditations upon the Bible Texts Used by our Presidents, from Lincoln to Truman, at Their Inaugurations*. Nashville, 1952. (Strengthening American people's idea of religious character of presidential office.)

5   WOLF, William J. *The Religion of Abraham Lincoln*. Rev. ed. New York, 1963. (Rev. of *The Almost Chosen People: A Study of the Religion of Abraham Lincoln*, 1959. (Lincoln's dynamic religion and its prophetic interpretation of American history.)

5. The "Catholic Question"

6   BARRET, Patricia. *Religious Liberty and the American Presidency: A Study in Church-State Relations*. New York, 1963. ("Catholic question" in election of 1960; extensive bibliog.; list of anti-Catholic propaganda.)

7   BLANSHARD, Paul. *American Freedom and Catholic Power*. Boston, 1958. (Can Catholicism be reconciled with a free culture? Controversial. Bibliog.)†

8   CUMMINS, Richard J., ed. *Catholic Responsibility in a Pluralistic Society*. Washington? 1961. (Controversial issues such as church-state relations, morals, education, with valuable bibliog.)

9   DULCE, Berton, Edward J. RICHTER. *Religion and the Presidency, a Recurring American Problem*. New York, 1962. (The "religious issue" in eight presidential elections; special emphasis on election of 1960; with bibliog. notes.)

10 GORMAN, Sister Mary Adele Francis. "Federation of Catholic Societies in the United States, 1870–1920." (Notre Dame), 1962. *Univ Mic* (1962), no. 62–2296. *Diss Abs*, XXIII (1962), 614. (Important because of effort to formulate Catholic public opinion and influence legislation.)

11 McMANAMIN, Francis G. "American Bishops and the American Electorate." *Am Eccles Rev*, CLI (1964), 217–229. (Examples of episcopal action in the U.S.)

12 ODEGARD, Peter H., ed. *Religion and Politics*. New Brunswick, N.J., 1960. (Collected essays and source documents, illustrating Catholic-Protestant issue in presidential campaigns.)

13 O'NEILL, James Milton. *Catholicism and American Freedom*. New York, 1952. (Reply to Paul Blanshard.)

14 SHIELDS, Currin V. *Democracy and Catholicism in America*. New York, 1958. (Argues that there is no incompatibility.)

1 SMYLIE, James Hutchinson. "The Roman Catholic Church, the State and Al Smith." *Church Hist*, XXIX (1960), 321–343. (Examines R. C. teaching on church and state for 30 years before election of 1928.)

6. Religion and the "Political Right"

2 CARLSON, John Roy. *Under Cover*. New York, 1943. (Father Coughlin as alleged Catholic "fascist" of the 1930's.)

3 DeSANTIS, Vincent P. "American Catholics and McCarthyism." *Cath Hist Rev*, LI (1965), 1–30. (Preponderance of pro-McCarthy sentiment due to isolationism, identified with Americanism and Catholicism.)

4 GUTERMAN, Norbert. "Portrait of the American Agitator." *Pub Opin Q*, XII (1948), 417–429. (Clear social-psychological analysis of "Christian-fascist" agitators.)

5 MASTERS, Nick Arthur. "Father Coughlin and Social Justice; a Case Study of a Social Movement." (Wis), 1956. *Univ Mic* (1956), no. 16,193; *Diss Abs*, XVI (1956), 987. (Bibliog.)

6 ROY, Ralph L. *Apostles of Discord*. Boston, 1953. (Gerald L. K. Smith as Protestant representative of "Christian fascism.")

7 SHENTON, James P. "The Coughlin Movement and the New Deal." *Pol Sci Q*, LXXIII (1958), 352–373. (Stresses division of opinion, Coughlin not able to "swing" whole Catholic vote.)

8 SWING, Raymond. *Forerunners of American Fascism*. New York, 1935. (Thorough study of religious fascist personality.)

9 TULL, Charles J. *Father Coughlin and the New Deal*. Syracuse, N.Y., 1965. (Scholarly analysis of reasons for failure of a priest to found a radical reform party.)

10 YOUNGER, George D. "Protestant Piety and the Right Wing." *Soc Act*, XVII (1951), 5–35. (Association between highly individualistic piety and extremely conservative politics and economics.)

7. Church and State. General History and Theory

11 ANTIEAU, Chester James; Phillip Mark CARROLL; and Thomas Carroll BURKE. *Religion under the State Constitutions*. Brooklyn, 1965. (Bibliog. refs. in footnotes.)

12 CARLSON, Carl Emanuel, and W. Barry GARRETT. *Religious Liberty; Case Studies in Current Church-State Issues*. Nashville, 1964. (Applying Baptist principles, but generally valuable from viewpoint of practical situations.)

13 COUGHLIN, Bernard John. "Church and State in Social Welfare." (Brandeis), 1963. *Univ Mic* (1964), no. 64–3088. *Diss Abs*, XXV (1964), 1386. (Relationship seems to portend historic changes in policy of separation.)

1 DIAMOND, Malcolm L. "Catholicism in America: The Emerging Dialogue." *Judaism*, IX (1960), 307–318. (Catholic doctrine shows signs of reinterpretation, accommodation to religious pluralism.)

2 DRINAN, Robert F. *Religion, the Courts, and Public Policy.* New York, 1963. (Review, Roman Catholic standpoint, of church-state relations, specifically in schools; Sunday legislation.)

3 FELLMAN, David. *Religion in American Public Law.* Boston, 1965. (Bibliog. footnotes.)

4 HOWE, Mark DeWolfe. *The Garden and the Wilderness. Religion and Government in American Constitutional History.* Chicago, 1965. (Lectures, questioning rightness of Supreme Court's exclusively political reading of the First Amendment.)†

5 HUEGLI, Albert George, ed. *Church and State under God.* Saint Louis, 1964. (Much on history of American "pattern" respecting religious liberty, education, chaplaincies, etc.)

6 HUSTON, Robert William. "Attitudes Toward Church and State Relationship of the Methodist Episcopal Church." (Bos), 1964. *Univ Mic* (1964), no. 64–11,131 *Diss Abs*, XXV (1964), 3139–3140. (Historical review, 1784–1939; statements and actions; no dogmatic theory of separation.)

7 KRINSKY, Fred, and Joseph BOSKIN, eds. *The Politics of Religion in America.* Beverly Hills, Calif., 1968. (Anthology of writings on church-state relations, Alexis de Tocqueville to Paul Blanshard.)†

8 KURLAND, Philip B. *Religion and the Law of Church and State and the Supreme Court.* Chicago, 1962. (Incl. bibliog.)

9 LOWELL, C. Stanley. *Embattled Wall; Americans United: An Idea and a Man.* Washington, 1966. (Detailed history of battles to defend "wall of separation.")

10 McALPIN, William Barr. "Presbyterians and the Relation of Church and State . . . 1789–1953." (Pitts), 1954. *Univ Mic* (1954), no. 7993; *Diss Abs*, XIV (1954), 1469–1470. (Covers very wide range of topics; from journal of General Assembly.)

11 MOEHLMAN, Conrad Henry. *The Wall of Separation Between Church and State; an Historical Study of Recent Criticism of the Religious Clause of the First Amendment.* Boston, 1951. (Uncompromising conservative and anti-Catholic attitude. Bibliog.)

12 MORGAN, Edmund Sears. *Roger Williams: The Church and the State.* New York, 1967. (Considered the best analysis of his thought on the subject; his stress on moral law.)†

13 MORGAN, Richard Ernest. "Backs to the Wall: A Study in the Contemporary Politics of Church and State." (Colo), 1967. *Univ Mic* (1967), no. 67–10,597. *Diss Abs*, XXVIII (1967), 743A. (The P.O.A.U. and its activity to preserve the "wall of separation.")

14 NORMAN, Edward R. *The Conscience of the State in North America.* Cambridge, Eng., 1968. (Comparison of the U.S. with Great Britain and Canada; alliance of religious dissent with radical constitutionalism.)

1 OAKS, Dallin H., ed. *The Wall Between Church and State*. Chicago, 1963. (Collection of papers representing variant views on problems, suggested solutions, ways of communication between groups.)†

2 PFEFFER, Leo. *Church, State, and Freedom*. Rev. ed. Boston, 1967. (Detailed history and consequences of experiment of "a free church in a free state;" numerous citations of decisions.)

3 POLIER, Shad. "Observations on Church-State Problems in America and the Interest of the American Jewish Community." *Jew J Socio*, I (1959), 69–79. (Judaism as beneficiary of separation, committed to it on many fronts.)

4 PRATT, John Webb. *Religion, Politics, and Diversity: The Church-State Theme in New York History*. Ithaca, N.Y., 1967. (Complete review from 1624, focussed on aid to Roman Catholic schools as a key issue.)

5 Protestants and Other Americans United for Separation of Church and State. *Studies in Church-state Relations: The American Way*. Washington, 1963. (Summary of historical background and present-day controversial issues; basic bibliog.)

6 "Recent Doctoral Dissertations in Church and State." *Church State*, VII (1965), 301–305. (See also other issues.)

7 REGAN, Richard J. *American Pluralism and the Catholic Conscience*. New York, 1963. (Tries to accommodate Catholicism in controversies raised by religious freedom and diversity.)

8 *Religion and the Public Order. An Annual Review of Church and State and of Religion, Law, and Society*. Ed. by Donald A. Giannella. Chicago, 1964– . (Broader ramifications of religion in law and society, objective review of events; no other such compilation.)

9 SHMIDMAN, Michael David. "Definitions of Religion, Religious Officials and Religious Activities in the Last Two Decades." (Colo), 1967. *Univ Mic* (1967), no. 67–9373. *Diss Abs*, XXVIII (1967), 745A–746A. (Special recognition and consideration accorded by government to religious institutions.)

10 STOKES, Anson Phelps. *Church and State in the United States*. 3 vols. New York, 1950. (Critical, selected bibliog.; first comprehensive treatment; arranged for "case study.")

11 TROUTMAN, William Fife, Jr. "Respecting the Establishment of Religion in Colonial America." (Duke), 1959. *Univ Mic* (1960), no. 60–475. *Diss Abs*, XX (1960), 3811–3812. (Variant attitudes toward church-state relations, important for future ideas and practice.)

12 WILCOX, William George. "New England Covenant Theology: Its English Precursors and Early American Exponents." (Duke), 1959. *Univ Mic* (1960), no. 60–1257. *Diss Abs*, XX (1960), 4195. (Close working relations between theoretically separated church and state, important in future U.S.)

13 WILSON, John Frederick. *Church and State in American History*. New York, 1965. (Primary and secondary accounts, colonial period to 1963.)†

8. Source Documents

1 McGRATH, J. J. *Church and State in American Law: Cases and Materials.* Milwaukee, 1962.

2 MOEHLMAN, Conrad Henry, comp. *The American Constitutions and Religion . . . a Sourcebook on Church and State in the United States.* Berne, Ind., 1938. (Massive compilation of constitutional provisions, federal and state laws.)

3 STOKES, Anson Phelps, and Leo PFEFFER. *Church and State in the United States.* Rev. one-volume ed. New York, 1964. (Source book, historical survey, interpretation of documents and events.)

4 TUSSMAN, Joseph. *The Supreme Court on Church and State.* New York, 1962. (Compilation of decisions relating to religion, 1815–1853.)†

5 WILSON, John Frederick, ed. *Church and State in American History.* Boston, 1965. (Brief, valuable selection of basic documents dealing with theory and practical, controversial issues.)†

6 ZOLLMAN, Carl Frederick Gustav. *American Church Law.* St. Paul, 1933. (Well-edited compilation, citing nearly 2,500 cases on many aspects.)

9. Religious Freedom

7 BLAU, Joseph Leon. *Cornerstones of Religious Freedom in America.* Rev. and enl. ed. New York, 1964. (Documentary sources, with comment and interpretation. Bibliog.)

8 CURRAN, Francis X. *Catholics in Colonial Law.* Chicago, 1963. (Example of former strict controls upon religious liberty.)

9 Fund for the Republic. *Religion and the Free Society.* New York, 1958. (Essays by writers of various faiths, stating problem of religion in a free society. Bibliog., and cases cited in notes.)

10 HOUGH, Richard Lee. "The Jehovah's Witnesses Cases in Retrospect." *W Pol Q,* VI (1953), 18–92. (Review of cases and philosophy of court decisions, 1938–1946; area and limits of freedom.)

11 Institute for Religious and Social Studies. Jewish Theological Seminary of America. *Well-springs of the American Spirit.* New York, 1964. (Essay considers Protestant and Jewish views of religious liberty.)

12 KATZ, Wilbur Griffith. *Religion and American Constitutions.* Evanston, Ill., 1964. (Bibliog. refs in "Notes," pp. 105–112.)

13 KIM, Richard Chong Chin. "Jehovah's Witnesses and the Supreme Court. An Examination of the Cases . . . 1938 to 1960." (Okla), 1963. *Univ Mic* (1963), no. 63–4896. *Diss Abs,* XXIV (1963), 371–372. (Witnesses bore brunt of securing religious liberty; bolstered Protestant ideal of supremacy of conscience.)

1 KONVITZ, M. R., ed. *First Amendment Freedoms: Selected Cases on Freedom of Religion, Speech, Press, Assembly.* Ithaca, N.Y., 1963.

2 MARNELL, William H. *The First Amendment; the History of Religious Freedom in America.* Garden City, N.Y., 1964. (Amendment an effort to preserve diversity of a religious tradition, spiritual although not legal support of government.)†

3 PFEFFER, Leo. *Creeds in Competition; a Creative Force in American Culture.* New York, 1958. (Diversity of belief as motive to richer cultural pluralism.)

4 ROTNEM, Victor W., and F. G. FOLSOM, Jr. "Recent Restrictions upon Religious Liberty." *Am Pol Sci Rev*, XXXVI (1942), 1053–1068. (Members of U.S. Dept. of Justice define restraint, citing many cases.)

5 SHRIVER, George H., ed. *American Religious Heretics; Formal and Informal Trials.* Nashville, 1966. (Protestant heresy trials, 1880–1905; conservative-liberal clash; issue of academic freedom.)

6 THORNING, Francis Joseph. *Religious Liberty in Transition; a Study of the Removal of Constitutional Limitations.* Washington, 1931. (Traces in detail the process in the states, 1789–1833. Bibliog.)

7 TORPEY, William George. *Judicial Doctrines of Religious Rights in America.* Chapel Hill, 1948. (Historical analysis, part of judiciary in defining rights. Bibliog.)

10. Religion in Wars

8 ABRAMS, Ray H. "The Churches and the Clergy in World War II." *Ann Am Acad Pol Soc Sci*, CCLVI (1948), 110–119. (Pacifism and neutrality yielding to belligerency in a "holy war.")

9 ABRAMS, Ray H. *Preachers Present Arms.* New York, 1933. (Sharply critical of clergy's part in World War I.)

10 BALDWIN, Alice Mary. *The New England Clergy and the American Revolution.* New York, 1958. (Discusses ideals of constitutional government, related to the Bible. Bibliog.)

11 BILLINGSLEY, Amos Stevens. *From the Flag to the Cross; or, Scenes and Incidents of Christianity in the War.* Philadelphia, 1872. (Religion in the armed forces.)

12 BRADSHAW, Marion John. *The War and Religion; a Preliminary Bibliography of Material in English, Prior to January 1, 1919.* New York, 1919. (Perhaps most complete list on relations of American churches to World War I.)

13 CHAMBERLIN, John Gordon. *The Church and Demobilization.* New York and Nashville, 1945. (Entire range of practical problems.)

14 DAVIDSON, Philip Grant. *Propaganda and the American Revolution, 1763–1783.* Chapel Hill, 1967. (Includes clergy as rival propagandists.)†

1   DOUGLASS, Harlan Paul. *The City Church in the War Emergency.* New York, 1945. (Social ministry to military personnel, defense workers, the demobilized.)

2   DURHAM, Chester Forrester. *The Attitude of the Northern Clergy toward the South, 1860–1865.* Toledo, 1942. (With bibliog.)

3   ELLSWORTH, Clayton Sumner. "American Churches and the Mexican War." *Am Hist Rev,* XLV (1940), 301–326. (Violent division of opinion, ardent clerical opposition.)

4   Federal Council of the Churches of Christ in America, Commission on the Relation of the Church to the War . . . *Atomic Warfare and the Christian Faith; Report.* New York, 1946. Also: *The Christian Conscience and Weapons of Mass Destruction; Report of a Special Commission.* New York, 1950. (Express general American Protestant opinion.)

5   FISHER, Miles Mark. "The Negro Church and the World War." *J Rel,* V (1925), 483–499. (New interest in social and political problems, racial consciousness, spirit of cooperation.)

6   GIFFORD, Frank Dean. "The Influence of the Clergy on American Politics from 1763 to 1776." *Hist Mag P E Ch,* X (1941), 104–123. (Clergy as apologists or opponents of revolution.)

7   HACKETT, Horatio Balch. *Christian Memorials of the War.* Boston and New York, 1864. (Extensive remarks on wartime evangelism.)

8   HENRY, James O. "History of the United States Christian Commission." (Md), 1959. *Univ Mic* (1960), no. 60–2272. *Diss Abs,* XXI (1960), 178–179. (Evangelical Protestant spiritual and medical ministry, 1861–1866.)

9   HICKS, Granville. "The Parsons and the War." *Am Mer,* X (1927), 129–142. (Unfavorable view of clergy who forsook pacifism and backed World War I.)

10   JOHNSON, Frederick Ernest. "The Impact of the War on Religion in America." *Am J Socio,* XLVIII (1942), 353–360. (Less crusading spirit than in World War I, deeper spirituality, parish system inadequate.)

11   JONES, John William. *Christ in the Camps; or, Religion in Lee's Army.* Richmond, 1887. (Evangelism in the army.)

12   JOYCE, Lester Douglas. *Church and Clergy in the American Revolution; a Study in Group Behavior.* New York, 1966. (Sociological study; clergy acted not from ideal motives, but from instinct of group survival.)

13   KARRAKER, William Archibald. "The American Churches and the Spanish-American War." (Chi), 1940. (Publ. in part, Chicago, 1943.)

14   KINSOLVING, Arthur Lee. "War and Our Religious Condition." *Va Q Rev,* XXI (1945), 355–367. (Religious revival in armed forces contrasted with home-front materialism; religion a support of democracy.)

15   LACY, Benjamin Rice, Jr. *Revivals in the Midst of the Years.* Richmond, Va., 1943. (In Confederate Army; debate between social and personal gospel.)

1 MILLER, John Chester. *Origins of the American Revolution.* Boston, 1943. (Discusses religious conflicts as causes of war, clergy as propagandists.)†

2 MOSS, Lemuel. *Annals of the United States Christian Commission.* Philadelphia, 1868. (Relief work, revivalism, morale-building.)

3 PRATT, Julius William. *The Expansionists of 1898.* . . . Baltimore, 1936. (Religious motivation and language of imperialists.)†

4 *Render unto Caesar, a Collection of Sermon Classics on all Phases of Religion in War-time.* New York, 1943. (Anthology of religious thought from four great American wars.)

5 "Sermons and Addresses on the Spanish American War," 1898–1902. Collection in Lib of Congress, Washington, D.C. (Some concern religious aspects, such as defection from Christian moral principles.)

6 SILVER, James Wesley. *Confederate Morale and Church Propaganda.* Tuscaloosa, Ala., 1957. (Bibliog., scholarly study of work for Confederate cause.)†

7 STANTON, Robert Livingston. *The Church and the Rebellion.* New York, 1964. (Completely reviews attitudes of churches on both sides.)

11. Chaplains in the Armed Forces

8 BARISH, Louis, ed. *Rabbis in Uniform. The Story of the American Jewish Military Chaplain.* New York, 1962. (History since official recognition in 1862, on service in World War II.)

9 CROSS, Christopher, and William R. ARNOLD. *Soldiers of God. True Story of the U.S. Army Chaplains.* New York, 1945. (Based largely upon personal experiences of chaplains in World War II.)

10 FRANK, Emma Lucile. *The Chaplaincy in the Armed Services, a Preliminary Bibliography.* Oberlin, 1945. (World War II and selected items on earlier wars.)

11 GERMAIN, Dom Aidan Henry. *Catholic Military and Naval Chaplains, 1776–1917.* Washington, 1929. (First essay ever written on a long-neglected subject, notes on governmental policy towards chaplains; bibliog.)

12 HONEYWELL, Roy John. *Chaplains of the United States Army.* Washington, 1958. (Detailed, scholarly; influence of wartime religious service in peace and civil life.)

13 Methodist Church (United States) Commission on Chaplains. *Chaplains of the Methodist Church in World War II. A Pictorial Record of Their Work.* Washington, 1948. (Records devotion and manifold ministries of over 1,700 chaplains.)

14 NORTON, Herman Albert. *Rebel Religion; the Story of Confederate Chaplains.* St. Louis, 1961.

1 PROEHL, Frederick C., comp. *Marching Side by Side. Stories from Lutheran Chaplains on the Far-flung Battlefronts.* Saint Louis, 1945. (Personal narratives of experiences in World War II; photos.)

2 SMITH, John Mortimer. "The Military Ordinariate of the United States of America." (Cath), 1966. *Univ Mic* (1967), no. 67–1271. *Diss Abs*, XXVII (1967), 2968A–2969A. (History of development into significant contribution to American life.)

3 Society for the Propagation of the Faith. *The Priest Goes to War. A Pictorial Outline of the Work of the Catholic Chaplains in the Second World War.* New York, 1945. (Collection of photos., many vivid, with captions and commentary.)

12. Pacifism, Peace Movements

4 American Civil Liberties Union. *A Report on the Treatment of Conscientious Objectors in World War II; Conscience and the War.* New York, 1943.

5 BROCK, Peter. *Pacifism in the United States from the Colonial Era to the First World War.* Princeton, 1968. (Dispassionate and discriminating, abundantly documented, religious origins stressed.)

6 BROOKS, Arle, and Robert J. LEACH. *Help Wanted! The Experiences of Some Quaker Conscientious Objectors.* Philadelphia, 1940. (Quakers as pacifists in World War I.)

7 BROWN, Robert McAfee; Abraham HESCHEL; and Michael NOVAK. *Vietnam: Crisis of Conscience.* New York, 1967.†

8 CARTLAND, Fernando Gale. *Southern Heroes; or, The Friends in War Time.* Cambridge, 1895. (Treatment of Quaker conscientious objectors in Confederate States.)

9 CURTI, Merle E. *The American Peace Crusade, 1815–1860.* Durham, N.C., 1965. (Significant internationalist manifestation of American Protestantism; bibliog.)

10 EISAN, Leslie. *Pathways of Peace, a History of the Civilian Public Service Program, Administered by the Brethren Service Committee.* Elgin, Ill., 1948. (Service in World War II.)

11 ELLIFF, Nathan T. "Jehovah's Witnesses and the Selective Service Act." *Va Law Rev*, XXXI (1945), 811–834. (Cases of violation and "ministerial exemption.")

12 FISHER, Robert Cameron ["Hatch Fletch"]. "The American Churches in the Twentieth Century and War." (Princeton Theol Sem), 1947. (Very thorough and frank review. Bibliog.)

13 GALPIN, W. Freeman. *Pioneering for Peace: A Study of American Efforts to 1846.* Syracuse, N.Y., 1933. (Considers Christian participation.)

14 GILPIN, Thomas, ed. *Exiles in Virginia; with Observations on the Conduct of the Society of Friends during the Revolutionary War.* Philadelphia, 1848. (Conscientious objectors.)

1 GINGERICH, Melvin. *Service for Peace.* Akron, Pa., 1949. (Scholarly study of conscientious objectors in World War II, Mennonites and affiliated groups.)

2 HALLOWAY, Vernon Howard. "American Pacifism Between Two Wars, 1919–1941." (Yale), 1949; abstract pub. in *Rel Life,* XIX (1950), 367–379. (Incl. religious philosophies of pacifism.)

3 HAMILTON, Michael Pollock, ed. *The Vietnam War: Christian Perspectives.* Grand Rapids, Mich., 1967. (Nine sermons presented by invitation of the Washington Cathedral, and two addresses, Mar. 12–Apr. 26, 1967.)†

4 HORST, Samuel. *Mennonites in the Confederacy: A Study in Civil War Pacifism.* Scottdale, Pa., 1968. (Based on contemporary sources; evidence of great strength of religiously inspired pacifism.)

5 LUND, Doniver A. "The Peace Movement Among the Major American Protestant Churches, 1919–1939." (Neb), 1956. *Univ Mic,* no. 16,243; *Diss Abs,* XVI (1956), 742. (Analyzes policies and activities, using largely original sources.)

6 MOELLERING, Ralph Luther. *Modern War and the American Churches.* New York, 1956. (Period since 1939, a sequel to Halloway. Bibliog.)

7 NEUHAUS, Richard John. "The War, the Churches, and Civil Religion." *Ann Am Acad Pol Soc Sci,* 387 (Jan., 1970), 128–140. (Religious opposition more concerned with civil religion than traditional theology and ethics; opposition between clergy and laity.)

8 O'CONNOR, John. *A Chaplain Looks at Vietnam.* Cleveland, 1968.

9 QUIGLEY, Thomas E., comp. *American Catholics and the Vietnam War.* Grand Rapids, Mich., 1968. (Considerations on war and religion and the Roman Catholic Church in Vietnam.)†

10 QUINLEY, Harold. "Hawks and Doves among the Clergy: Protestant Reaction to the War in Vietnam." *Ministry Studies,* 3, no. 3 (1969). (Survey in 1968 shows dramatic cleavage between clergy and laity, latter far more "hawkish.")

11 ROHRER, Peter Lester, and Mary E. *The Story of the Lancaster County Conference Mennonites in Civilian Public Service. . . .* Lancaster, Pa., 1946. (Actual treatment of conscientious objectors.)

12 RUSSO, Paul Gia. "The Conscientious Objector in American Law." *Rel Life,* X (1941), 333–345. (Notes on legislative power over religious objectors.)

13 SIBLEY, Mulford Quickert. *Conscription of Conscience; the American State and the Conscientious Objector, 1940–1947.* Ithaca, 1952. (Impartial, objective, yet sympathetic toward the "C.O." viewpoint.)

14 SWOMLEY, John M., Jr. *The Military Establishment.* Boston, 1964. (Relations with religion and the churches, pacifist viewpoint.)

15 WHITNEY, Edson L. *The American Peace Society: A Centennial History.* Washington, 1928. (Refs. to religious support.)

1 WRIGHT, Edward Needles. *Conscientious Objectors in the Civil War.* Philadelphia, 1931. (Scholarly study of Quakers and others, stressing legal aspects.)†

2 ZAHN, Gordon C. "Catholic Conscientious Objectors: A Portrait." *Continuum,* III (1965), 329–337. (Sympathetic toward a forgotten group; comment on objectors in American society.)

13. Religion and Foreign Relations

3 COLE, Patricia Ann. "The Function of the Church as Critic of Society Exemplified in the Area of United States International Policy." (Bos), 1963. *Univ Mic* (1964), no. 64–375. *Diss Abs,* XXIV (1964), 4828–4829. (From 1948, lobbying for application of Christian ethics to world politics.)

4 DARKEN, Arthur H. "The National Council of Churches and Our Foreign Policy." *Rel Life,* XXIV (1954–1955), 113–126. (Criticism of lack of realism.)

5 GEYER, Alan Francis. *Piety and Politics: American Protestantism in the World Arena.* Richmond, 1963. (Influence of Anglo-American Protestant morality upon foreign policy-making, since about 1898.)†

6 LE FEVER, Ernest Warren. "Protestants and United States Foreign Policy, 1925–1954." (Yale). (Excellent review of attitudes and influence regarding responsibility for world order.)

7 MacKENZIE, Kenneth M. "American Methodism and Imperialism (1865–1900)." (NY), 1957. *Univ Mic* (1959), no. 59–6680. *Diss Abs,* XXI (1960), 180–181. (Imperialism justified as outcome of divine providence in American history.)

8 ROOTS, John McCook, ed. *Modernizing America; Action Papers of National Purpose.* Los Angeles, 1965. (Application of Christian principles to international affairs, under leadership of the U.S.)

9 STRONG, Josiah. *Our Country.* Ed. by Jorgen Herbst. Cambridge, Mass., 1963. (National and international mission of Anglo-American Protestantism for evangelizing and meliorating.)

10 TUVESON, Ernest Lee. *Redeemer Nation: The Idea of America's Millenial Role.* Chicago, 1968. (Best study of religious elements in idea of American mission, traced to Book of Revelation; plays down secular motives.)

XVI. Sociology of Religion

1. General Works

11 AHLSTROM, Sydney E. "The Radical Turn in Theology and Ethics: Why it Occurred in the 1960's." *Ann Am Acad Pol Soc Sci,* 387 (Jan., 1970), 1–13. (Influence of demographic, technological, urban and racial crises in upsetting long-established attitudes and loyalties.)

1   American Academy of Political and Social Science. *Not Many Wise, a Reader on Religion in American Society.* Boston, 1962. (Essays selected from Nov. 1960 issue of the *Annals.*)

2   BOISEN, Anton T. *Religion in Crisis and Custom, a Sociological and Psychological Study.* New York, 1955. (Profound study of relations of sociological factors and personal crises to familiar features of Protestant religious life.)

3   CAHOON, Sister M. Janelle. "Tensions and Dilemmas Facing Organized Christianity in the Contemporary United States as Recognized in Official Church Statements." (Fordham), 1963. *Univ Mic* (1964), no. 64-2422. *Diss Abs,* XXV (1964), 2648. (Tension between faith and society; how to make faith relevant without losing its essence.)

4   COGLEY, John, ed. *Religion in America. Original Essays on Religion in a Free Society.* New York, 1958. (Essays based on seminar talks, incl. men of varying shades of belief.)†

5   COX, Harvey Gallagher. *The Secular City: Secularization and Urbanization in Theological Perspective.* New York, 1965. (City and town life and the problems of city churches in a secularized society.)†

6   GARDNER, Edward Clinton. *The Church as a Prophetic Community.* Philadelphia, 1967. (Necessity of renewal by engagement in modern American culture.)

7   GLOCK, Charles Y., and Rodney STARK. *Religion and Society in Tension.* Chicago, 1965. (Religion in social-scientific perspective, role in social change, contrast with humanist perspectives.)

8   HERBERG, Will. *Protestant, Catholic, Jew; an Essay in American Religious Sociology.* Rev. ed. Garden City, N.Y., 1955. (Stresses growth of accepted "cultural pluralism" in religion. Bibliog.)†

9   HOOK, Sidney. *Religion in a Free Society.* Lincoln, Neb., 1967. (Difficulty of relations between religion and increasingly secular society, with politically affected judiciary as arbiter.)

10 LEE, Robert, and Martin E. MARTY, eds. *Religion and Social Conflict.* New York, 1964. (Religion involved in technological, ethical, racial, political, theological, church and state and other conflicts.)†

11 LENSKI, Gerhard Emmanuel. *The Religious Factor; a Sociological Study of Religion's Impact on Politics, Economics, and Family Life.* Garden City, N.Y., 1961. (Based upon survey of Detroit in 1958, revealing mutual impact between religion and the world.)†

12 LENSKI, Gerhard Emmanuel. "The Sociology of Religion in the United States: A Review of Theoretically Oriented Research." *Soc Com,* IX (1962), 307-337. (Surveys many topics in literature of past two decades.)

13 MIYAKAWA, Tetsuo Scott. *Protestants and Pioneers; Individualism and Conformity on the American Frontier.* Chicago, 1964. ("Popular denominations" of the Ohio Valley, 1800-1836, as voluntary lay groups.)

1   MOBERG, David O. *The Church as a Social Institution; the Sociology of American Religion.* Englewood Cliffs, N.J., 1962. (Church's part in contemporary life, with broad historical background; extensive bibliog.)

2   OBENHAUS, Victor. *The Church and Faith in Mid-America.* Philadelphia, 1963. (Analysis of typical "Cornbelt" county; cultural uniformity and denominational peculiarities influence religion.)

3   O'BRIEN, John Francis. "The Socialization of the American Church in the Last Quarter of the Nineteenth Century." *Soc Forces*, II (1924), 700–705; III (1925), 297–304. (Period 1870's to 1900; analysis of causes and description of one of the most far-reaching changes in history of religion.)

4   PARSONS, Talcott. "The Pattern of Religious Organization in the United States." *Daedalus*, LXXXVII (1959), 65–85. (Society organized about Christian values, trend toward integration of varying elements.)

5   PHARES, Ross. *Bible in Pocket, Gun in Hand; the Story of Frontier Religion.* Garden City, N.Y., 1964. (On a type of Anglo-American Protestantism, "narrow in its concept, and rough-hewn, but it was never dull.")

6   SALISBURY, W. Seward. *Religion in American Culture, a Sociological Interpretation.* Homewood, Ill., 1964. (Studies intensively structure of religion, substance and processes of change, individual religious experiences. Large bibliog.)

7   SCHROEDER, W. Widick, and Victor OBENHAUS. *Religion in American Culture; Unity and Diversity in a Midwestern County.* New York, 1964. (Interviews and statistics reveal religion's impact upon life.)

8   STAHMER, Harold, ed. *Religion & Contemporary Society.* New York and London, 1963. (Essays by Jewish, R. C. and Protestant writers, critical of tendency to identify religious heritage with national purposes and secularism.)†

9   THOMAS, John Lawrence. *Religion and the American People.* Westminster, Md., 1963. (Based upon extensive survey questionnaire, thoroughly investigates, describes, analyzes religious beliefs, practices, and attitudes of "average" adults.)

10 VOGT, Von Ogden. *Cult and Culture, a Study of Religion and American Culture.* New York, 1951. (Sees religion as element that creates and unifies culture.)

11 WILLIAMS, John Paul. *What Americans Believe and How They Worship.* New York, 1952. (Distinctive group qualities, their place in society and religious life.)

12 WILLIAMS, Robin Murphy, Jr. *American Society: A Sociological Interpretation.* New York, 1951. (Relation of religion to general social structure.)

13 YINGER, J. Milton. *Religion in the Struggle for Power. A Study in the Sociology of Religion.* Durham, N. C., 1946. (Scientific treatise on religion's relations to economics, social structure, nationalism, industrialism, war. Large bibliog.)

1 ZAHN, Jane C., ed. *Religion and the Face of America.* Berkeley, Calif., 1958. (Six essayists discuss social problems of religion; religion as cultural institution.)

2. Religious Ideals in Life

2 BRANSCOMB, Bennett Harvie. *The Contribution of Moral and Spiritual Ideas to the Making of the American Way of Life.* . . . Madison, Wis., 1952.

3 EDDY, George Sherwood. *The Kingdom of God and the American Dream; the Religious and Secular Ideals of American History.* New York and London, 1941.

4 LATOURETTE, Kenneth Scott. "The Contribution of the Religion of the Colonial Period to the Ideals and Life of the United States." *Americas,* XIV (1958), 340–355. (Influences from extreme Protestantism.)

5 LIPSET, Seymour Martin. "Religion and American Values," in *The First New Nation. The United States in Historical and Comparative Perspective.* New York, 1963, pp. 140–169. (On pervasiveness, secularity, voluntarism; quotes from American and foreign observers.)†

6 McLOUGHLIN, William Gerald, Jr. "Pietism and the American Character." *Am Q,* XVII (1965), 163–186. (Americans committed to moralistic approach to life because of Puritan Protestant background.)

7 SHEA, Daniel Bartholomew, Jr. "Spiritual Autobiography in Early America." (Stan), 1966. *Univ Mic* (1966), no. 66–14,718. *Diss Abs,* XXVII (1967), 2135A. (Revelation of American religious experience, mostly Puritan and Quaker.)

8 SHINN, Roger L., ed. *The Search for Identity: Essays on the American Character.* New York, 1964. (Essay by Joseph L. Blau, "Religion and the Two Faces of America," pp. 29–38, stresses opposition between priestly or cultural and prophetic religion.)

9 WITTKE, Carl. "Religious Influence in American History." *Calif Univ Chron,* XXVI (1924), 451–477. (Shaping influences upon ideals and culture.)

3. Religion and Economics

10 ALLINSMITH, Wesley and Beverly. "Religious Affiliation and Politico-Economic Attitude: A Study of Eight Major U.S. Religious Groups." *Pub Opin Q,* XII (1948), 377–389.

11 BURSK, Edward C., ed. *Business and Religion: A New Depth Dimension in Management.* New York, 1959. (Essays by 12 authors from *Harvard Business Review,* showing rise of concern about ethical, moral and religious problems.)

12 EVERETT, John Rutherford. *Religion in Economics, a Study of John Bates Clark, Richard T. Ely* [and] *Simon N. Patton.* New York, 1946. (Religious influence upon Protestant formulators of most potent American economic theories; selected bibliog.)

1   Federal Council of Churches of Christ in America, Dept. of Research and Education. "Christianity and the Economic Order." Study no. 10, "Social-Economic Status and Outlook of Religious Groups in America." *Information Service*, no. 27 (May 15, 1948), 1–8.

2   Guild of St. Ives. "Report on Churches and Taxation." *The Religious Situation: 1968.* Ed. by Donald R. Cutler. Boston, 1968, pp. 931–960. (Refs., and a commentary by Jack Mendelsohn.)

3   JENNINGS, William Hansell. "Property in American Protestant Thought, 1929–1965." (Yale), 1966. *Univ Mic* (1966), no. 67–92. *Diss Abs*, XXVII (1967), 2601A–2602A. (Liberal and conservative Protestant economic thought.)

4   KELLER, Edward A. *Christianity and American Capitalism.* Chicago, 1953. (Defense of Christianized capitalism from viewpoint of Catholic theology and ethics.)

5   MOORE, William Hoyt. "Religion and the Consumer's Cooperative Movement." (Chi), 1938. Priv. ed, 1940. (Summary. Involvement of religious people in support of specific panacea for economic ills of the depression.)

6   NELSON, Clyde K. "Russell H. Conwell and the 'Gospel of Wealth.'" *Foundations*, V (1962), 39–51. (Baptist preacher, who believed in stewardship and sharing.)

7   TROTT, Norman L. and Ross W. SANDERSON. *What Church People Think about Social and Economic Issues; Report of an Opinion Survey Made in Baltimore. . . .* New York, 1938. (Intended as representative cross section of opinion. Bibliog.)

8   WILLIAMS, John Paul. *What Americans Believe and How They Worship.* New York, 1952. (Impact of churches on economic affairs, especially by political pressure.)

4. Religion and Class

9   BALTZELL, Edward Digby. *Philadelphia Gentlemen: The Making of a National Upper Class.* Glencoe, Ill., 1958. (Relation of religion to upper class.)†

10 BALTZELL, Edward Digby. *The Protestant Establishment: Aristocracy and Caste in America.* New York, 1964. (Place of religion in class system.)†

11 BURCHINAL, Lee G. "Some Social Status Criteria and Church Membership and Church Attendance." *J Soc Psycho*, XLIX (1959), 53–64. (Sampling of husbands and wives in Midwestern rural and small-town settings.)

12 CANTRIL, Hadley. "The Educational and Economic Composition of Religious Groups." *Am J Socio*, XLVIII (1943), 574–579. (Ample evidence based upon polling techniques.)

13 DANIEL, Vattel Elbert. "Ritual and Stratification in Chicago Negro Churches." (Chi), 1940. Partly pub. in *Am Socio Rev*, VII (1942), 352–361. (Relations between ritual and social class.)

1 DAVIES, J. Kenneth. "The Mormon Church: Its Middle-Class Propensities." *Rev Rel Res*, IV (1963), 84–95. (Middle-classness and less sympathy with labor and unions, result of urbanism and industrialism.)

2 DEMERATH, Nicholas Jay, III. *Social Class in American Protestantism.* Chicago, 1965. (Examination of five Protestant denominations to determine factors in churchlike and sectlike involvement.)†

3 DILLINGHAM, Harry C. "Protestant Religion and Social Status." *Am J Socio*, LXX (1965), 416–422. (Protestant members of higher status than non-members, status related to attendance rates.)

4 DOLLARD, John. *Caste and Class in a Southern Town.* New York, 1949. (Church affiliations of classes and Negroes, religion in social control, Negro acculturation.)†

5 DOUGLASS, Harlan Paul. "Cultural Differences and Recent Religious Divisions." *Christendom*, X (1945), 89–105. (Variances between standard Protestantism and lower class evangelistic splinters.)

6 ELINSON, Howard. "The Class Implications of Pentecostal Religion for Intellectualism, Politics and Race Relations." *Am J Socio*, LXX (1965), 403–415. (Aloofness from science and politics, opposition to segregation, personalistic faith.)

7 FORD, Thomas R. "Status, Residence and Fundamentalist Religious Beliefs in the Southern Appalachians." *Soc Forces*, XXXIX (1960), 41–49. (Components vary with different social conditions, no pattern to fit strict theory.)

8 FRY, Charles Luther. "The Religious Affiliations of American Leaders." *Sci Mo*, XXXVI (1933), 241–249. (Statistics and comment on relation of religious preference to occupation and social class.)

9 GOLDSCHMIDT, Walter R. "Class Denominationalism in Rural California Churches." *J Socio*, XLIX (1944), 348–360.

10 LAZERWITZ, Bernard. "A Comparison of Major United States Religious Groups." *J Am Stat Assn*, LVI (1961), 568–579. (Demographic study indicating social stratification.)

11 MAYER, Albert J., and Harry SHARP. "Religious Preference and Worldly Success." *Am Socio Rev*, XXVII (1962), 218–277. (Metropolitan Detroit; most Protestant groups far ahead of Catholics; high achievement of Jews and Eastern Orthodox.)

12 NIEBUHR, H. Richard. *The Social Sources of Denominationalism.* New ed. New York, 1940. (Tendency of denominations to follow social class lines.)†

13 ORGANIC, Harold Nathan. "Religious Affiliation and Social Mobility in Contemporary American Society: A National Study." (Mich), 1963. *Univ Mic* (1964), no. 64–6730. *Diss Abs*, XXV (1964), 679–680. (Shows tendency of Protestants to be a social and economic élite.)

14 PITCHER, Alvin. "The Church and the American Achievement Culture." *Foundations*, III (1960), 292–305. (Critique of character structure the culture encourages, and of church as status symbol.)

1 POPE, Liston. *Millhands and Preachers; a Study of Gastonia.* New Haven, 1942. (Exceptionally able studies of class denominationalism.)†

2 QUINNEY, Richard V. "Political Conservatism, Alienation, and Fatalism: Contingencies of Social Status and Religious Fundamentalism." *Sociometry,* XXVII (1964), 372–381. (Analysis of residents in southern Appalachia.)

3 SMALL, Albion W. "The Church and Class Conflicts, An Open Letter to the Laymen's Committee on Interchurch Survey." *Am J Socio,* LX (1955), 54–74. (Suggests definite policy to overcome barrier between churches and wage-earners.)

4 SWAN, Charles Lundeen. "The Class-related Characteristics of Lay Leaders in the Churches of a Small Midwestern City." (N W Univ), 1955. *Univ Mic* (1955), no. 13–142. *Diss Abs,* XV (1955), 2322. (Three Rivers, Mich.)

5 VERNON, Glenn M. "Religious Groups and Social Class—Some Inconsistencies." *Pap Mich Acad Sci Arts and Letters,* XLV (1960), 295–301. (Confused picture; student sentiment, improved social status and "improved" religion not necessarily compatible.)

6 WATSON, Kenneth. "The Religious Affiliation, Motivation and Opinions of Business and Labor Leaders in the United States." (S Calif Sch Theol), 1960. *Univ Mic* (1963), no. 63–4473. *Diss Abs,* XXIV (1963), 1267–1268. (Shows firm hold of religion on both; labor more favorable to Social Gospel.)

7 WEST, James. *Plainville, U.S.A.* New York, 1945. (Chap. IV considers relation of religious denominationalism to social class.)†

8 YINGER, J. Milton. *Religion in the Struggle for Power.* Durham, N.C., 1946. (Social stratification of religion, prop of class.)

5. Acculturation and Americanization

9 GORDON, Milton M. *Assimilation in American Life: The Role of Race, Religion and National Origins.* New York, 1964. (Many refs. to Jews, Catholics, White Protestants in acculturation.)†

10 LEE, J. Oscar. "Religion Among Ethnic and Racial Minorities." *Ann Am Acad Pol Soc Sci,* CCCXXXII (1960), 112–124. (Movement toward desegregation and integration.)

11 MOL, J. J. "Churches and Immigrants (A Sociological Study of the Mutual Effect of Religion and Immigrant Adjustment)" *Bull Res Group Europ Mig Prob,* no. 9 (Supplement 5), May, 1961. (Thorough sociological analysis of acculturation problems; summarizes literature, 1900–1960; large bibliog.)

12 ROBBINS, Richard. "American Jews and American Catholics: Two Types of Social Change." *Socio Anal,* XXVI (1965), 1–17. Thomas F. O'Dea, "Comment," 18–20. (Study of assimilation and acculturation, upward trend from ethnic ghetto.)

1   SPIRO, M. E. "The Acculturation of American Ethnic Groups." *Am Anthro*, LVII (1955), 1240–1252. (Including religious acculturation.)

2   VEROFF, Joseph; Sheila FIELD; and Gerald GURIN. "Achievement Motivation and Religious Background." *Am Socio Rev*, XXVII (1962), 205–217. (Nationwide sample survey, with refs. and statistical tables. Jews and Catholics feel urge to rise; drive of economic hardships.)

A. Jews

3   AGUS, Jacob Bernard. *Guideposts in Modern Judaism, An Analysis of Current Trends in Jewish Thought.* New York, 1954. (Impact of American culture; Jewish community as a creative minority.)

4   CLARK, Kenneth B. "Jews in Contemporary America. Problems in Identification." *Jew Soc Serv Q*, XXXI (1954), 12–22. (Stresses of anti-semitism and assimilationism, patterns of adjustment, degrees of in-group identification.)

5   COHEN, Arthur Allen. *The Natural and the Supernatural Jew: An Historical and Theological Introduction.* London, 1967. (Incl. realistic discussion of American Judaism's chance of survival as a culture [natural] and/or religion [supernatural].)†

6   GANS, Herbert J. "American Jewry: Present and Future." *Commentary*, XXI (1956), 422–430, 555–563. (Doubt of ability of religious Judaism to survive pressures of acculturation and assimilation.)

7   GINZBERG, Eli. *Agenda for American Jews.* New York, 1950. (Emergence of an American and not specifically religious communal life. Bibliog.)†

8   GLAZER, Nathan. *American Judaism.* Chicago, 1957. (Religious socio-logist on the inner dilemma of American Jews; revival.)

9   SKLARE, Marshall, ed. *The Jews: Social Patterns of an American Group.* Glencoe, Ill., 1958. (Essays on accommodation to American life.)†

10   STEINBERG, Milton. *A Partisan Guide to the Jewish Problem.* Indianapolis and New York, 1963. (Problem of anti-Semitism; positive program of adjustment to American pattern.)†

B. Protestants

11   CAIN, Leonard D., Jr. "Japanese-American Protestants. Acculturation and Assimilation." *Rev Rel Res*, III (1962), 113–121. (Tendency to adopt middle-class American religiosity.)

12   DEITZ, Reginald W. "Eastern Lutheranism in American Society and American Christianity, 1870–1914: Darwinism, Biblical Criticism, the Social Gospel." (Penn), 1958. *Univ Mic* (1958), no. 58–317; *Diss Abs*, XIX (1958), 784–785. (Church's effort to be American, evangelical, relevant.)

1   DOUGLASS, Paul Franklin. *The Story of German Methodism; Biography of an Immigrant Soul.* New York and Cincinnati, 1939. (Typical story of Americanization of immigrants. Bibliog.)

2   GRAEBNER, Alan Niehaus. "The Acculturation of an Immigration Lutheran Church: The Lutheran Church—Missouri Synod, 1917–1929." (Colum), 1965. *Univ Mic* (1965), no. 65–9161. *Diss Abs*, XXVI (1965), 3263–3264. (Historical process of assimilation of a "foreign" religious group.)

3   LUND, Gene Jessie. "The Americanization of the Augustana Lutheran Church." (Princeton Theol Sem), 1954. (Transformation to English-speaking community, factors in the change.)

4   MARTY, Myron A. *Lutherans and Roman Catholicism: The Changing Conflict, 1917–1963.* Notre Dame and London, 1968. (Based on primary sources; relations between two "foreign" groups, attempted assimilation to American tolerance.)

5   MEYER, Carl Stamm. "Lutheran Immigrant Churches Face the Problem of the Frontier." *Church Hist*, XXIX (1960), 440–462. (Similarity of approach to acculturation in various denominations, 1840–1870.)

6   NYHOLM, Paul C. *The Americanization of the Danish Lutheran Churches in America, a Study in Immigrant History.* Copenhagen, Minneapolis, 1963. (Cultural and religious assimilation in two Danish synods.)

7   SPAUDE, Paul W. *The Lutheran Church under American Influence . . . Its Relation to Various Modifying Forces in the United States.* Burlington, Iowa, 1943. (Close study of assimilation.)

8   WHYMAN, Henry C. "The Conflict and Adjustment of Two Religious Cultures—The Swedish and the American as Found in the Swede's Relation to American Methodism." (N Y), 1937.

9   WOLF, Richard Charles. "The Americanization of the German Lutherans, 1683–1829." (Yale), 1947. (Earlier immigrants becoming truly American and truly Lutheran.)

C.   Roman Catholics

10   CADA, Joseph. *Czech-American Catholics, 1850–1920.* Chicago, 1964. (Scholarly study of growth, culture, and gradual assimilation.)

11   CALLAHAN, Daniel J. "Contraception and Abortion: American Catholic Responses." *Ann Am Acad Pol Soc Sci*, 387 (Jan., 1970), 109–117. (Reflection of theological and social change; controversy due to Roman Catholic assimilation to American life.)

12   CALLAHAN, Daniel J., ed. *Generation of the Third Eye.* New York, 1965. (Twenty-four vivid intellectual and spiritual autobiographies, pointing up important changes in Catholic thinking since 1945.)

13   College of New Rochelle. *Catholicism in American Culture, Semicentenary Lecture Series, 1953–1954.* New Rochelle, N.Y., 1955. (Church can be American and retain general supranational culture.)

1 CROSS, Robert D. "Changing Image of Catholicism in America." *Yale Rev*, XLVIII (1959), 562–575. (Shifting Protestant attitude, from enmity to acceptance of Catholicism as part of American way.)

2 GETLEIN, Frank. *"The Trouble with Catholics. . . ."* Baltimore, 1964. (Agonies of emerging from long isolation in clericalism into reality of a lay world.)

3 GREELEY, Andrew M. *Religion and Career. A Study of College Graduates.* New York, 1963. ("Inferiority" as a group passing as R.C.'s take place in American culture.)

4 KANE, John Joseph. "The Social Structure of American Catholics." *Am Cath Socio Rev*, XVI (1955), 23–40. (Gradual assimilation; rise in social and economic scale.)

5 KOSA, J. "Patterns of Social Mobility among American Catholics." *Soc Com*, IX (1962), 361–371. (Rise of socio-economic level comparable to that of Protestants. Refs. in footnotes.)

6 McAVOY, Thomas Timothy. *The Formation of the American Catholic Minority, 1820–1860.* Philadelphia, 1967. (On development of American Catholic culture thru assimilation of non-English speaking immigrants.)†

7 MacEOIN, Gary. *New Challenges to American Catholics.* New York, 1965. (Necessity of sloughing off old attitudes and practices to adjust to change, without sacrificing *essential* Catholicism.)

8 NOVAK, Michael. *A New Generation, American and Catholic.* New York, 1964. (Frank discussion of problems that face young American Roman Catholics in adjusting to dynamic, secular, technological culture.)

9 SHANNON, James P. *Catholic Colonization on the Western Frontier.* New Haven, 1957. (Immigrant societies, land companies, Church as an American-izer. Essay on sources.)

10 WAKIN, Edward, and Joseph F. SCHEUER. *The de-Romanization of the American Catholic Church.* New York, 1966. (Discussion of Americanization and laicizing of a hitherto "closed" society.)

11 WARD, Leo Richard, ed. *The American Apostolate; American Catholics in the Twentieth Century.* Westminster, Md., 1952. (Essays, stressing effort to interpret Catholic thought and action to Americans.)

6. Social Gospel

A. General Histories

12 BARCLAY, Wade Crawford. "To Reform the Nation." Vol. II of *Early American Methodism 1769–1844.* New York, 1949. (Influence of "holiness" piety on social movements.)

13 BEARDSLEY, Frank Grenville. *Religious Progress through Religious Revivals.* New York, 1943. (Detailed evidence that results are primarily social.)

1 CARTER, Paul Allen. *The Decline and Revival of the Social Gospel.* Ithaca, N.Y., 1954. (Covers 1920–1940, reasons for decline and upswing. Bibliog.)

2 HANDY, Robert T., ed. *The Social Gospel in America, 1870–1920.* New York, 1966. (Selections from writings of Washington Gladden, Richard T. Ely, Walter Rauschenbusch; historical introduction; brief biogs.)

3 HOPKINS, Charles Howard. *The Rise of the Social Gospel in American Protestantism, 1865–1915.* New Haven and London, 1940. (Classic history, seeing it as part of much broader reform movement.)†

4 McGOWAN, Chester C. *The Genesis of the Social Gospel.* New York and London, 1929. (American phase as one of latest adjustments of Christian ethic to history.)

5 MILLER, Robert Moats. *American Protestantism and Social Issues, 1919–1939.* Chapel Hill, 1958. (Painstaking, comprehensive survey of history of attitudes and action. Bibliog.)

6 MORRISON, Charles Clayton. *The Social Gospel and the Christian Cultus.* New York, 1933. (Reasons for recent decline of social emphasis.)

7 RYLEY, Thomas Woodman. "The Social Gospel Movement during the Period of American Reform 1880–1910." (N Y), 1965. *Univ Mic* (1965), no. 65–7308. *Diss Abs*, XXVI (1966), 3915–3916. (Close relations between Social Gospel and Progressive Movement.)

8 SMITH, Timothy Lawrence. *Revivalism and Social Reform in Mid-Nineteenth-Century America.* New York, 1957. (New view of origins of Social Gospel, 1840–1857.)†

9 TYLER, Alice Felt. *Freedom's Ferment; Phases of American Social History to 1860.* Minneapolis, 1944. (Religious optimism as motive force in religious and secular reform movements. Bibliog.)†

B. Ideals and Theory

10 BECHMAN, Everett Gladstone. "The Changing Conceptions of the Role of Religion with Reference to Social Justice, as Reflected in the *Congressional Record*, 1930–1960." (Pitts), 1965. *Univ Mic* (1965), no. 65–10,503. *Diss Abs*, XXVI (1966), 4470. (More than 500 entries covering many topics.)

11 COMMONS, John R. *Social Reform and the Church.* New York, 1967. (Repr. of 1894 pioneer essays on relevance of sociology for Christianity, responsibility of church to redeem society.)

12 CROWELL, George H. "American Cultural Values Obstructing Christian Social Action." *Univ Mic* (1966), no. 66–11,548; *Diss Abs*, XXVII (1966), 1909A–1910A. (Churches are basically of the "establishment," the impetus must come from individuals.)

13 CURTI, Merle E. *The Growth of American Thought.* 3rd ed. New York, 1964. (Chap. XXV reviews individualistic philosophy opposed to the Social Gospel.)

1 DURFEE, Harold Allen. "The Theologies of the American Social Gospel, a Study of the Theological and Philosophical Presuppositions of the American Social Gospel." (Colum), 1950. *Univ Mic*, no. 2809; *Mic Abs* XI (1951), 1059–1060. (A close analysis.)

2 GABRIEL, Ralph Henry. *The Course of American Democratic Thought*. 2nd ed. New York, 1956. (Describes the "gospel of wealth" in the post-Civil War period.)

3 GREER, Thomas H. *American Social Reform Movements; Their Pattern Since 1865*. New York, 1949. (Religious thought currents. Bibliog.)

4 JOHNSON, Frederick Ernest. *The Social Gospel Re-examined*. New York and London, 1940. (Attempts to meet criticism by religious and economic conservatives, and by theologians.)

5 KENNEDY, Gail, ed. *Democracy and the Gospel of Wealth*. Boston, 1949. (Readings on doctrine of Christian stewardship of riches.)†

6 McGIFFERT, Arthur C., Jr. *The Rise of Modern Religious Ideas*. New York, 1929. (Origin of Social Gospel in liberal theology of Horace Bushnell.)

7 McKEE, William Finley. "The Social Gospel and the New Social Order, 1919–1929." (Wis), 1961. *Univ Mic* (1961), no. 61–2965. *Diss Abs*, XXII (1961), 852–853. (Optimism, utopianism, quest for Kingdom of God, service, brotherhood, pacifism.)

8 NIEBUHR, H. Richard. *The Kingdom of God in America*. Chicago and New York, 1937. (Origins of Social Gospel in Puritan ideal of a godly commonwealth, and equalitarian democracy.)†

9 NOBLE, David W. "The Religion of Progress in America, 1890–1914." *Soc Res*, XXII (1955), 417–440. (Inspiration of Social Gospel in secular optimism.)

10 SCHLESINGER, Arthur M., Jr. *The American as Reformer*. Cambridge, Mass., 1968. (Christian basis of many reform impulses.)†

C. *Protestant*

11 BOCK, Paul John. "The Social Pronouncements of the United Church of Christ." (W Res), 1965. *Univ Mic* (1966), no. 66–5180. *Diss Abs*, XXVI (1966), 7468. (1934–1962, liberal and conservative, contemporary theological trends.)

12 BRILL, Earl Hubert. *The Creative Edge of American Protestantism*. New York, 1966. (Adaptation of progressive Protestantism to Christian solution of social problems.)

13 BROWN, Kenneth Lee. "Washington Gladden: Exponent of Social Christianity." (Duke), 1964. *Univ Mic* (1966), no. 66–13,753. *Diss Abs*, XXVII (1966), 1908A. (Pioneer of present-day religious-social thought; Kingdom of God philosophy.)

14 COLE, Charles Chester, Jr. *The Social Ideas of the Northern Evangelists, 1826–1860*. New York, 1966. (Opinions of a rather diverse group.)

1   CROSS, Robert D., ed. *Walter Rauschenbusch: Christianity and the Social Crisis.* New York, 1964.†

2   DORN, Jacob Henry, III. *Washington Gladden: Prophet of the Social Gospel.* Columbus, Ohio, 1967. (First full biographical study, thoroughly documented; about half concerns his views on social topics.)

3   FARNHAM, Henry May. *Protestant Churches and Industrial America.* New York, 1949. (Protestant intellectual and moral leadership in reform. Bibliog.)

4   GUTHRIE, Robert Verus. "A Sociological Inquiry into the Origin, Nature, and Significance of the Social Creed of the Methodist Church in America." (New School of Soc Res), 1964. *Univ Mic* (1965), no. 65–1100. *Diss Abs,* XXVI (1965), 1202–1203. (Socializing of Methodist morality to minister to conditions.)

5   KELSEY, George D. "The Social Thought of Contemporary Southern Baptists." (Yale), 1946. *Univ Mic* (1966), no. 65–2492. *Diss Abs,* XXVII (1966), 1915A. (1917–1944, relation of thought to history and culture of South.)

6   KNUDTEN, Richard D. *The Systematic Thought of Washington Gladden.* New York, 1969. (Handbook of theological and social ideas, from sermons and addresses.)

7   PIPER, John Franklin, Jr. "The Social Policy of the Federal Council of the Churches of Christ in America During World War I." (Duke), 1965. *Univ Mic* (1965), no. 65–7279. *Diss Abs,* XXVI (1965), 515. (Influential pronouncements and leaders.)

8   RAUSCHENBUSCH, Walter. *A Rauschenbusch Reader; the Kingdom of God and the Social Gospel,* comp. by Benson Y. Landis. New York, 1957. (With interpretation of life and works, by Harry Emerson Fosdick.)

9   RUSS, Charles Trumbull. "The Theological Views of Graham Taylor, with Reference to the Social Gospel, and Its Applications to Industry, also a Bibliography of Graham Taylor's Works." (Hart Sem Found), 1964. *Univ Mic* (1965), no. 65–2678. *Diss Abs,* XXV (1965), 7401–7402. (Strove to reform, not replace social order.)

10 SPAIN, Rufus Buin. "Attitudes and Reactions of Southern Baptists to Certain Problems of Society, 1865–1900." (Vanderbilt), 1961. *Univ Mic* (1961), no. 61–3604. *Diss Abs,* XXII (1961), 1148. (Wide range of problems and opinions, increasing sense of social responsibility.)

11 SVENDSBY, Lloyd. "The History of a Developing Social Responsibility among the Lutherans in America from 1930 to 1960. . . ." (Un Theol Sem), 1966. *Univ Mic* (1967), no. 66–11,544. *Diss Abs,* XXVIII (1967), 290A–291A. (General conservatism, no uniform, adequate theology for social action.)

12 VULGAMORE, Melvin L. "Social Reform in the Theology of Charles Grandison Finney." (Bos), 1963. *Univ Mic* (1964), no. 64–391. *Diss Abs,* XXIV (1963), 2600. (Effect of teaching in reform following conversion, social and personal.)

D. Roman Catholic

1 BRODERICK, Francis L. *Right Reverend New Dealer, John A. Ryan.* New York, 1963. (Scholarly life of pioneer in Roman Catholic progressive social thought and reform.)

2 Catholic Church in the U.S. *Our Bishops Speak: National Pastorals and Annual Statements of the Hierarchy of the United States . . . 1919–1951.* Milwaukee, 1952. (Pronouncements on social problems and policy.)

3 CERNY, Karl Hubert. "Monsignor John A. Ryan and the Social Action Department: An Analysis of a Leading School of American Catholic Social Thought." (Yale), 1955. *Univ Mic* (1965), no. 65–2337. *Diss Abs*, XXV (1965), 4232–4233. (Creation of Catholic tradition of social thought, related to Progressivism's economic democracy.)

4 CRONIN, John Francis. *Catholic Social Principles; the Social Teaching of the Catholic Church Applied to American Economic Life.* Milwaukee, 1950. (Comprises whole Christian social order; annotated reading list.)

5 DERRIG, James Raymond. "The Political Thought of the Catholic Press, 1880 to 1920." (St. Louis), 1960. *Univ Mic* (1961), no. 61–746. *Diss Abs*, XXI (1961), 3504. (Emphasis upon social and political reform.)

6 KLINE, Omer Urban. "The Public Address of James Cardinal Gibbons as a Catholic Spokesman on Social Issues in America." (Colo), 1963. *Univ Mic* (1964), no. 64–1486. *Diss Abs*, XXIV (1964), 3461. (His influential thought, ahead of his time and church.)

7 O'BRIEN, David Joseph. *American Catholics and Social Reform: The New Deal Years.* New York, 1968. (Application of official teachings lagged behind acceptance; widely variant views. Richly documented.)

7. Social Action of Churches

8 ABELL, Aaron Ignatius. *American Catholicism and Social Action: A Search for Social Justice, 1865–1950.* Notre Dame, Ind., 1963. (Bibliog.)†

9 ABELL, Aaron Ignatius. "The Reception of Leo XIII's Labor Encyclical in America, 1891–1919." *Rev Pol*, VII (1945), 464–495. (Review of Catholic thought, writings and organizations regarding social problems.)

10 COSSETTE, J. P. *Catholic Social Work and Catholic Action: A Comparative Study on the Basis of the Lay Apostolate.* Washington, 1952. (Microcard HN37.C3.)

11 DAVIS, Jerome. "The Social Action Pattern of the Protestant Religious Leader." *Am Socio Rev*, I (1936), 105–114. (Analysis of 4,700 cases; tension between activists and community.)

1   DIRKS, Lee E. *Religion in Action; How America's Faiths Are Meeting New Challenges.* Silver Spring, Md., 1965. (Militant efforts to confront and solve urgent religious and social problems.)†

2   EIGHMY, John Lee. "The Social Conscience of Southern Baptists from 1900 to the Present as Reflected in Their Organized Life." (Mo), 1959. *Univ Mic* (1959), no. 59–5636. *Diss Abs,* XX (1960), 2770–2771. (Slow progress due to individualism and local autonomy.)

3   GANNON, Michael V. "Augustin Verot and the Emergence of American Catholic Social Consciousness." (Fla), 1962. *Univ Mic* (1963), no. 63–2668. *Diss Abs,* XXIII (1963), 2888–2889. (Period 1861–1870, earlier than is usually supposed; Verot a pace-setter.)

4   GROVER, Norman L. "The Church and Social Action: The Idea of the Church and Its Relation to Christian Social Strategy in Charles G. Finney, Horace Bushnell, and Washington Gladden." (Yale), 1957. *Univ Mic* (1967), no. 67–3735. *Diss Abs,* XXVII (1967), 3109A. (History of Social Gospel theology, individualistic moralism to direct church action.)

5   LACY, Creighton. *Frank Mason North: His Social and Ecumenical Mission.* Nashville, 1967. (Readable biography of beloved missionary and poet, whose life summarizes Social Gospel in practice.)

6   LANDIS, Judson T. "Social Action in American Protestant Churches." *Am J Socio,* LII (1947), 517–522. (Churches feel responsibility; programs mostly embryonic; meager financial support; inadequate personnel and leaders.)

7   LA NOUE, George R. "Church-State Relations in the Federal Policy Process." (Yale), 1966. *Univ Mic* (1966), no. 66–13,889. *Dis Abs,* XXVII (1967), 2575A. (Leaders in church and state cooperate to alleviate need and promote social justice.)

8   MILLER, Haskell M. *Compassion and Community: An Appraisal of the Church's Changing Role in Social Welfare.* New York, 1961. (Development of church work; many refs. to specific activities.)

9   O'NEILL, William Lawrence. "The Divorce Crisis of the Progressive Era." (Calif, Berkeley), 1963. *Univ Mic* (1964), no. 64–5275. *Diss Abs,* XXIV (1964), 5363–5364. (Religious, conservative opposition to divorce, 1890–1920, failed in changing moral climate.)

10   PAULSELL, William Oliver. "The Disciples of Christ and the Great Depression 1929–1936." (Vanderbilt), 1965. *Univ Mic* (1965), no. 65–10,482. *Diss Abs,* XXVI (1965), 2359. (Lack of preparedness and constructive social role; no consistent policy.)

11   RIEGLER, Gordon Arthur. *Socialization of the New England Clergy, 1800 to 1860.* Greenfield, Ohio, 1945. (Reveals increasing concern with application of doctrine to social conditions. Bibliog.)

12   SAPPINGTON, Roger Edwin. "The Development of Social Policy in the Church of the Brethren: 1908–1958." (Duke), 1959. *Univ Mic* (1960), no. 60–270. *Diss Abs,* XX (1960), 3715–3716. (Progress from in-group to social responsibility, stress on antiwar and civilian service causes.)

1 THOMPSON, Ernest Trice. *Plenty and Want; the Responsibility of the Church.* Nashville, 1966. (History of Christian ministry, facts about the U.S., duty and accomplishment of the churches.)

8. Slavery Question

2 BARNES, Gilbert H. *The Antislavery Impulse, 1830–1844.* New York, 1933. (Sees a cause in strong ethical impulse of evangelism.)†

3 DRAKE, Thomas E. *Quakers and Slavery in America.* New Haven, 1950. ("Gradualism" of Quaker emancipation policy.)

4 DUMOND, Dwight L. *Anti-Slavery Origins of the Civil War in the United States.* Ann Arbor, 1939. (Evangelical attack upon slavery.)†

5 ENGELDER, Conrad James. "The Churches and Slavery. A Study of the Attitudes Toward Slavery of the Major Protestant Denominations." (Mich), 1964. *Univ Mic* (1964), no. 64–12589. *Diss Abs* (1964), 3533. (Significance of Bible in making policy, which was often vacillating.)

6 FIFE, Robert Oldham. "Alexander Campbell and the Christian Church in the Slavery Controversy." (Ind), 1960. *Univ Mic* (1960), no. 60–6289. *Diss Abs*, XXI (1961), 2689. (Stresses conversion of individual to antislavery rather than church action.)

7 FORTENBAUGH, Robert. "American Lutheran Synods and Slavery, 1830–1860." *J Rel*, XIII (1933), 79–92. (Closely examines official attitudes; no consensus of opinion.)

8 JENKINS, William Sumner. *Pro-Slavery Thought in the Old South.* Chapel Hill, N.C., 1935. (Religious views and Biblical arguments.)

9 JOHNSON, Clifton Herman. "The American Missionary Association, 1846–1861: A Study of Christian Abolitionism." (NC), 1959. *Univ Mic* (1959), no. 59–5561. *Diss Abs*, XX (1960), 2774–2775. (Significant contribution to religiously-inspired anti-slavery cause.)

10 KULL, Irving Stoddard. "Presbyterian Attitudes Toward Slavery." *Church Hist*, VII (1938), 101–114. (Split in church due to conflicting religious attitudes.)

11 LYONS, Adelaide Avery. "Religious Defense of Slavery in the North." *Trinity Col Hist Soc Pap*, ser. 13. Durham, N.C., 1919.)

12 MATHEWS, Donald Gene. *Slavery and Methodism; A Chapter in American Morality, 1780–1845.* Princeton, N.J., 1965. (Conflict between ideals and social conditions. Bibliog.)

13 MILLER, Richard Roscoe. *Slavery and Catholicism.* Durham, N.C., 1957. (Thorough, scholarly review of history in U.S.)

14 PARKER, Russell Dean. " 'Higher Law': Its Development and Application to the American Antislavery Controversy." (Tenn), 1966. *Univ Mic* (1967). no. 67–1373. *Diss Abs*, XXVII (1967), 2996A–2997A. (Slavery versus law of God, example of religious influence on political controversy.)

1 POSEY, Walter Brownlow. "The Baptists and Slavery in the Lower Mississippi Valley." *Negro Hist*, XLI (1956), 117–130. (Growing pro-slavery feeling and schisms on the question.)

2 POWELL, Milton Bryan. "The Abolitionist Controversy in the Methodist Episcopal Church, 1840–1864." (St Univ Iowa), 1963. *Univ Mic* (1964), no. 64–3415. *Diss Abs*, XXIV (1964), 4661. (Re-evaluation by Methodists of their adjustment to American society.)

3 PURIFOY, Lewis McCarroll. "The Methodist Episcopal Church, South, and Slavery, 1844–1865." (NC), 1965. *Univ Mic* (1966), no. 66–4728. *Diss Abs*, XXVI (1966), 6005. (Departure from early anti-slavery stand to conform to Southern society.)

4 SENIOR, Robert Cholerton. "New England Congregationalists and the Anti-Slavery Movement, 1830–1860." (Yale), 1954. *Univ Mic* (1967), no. 67–9158. *Diss Abs*, XXVIII (1967), 606A. (A moderate movement, never committed to abolitionism.)

5 SHERWIN, Oscar. "The Armory of God." *N Eng Q*, XVIII (1945), 70–82. (Use of Biblical sanctions by both sides in the slavery argument.)

9. Labor Problem

6 BLACHLY, Clarence Dan. *The Treatment of the Problem of Capital and Labor in Social Study Courses in the Churches*. Chicago, 1920. (Contemporary attitudes, historically important.)

7 BROWNE, Henry Joseph. *The Catholic Church and the Knights of Labor*. Washington, D.C., 1949. (Beginning of greater concern about social and labor questions.)

8 DANIEL, John. *Labor, Industry, and the Church; a Study of the Inter-relationships Involving the Church, Labor and Management*. St. Louis, 1957. (Bibliog.)

9 DAVIS, Jerome, ed. *Labor Speaks for Itself on Religion; a Symposium of Labor Leaders Throughout the World*. New York, 1929. (American union leaders; possibility of cooperation to secure social justice.)

10 Federal Council of the Churches of Christ in America. *The Church and Modern Industry*. New York, 1908. (New "social creed," epoch-making.)

11 GRIFFITHS, Carl Warren. "Attitudes of the Religious Press toward Organized Labor, 1877–1896." (Chi), 1942. (Pub. in part in *Church Hist*, XI (1942), 138–148, bibliog. footnotes.)

12 Jewish Theological Seminary of America, Institute for Religious and Social Studies. *Labor's Relation to Church and Community, a Series of Addresses*. Ed. by Liston Pope. New York, 1947. (Liberal Protestant view.)

13 McQUADE, Vincent Augustine. *The American Catholic Attitude on Child Labor Since 1891*. Washington, 1938. (About legislation; with bibliog.)

1 MUELDER, Walter G. "The Church and the Labor Movement." *Rel Life*, XVI (1947), 483–493. (Recent relations, showing maturity of outlook.)

2 MUNIER, John David. *Some American Approximations to Pius XI's Industries and Professions.* Washington, 1943. (Applications of the Pope's encyclical on labor.)

3 RYAN, John A. and Joseph HUSSLEIN. *The Church and Labor.* New York, 1920. (Primarily documentary, quotes pronouncements by American hierarchy. Bibliog.)

4 THOMAS, Stanley Whitaker. "The Image of Labor Organization in Church and Trade Union, 1945–1955. . . ." (Bos), 1960. *Univ Mic* (1960), no. 60–3488. *Diss Abs*, XXI (1960), 979–980. (Development of Protestant and Roman Catholic Labor policies.)

5 WARD, Harry Frederick. *The Gospel for a Working World.* New York, 1918. (Contemporary labor conditions and planting of Gospel in industrial world. Bibliog.)

6 WILSON, John Moran Cochran. *The Labour Movement and the Church.* Boston, 1922. (Papers on Christianizing labor relations.)

10. Christian Socialism

7 BARKAT, Anwar Masih. "The Fellowship of Socialist Christians and Its Antecedents." (Duke), 1965. *Univ Mic* (1966), no. 66–80. *Diss Abs*, XXVI (1966), 5523. (Continued and modified Social Gospel movement, 1930–1963.)

8 BESTOR, Arthur. *Backwoods Utopias, the Sectarian and Owenite Phases of Communitarian Socialism in America, 1663–1829.* Philadelphia, 1950. (Scholarly treatment of religious communism; bibliog. essay.)†

9 DOMBROWSKI, James. *The Early Days of Christian Socialism in America.* New York, 1936. (Diverse origins and Society of Christian Socialists. Bibliog.)

10 HANDY, Robert T. "Christianity and Socialism in America, 1900–1920." *Church Hist*, XXI (1952), 39–54. (Christians in Socialist ranks; many refs.)

11 LAUBENSTEIN, Paul F. *A History of Christian Socialism in America.* New York, 1925. (Valuable bibliog. and notes on Christian Socialist periodicals.)

12 NORDHOFF, Charles. *The Communistic Societies of the United States: From Personal Visit and Observation.* New York, 1875. (Includes those of Christian inspiration. Bibliog.)†

13 PERSONS, Stow. "Christian Communitarianism in America." Vol. I of *Socialism in American Life.* Ed. by Donald Drew Egbert and Stow Persons. Princeton, 1952, pp. 127–151. (With bibliog.)

14 WEBBER, Christopher L. "William Dwight Porter Bliss (1856–1926) Priest and Socialist." *Hist Mag P E Ch*, XXVIII (1959), 9–39. (Documented account of Christian Socialist movement.)

15 WHITNEY, Norman Jehiel. *Experiments in Community. . . .* Wallingford, Pa., 1966. (Captures motives and spirit of exclusive religious societies.)†

11. Race Question

1 CAMPBELL, Ernest Queener, and Thomas F. PETTIGREW. *Christians in Racial Crisis: A Study of Little Rock's Ministry.* Washington, D.C., 1959. (Systematic study of part of clergy and church in civil rights struggle; statements on race question by leading denominations.)

2 CULVER, Dwight W. *Negro Segregation in the Methodist Church.* New Haven, 1953. (Study of attitudes.)

3 EDWARDS, Lyford P. "Religious Sectarianism and Race Prejudice." *Am J Socio*, XLI (1935), 167–179. (Prejudice generally dominant over religious beliefs.)

4 EIGHMY, John Lee. "Recent Changes in the Racial Attitudes of Southern Baptists." *Foundations*, V (1962), 354–360. (Little overt action against discrimination, creation of favorable climate of opinion.)

5 GRIMES, Alan P. *Equality in America: Religion, Race and the Urban Majority.* New York, 1964. ("Religion," pp. 3–40, development of religious toleration and freedom.)†

6 HARTE, Thomas J. "Scalogram Analysis of Catholic Attitudes toward the Negro." *Am Cath Socio Rev*, XII (1951), 66–74. (More favor to religious than economic or social equality.)

7 HILL, Samuel S. "Southern Protestantism and Racial Integration." *Rel Life*, XXXIII (1964), 421–429. (Sociological, cultural, doctrinal background of mere token progress since 1840's.)

8 KAY, Toombs Hodges, Jr. "The Role of Selected Protestant Churches in Emancipation and Integration." (N Y), 1962. *Univ Mic* (1962), no. 62–5336. *Diss Abs*, XXIII (1963), 2606–2607. (Gradual liberalization of attitude since 1830; church leadership in work for better relations.)

9 KRAMER, Alfred S. "Patterns of Racial Inclusion among Selected Congregations of Three Protestant Denominations." (N Y) *Univ Mic* (1955), no. 13,621; *Diss Abs*, XV (1955), 1928. (General practice of segregation. Bibliog.)

10 MANSCHRECK, Clyde L. "Religion in the South: Problem and Promise." *The South in Perspective, Institute of Southern Culture Lectures at Longwood College, 1958.* Ed. by Francis B. Simkins. Farmville, Va., 1958. (Struggles of Christian conscience regarding race question.)

11 MAY, William Wright. "The Methodist Church and the Present Racial Crisis: A Study of Response and Action." (Drew), 1967. *Univ Mic* (1967), no. 67–14,377. *Diss Abs*, XXVIII (1967), 1890A–1891A. (History of attitudes and action since 1939.)

12 MOELLERING, Ralph Luther. *Christian Conscience and Negro Emancipation.* Philadelphia, 1965. (Record of churches in race relations; dilemma and duty in light of past conflicts over morality of slavery and racism.)

1 National Conference on Race and Religion. *Race: Challenge to Religion, Original Essays and an Appeal to the Conscience.* Chicago, 1963. (Protestant, Roman Catholic, Jewish writers discuss the problem, with historic background.)

2 OSBORNE, William Audley. *The Segregated Convenant: Race Relations and American Catholics.* New York, 1967. (History of relations, crisis of conscience regarding education and housing.)

3 PARSONS, Talcott. "Racial and Religious Differences as Factors in Group Tensions." Vol V (1944) of *Conference on Science, Philosophy and Religion, A Symposium.* New York, 1945. (Doubtful whether universalistic element has reduced group clashes, because of ingrown communalism, pp. 182–199.)

4 REIMERS, David M. *White Protestantism and the Negro.* New York, 1965. (Scholarly review of relations, beginning of 19th century to 1960's.)

5 SPIKE, Robert Warren. *The Freedom Revolution and the Churches.* New York, 1965. (They generally "have aided and abetted the Anglo-Saxon white conspiracy.")

6 STARK, Rodney, and Charles Y. GLOCK. "Prejudice and the Churches." *Prejudice, U.S.A.* Ed. by Charles Y. Glock and Ellen Siegelman. New York, 1969. (Those involved in religious institutions are not less racist than others; in fact, more so.)†

7 WARNOCK, Henry Young. "Moderate Racial Thought and Attitudes of Southern Baptists and Methodists, 1900–1921." (N W), 1963. *Univ Mic* (1964), no. 64–2539. *Diss Abs*, XXIV (1964), 3724. (Contribution to climate favorable to raising Negro status and for better relations.)

8 WASHINGTON, Joseph R., Jr. *The Politics of God.* Boston, 1967. (Relations between Negro religiosity and history of attitude of "white folk religion" toward Negroes.)

12. Church in the City

9 ABELL, Aaron Ignatius. "The Catholic Factor in Urban Welfare: The Early Period, 1850–1880." *Rev Pol*, XIV (1952), 289–324. (Detailed history of Catholic action, charity, social reform.)

10 ABELL, Aaron Ignatius. *The Urban Impact on American Protestanism, 1865–1900.* Cambridge, Mass., and London, 1943. (Origins and development of efforts to adjust to urbanism; bibliog. essays.)

11 BLUMHORST, Roy. *Faithful Rebels; Does the Old-Style Religion Fit the New Style of Life?* Saint Louis, 1967. (Experience of a minister in typical high-rise apartment living.)

12 CROSS, Robert D. "The Changing Image of the City Among American Catholics." *Cath Hist Rev*, XLVIII (1962), 33–52. (Influential opinion over 80 years, development of urban sociology.)

13 CROSS, Robert D., ed. *The Church and the City, 1865–1910.* Indianapolis, 1967. (Selections from writings of 16 leaders, on problems and ministries of urban churches.)†

1 DOUGLASS, Harlan Paul. *1000 City Churches; Phases of Adaptation to Environment.* New York, 1926. (Church work in all cities of 100,000 or more.)

2 DOUGLASS, Harlan Paul. *Protestant Cooperation in American Cities.* New York, 1930. (Based on case studies over nearly a decade.)

3 DUNSTAN, John Leslie. *A Light to the City; 150 Years of the City Missionary Society of Boston, 1816–1966.* Boston, 1966. (Very detailed story of first such American society.)

4 FICHTER, Joseph Henry. *Social Relations in the Urban Parish.* Chicago, 1954. (Adaptation for apostolic urban missionary action.)

5 HALLENBACH, Wilbur Chapman. "The Organization of Religion." *American Urban Communities.* New York, 1951. (Gradual dispersal of Protestant communities, parochial disintegration.)

6 HALLENBACH, Wilbur Chapman. *Urban Organization of Protestantism.* New York, 1934. (Interchurch and interdenominational cooperation.)

7 HENRY, John Robertson. *Fifty Years on the Lower East Side of New York.* N.p. 1966. (Personal recollections of social-gospel pastor among the poor; vivid pictures of immigrant life, society, politics, reform.)

8 LEE, Robert, ed. *The Church and the Exploding Metropolis.* Richmond, 1965. (Theological, social, strategic adjustment to urbanization, in historical perspective.)†

9 LEE, Robert, ed. *Cities and Churches: Readings on the Urban Church.* Philadelphia, 1962. (About 30 authors; problem since about 1916; stories of parishes.)†

10 LEIFFER, Murray Howard. *City and Church in Transition; a Study of the Medium-sized City and Its Organized Religious Life.* Chicago and New York, 1938. (With maps.)

11 MARIE LUCITA, Sister. *Manhattan Mission.* Garden City, N.Y., 1967. (Experiences of Roman Catholic missionary order among depressed and alienated urban folk.)

12 Methodist Church, Board of Missions, Joint Section of Education and Cultivation. *Crowded Ways; a Symposium.* New York, 1954. (Problems of city missions.)

13 MILLER, Kenneth Dexter. *Man and God in the City.* New York, 1954. (Survey of methods and influence of city missions.)†

14 MILLER, Kenneth Dexter and Ethel Prince. *The People Are the City; 150 years of Social and Religious Concern in New York City.* New York, 1962. (New York City Mission Society, philanthropic individuals, response to new challenges.)

15 MOORE, Richard E., and Duane L. DAY. *Urban Church Breakthrough.* New York, 1966. (Church's theological and practical problems in urban ministry; efforts to meet them.)

16 National Conference of Catholic Charities, ed. *The Church and Neighborhood Conservation.* Washington, 1955. (Experience of Chicago pastors in developing positive social program.)

1 SANDERSON, Ross W. *The Church Serves the Changing City.* New York, 1955. (Experimental ministries of Protestant churches in "blighted" urban areas.)

2 YOUNGER, George D. *The Church and Urban Renewal.* Philadelphia, 1965. (Presbyterian study, discussing approaches to problem, case histories of churches that solved it.)

13. Church in Suburbia

3 DODSON, Dan W. "Religion in Suburbia." *J Educ Socio,* XXXII (1959), 365–373. (Danger of becoming mere servant of ideals of middle-class life.)

4 GORDON, Albert I. *Jews in Suburbia.* Boston, 1959. (Significance for American society of new type of middle-class Jewish religious life, Chaps. IV–VI.)

5 GREELEY, Andrew M. *The Church and the Suburbs.* New York, 1959. (Adjustment of Catholicism to new suburban living.)

6 MAYS, William Egli. "A Study of the Factors Influencing the Geographical Movement of Churches in a Metropolitan Area." (Pitts), 1956. *Univ Mic* (1956), no. 18–246; *Diss Abs,* XVI (1956), 2548. (Flight to the suburbs and its problems.)

7 MILLER, Kenneth Dexter. "Our Growing Suburbs and Their Churches." *Rel Life,* XXIV (1955), 516–523. (Deeper seriousness may be threatened by "social" and complacent religion.)

8 NASH, Dennison, and Peter L. BERGER. "The Child, the Family and the 'Religious Revival' in Suburbia." *J Sci Stud Rel,* II (1962), 85–93. (Joining church a "rite of passage" in middle-class child-centered family.)

9 REISMAN, David. *The Organization Man.* New York, 1956. (Incl. criticism of identification of religion with social class.)

10 SENN, Milton. "Race, Religion and Suburbia." *J Intergr Relat,* III (1962), 159–170. (Mainly on self-ghettoization of Jews, adopting general middle-class character.)

11 SHIPPEY, Frederick A. *Protestantism in Suburban Life.* New York, Nashville, 1964. (Suburban trend since 1945, basic problems in relations with minorities; large bibliog.)

12 WINTER, Gibson. *The Suburban Captivity of the Churches: An Analysis of Protestant Responsibility in the Expanding Metropolis.* Garden City, N.Y., 1961. (Seen against background of growth of metropolitan society, 1870–1950.)†

14. Rural Churches

13 DAVIDSON, Walter S. "The Plight of Rural Protestantism." *Rel Life,* XV (1946), 337–390. (Decline of small country church; efforts to solve problem.)

1   HARRIS, Marshall D., and Joseph ACKERMAN. *Town and Country Churches and Family Farming.* New York, 1960. (Review of effort, 1940–1955, to meliorate Christian rural life in a democracy.)

2   McBRIDE, Charles R. *Protestant Churchmanship for Rural America.* Valley Forge, Pa., 1962. (Readjustment of rural church to recent changes in agricultural and general economy.)

3   MUELLER, Elwin W., and Giles C. EKOLA, eds. *The Silent Struggle for Mid-America: The Church in Town and Country Today.* Minneapolis, 1963. (Problem in historical perspective of changes in country and small-town since 1920. Bibliog.)†

4   North Carolina University, Institute for Research in Social Science. *Church and Community in the South.* Richmond, 1949. (Essays on church-community relations in urban and rural areas.)

5   ODUM, Howard W. *American Social Problems.* New York, 1939. (Chap. XXII discusses problems of rural churches.)

6   SKRABANEK, R. L. "The Rural Church: Characteristics and Problems," *Rural Sociology: An Analysis of Contemporary Rural Life.* Ed. by Alvin Lee Bertrand. New York, 1958. (Historic factors in plight of rural church, efforts to adjust to changed conditions, pp. 237–252. Bibliog.)

7   WEST, James. *Plainville, U.S.A.* New York, 1945. (Chap. IV studies social and religious problems of modern rural church.)†

XVII. Special Ministries

1. Evangelism and Revivalism. General Histories

8   JOHNSON, Charles A. *The Frontier Camp Meeting; Religion's Harvest Time.* Dallas, 1955. (Dispels derogatory misconceptions; a civilizing force. Large bibliog.)

9   MUNCY, William Luther. *A History of Evangelism in the United States.* Kansas City, Kan., 1945. (Heavily accents social influences.)

10 SCHARPFF, Paulus. *History of Evangelism; Three Hundred Years of Evangelism in Germany, Great Britain, and the United States of America.* Grand Rapids, 1966. (American evangelism from origins in Continental European Pietism, connection with similar movements abroad.)

11 SHELLEY, Bruce Leon. *Evangelicalism in America.* Grand Rapids, 1967. (Movement stressing true decision for Christ, from origins in colonial Pietism and revivals.)

12 SWEET, William Warren. *Revivalism in America, Its Origin, Growth, and Decline.* Gloucester, Mass., 1965. (Appeal to individual, association with common man, social reform, decline because of institutionalizing.)†

2. The Great Awakening

1 ARMSTRONG, Maurice W. "Religious Enthusiasm and Separatism in Colonial New England." *Har Theol Rev*, XXXVIII (1945), 111–140. (Effects in democratizing religion, freedom, toleration, church-state separation.)

2 BRYNESTAD, Lawrence E. "The Great Awakening in the New England and Middle Colonies." *J Presby Hist Soc*, XIV (1930), 80–91, 104–141. (Transformations in secular and religious culture, humanitarian aspects.)

3 FRELINGHUYSEN, Peter H. B. *Theodorus Jacobus Frelinghuysen*. Princeton, 1938. (Forerunner of Great Awakening, indebted to Pietism. Bibliog.)

4 GAUSTAD, Edwin Scott. *The Great Awakening in New England*. New York, 1957. Gloucester, Mass., 1965. (Stresses effects of religious democracy. Bibliog.)†

5 GOEN, C. C. *Revivalism and Separatism in New England, 1740–1800; Strict Congregationalists and Separate Baptists in the Great Awakening*. New Haven, 1962. (Shows influence of Separatism in growth of Baptist beliefs, ideal of a pure church, decline of state-churchism.)

6 HEIMERT, Alan E., and Perry MILLER, eds. *The Great Awakening: Documents Illustrating the Crisis and Its Consequences*. Indianapolis, 1967. (Sermons and tracts on origins, progress, and opinions; indispensable for study.)†

7 HENRY, Stuart Clark. *George Whitefield: Wayfaring Witness*. New York and Nashville, 1957. (Best modern critical study, correcting much in earlier biographies. Selected bibliog.)

8 KENNEY, William Howland, III. "George Whitefield and Colonial Revivalism: The Social Sources of Charismatic Authority, 1737–1770." (Penn), 1966. *Univ Mic* (1967), no. 67–3080. *Diss Abs*, XXVII (1967), 3399A–3400A. (Revival brought spiritual consensus, society of separate and equal faiths.)

9 LODGE, Martin Ellsworth. "The Great Awakening in the Middle Colonies." (Calif, Berkeley), 1964. *Univ Mic* (1965), no. 65–3027. *Diss Abs*, XXV (1965), 6572. (Evangelism laid foundations of independent American churches.)

10 MILLER, John Chester. "Religion, Finance, and Democracy in Massachusetts." *N Eng Q*, VI (1933), 29–58. (Association of class conflict with pro- and anti-evangelistic parties.)

11 MILLER, Perry. "Jonathan Edwards' Sociology of the Great Awakening." *N Eng Q*, XXI (1948), pp. 50–77. (Penetrating study of social views springing from pietist evangelism.)

12 PARKES, Henry B. "New England in the Seventeen-Thirties." *N Eng Q*, III (1930), 397–419. (Mental and spiritual ferment preceding and accompanying Awakening; change in culture.)

1 TANIS, James. *Dutch Calvinistic Pietism in the Middle Colonies.* The Hague, 1967. (Comprehensive view of ministry of Rev. T. J. Frelinghuysen and its influence.)

2 TOLLES, Frederick B. "Quietism Versus Enthusiasm: The Philadelphia Quakers and the Great Awakening." *Penn Mag Hist Biog*, LXIX (1945), 26–49. (Unfavorable, conservative Quaker religious and social attitude.)

3. Later Revivals. Decline

3 CLEVELAND, Catharine C. *The Great Revival in the West, 1797–1805.* Chicago, 1916. (Original narratives; explained in modern psychological terms. Bibliog.)

4 CROSS, Whitney Rogers. *The Burned-Over District, the Social and Intellectual History of Enthusiastic Religion in Western New York, 1800–1850.* Ithaca, N.Y., 1950. (Relation to social environment and reform movements. Bibliog.)†

5 EMMONS, Irvin Willetts. "A History of Revivalism in America Since the Civil War." Th.M. thesis, Princeton Theol Sem., 1944. Typ. (Bibliog.)

6 LOETSCHER, Lefferts A. *Presbyterianism and Revivals in Philadelphia Since 1875.* Philadelphia, 1944. (Typical account of decline of urban revivalism; causes.)

7 LOUD, Grover C. *Evangelized America.* New York, 1928. (Urban adaptation of revival techniques.)

8 McLOUGHLIN, William Gerald, Jr. *Modern Revivalism: Charles Grandison Finney to Billy Graham.* New York, 1959. (Well-documented analysis of professional revivalism since 1825, related to American life.)

9 PRIME, Samuel Irenaeus. *Five Years of Prayer, with the Answers.* New York, 1864. (Morale-sustaining influence of revivals in the Civil War.)

10 SPEER, William. *The Great Revival of 1800.* . . . Philadelphia, 1872. (Ultimate effects upon missions, humanitarianism, reforms, education, literature.)

11 STELZLE, Charles. "The Passing of the Old Evangelism." *World's Work*, LV (1927), 195–202; and "The Evangelist in Present-Day America." *Current Hist*, XXXV (1931), 224–228. (Excellent reviews of reasons for decline in 20th century.)

12 STRAUSS, Preston Franklin. "The Revivals of Religion in the State of New York (1825–1835) under the Leadership of Charles G. Finney." Princeton Theol Sem. 2 vols. Ca. 1940. Typ. (Large bibliog.)

13 STRICKLAND, Arthur B. *The Great American Revival; A Case Study in Historical Evangelism with Implications for Today.* Cincinnati, 1934. (Defends revivals as props of national morale, social and economic betterment. Bibliog.)

14 SWEET, William Warren. *Religion on the American Frontier, 1783–1840.* 4 vols. New York and Chicago, 1931–1946. (Source materials on frontier revivalism, with bibliogs.)

4. Evangelists

1 CARTWRIGHT, Peter. *Autobiography of Peter Cartwright, the Backwoods Preacher.* Ed. by W. P. Strickland. Nashville, 1956. (Symbolic figure of revivalistic frontier religion.)

2 CURTIS, Richard Kenneth. *They Called Him Mister Moody.* Garden City, N.Y., 1962. (Favorable, but not uncritically laudatory; his educational and evangelistic work.)†

3 FINDLAY, James Franklin, Jr. *Dwight L. Moody: American Evangelist, 1837–1899.* Chicago, 1969. (Stresses his effort to "urbanize" revivalism and adapt traditional faith to rapidly altering social environment. Supersedes other biographies.)

4 HALL, Gordon Langley. *The Sawdust Trail; the Story of American Evangelism.* Philadelphia, 1964. (Popular sketches of twelve evangelists, from Great Awakening to Billy Graham.)

5 HIGH, Stanley. *Billy Graham, the Personal Story of the Man, His Message, and His Mission.* New York, Toronto, London, 1956. (Socially "respectable" evangelism for a "sophisticated" era.)

6 JOHNSON, James E. "The Life of Charles Grandison Finney." (Syracuse), 1959. *Univ Mic* (1959), no. 59–6306. *Diss Abs,* XX (1960), 2763–2764. (Proponent of Christian perfectionism; linked revivalism to social reform.)

7 McLOUGHLIN, William Gerald, Jr. *Billy Sunday Was His Real Name.* Chicago, 1955. (Only competent life, largely from personal records and interviews.)

8 MOODY, William Revell. *D. L. Moody.* New York, 1930. (Most authoritative life, emphasis on part in melioration of society. Large bibliog.)

9 NELSON, Daniel Wilhelm. "B. Fay Mills: Revivalist, Social Reformer and Advocate of Free Religion." (Syracuse), 1964. *Univ Mic* (1965), no. 65–3427. *Diss Abs,* XXV (1965), 6090–6091. (Tried to combine individual conversion and Social Gospel, important for future developments.)

10 POLLOCK, John Charles. *Billy Graham; the Authorized Biography.* Grand Rapids, 1967. (First major biography, based mostly on tape-recorded interviews and private papers.)†

11 POLLOCK, John Charles. *Moody: A Biographical Portrait of the Pacesetter in Modern Mass Evangelism.* New York, 1963, Grand Rapids, 1967. (Development and impact of his personality, ecumenicity, inspiration of movements.)†

12 RAMSAY, John Cummins. *John Wilbur Chapman, the Man, His Methods and His Message.* Boston, 1962. (Scholarly but popular life of world-famous Presbyterian evangelist.)

13 STOWE, Lyman Beecher. *Saints, Sinners and Beechers.* Indianapolis, 1934. (Appreciation of Lyman Beecher as an evangelist.)

1 WEISBEGER, Bernard A. *They Gathered at the River: The Story of the Great Revivalists and Their Impact upon Religion in America.* Boston and Toronto, 1958. (Relation to contemporary movements of thought.)†

2 WRIGHT, George Frederick. *Charles Grandison Finney.* Boston, 1891. (Still authoritative appraisal of the evangelist and his work.)

5. *Home Missions*

3 Christian Commission for Camp and Defense Communities. *A Guide to Church Volunteer Service in Defense Areas.* New York, 1944. (Special ministries in war-created settlements. Bibliog.)

4 CLARK, M. Edward; William L. MALCOMSON; and Warren Lane MOLTON, eds. *The Church Creative: A Reader on the Renewal of the Church.* Nashville and New York, 1967. (Essays on origins and histories of special types of ministries in different communities across the nation.)

5 DAWBER, Mark A. *America's Changing Frontiers.* New York, 1945. (Home missions and internal migration.)

6 DOUGLASS, Truman B. *Mission to America.* New York, 1951. (Needs and strategy for Protestants, in light of modern sociological changes and attitudes; valuable bibliog.)

7 ELSBREE, Oliver Wendell. *The Rise of the Missionary Spirit in America, 1790–1815.* Williamsport, Pa., 1928. (Strong impulse from revivals broadening into many benevolences. Bibliog.)

8 GOODWIN, R. Dean. *There Is No End.* New York, 1956. (Home missions, religion and social conditions.)

9 GOODYKOONTZ, Colin B. *Home Missions on the American Frontier, with Particular Reference to the American Home Missionary Society.* Caldwell, Idaho, 1939. (Emphasizes cooperative work. Selected bibliog.)

10 GUNTHER, Peter F., ed. *The Fields at Home: Studies in Home Missions.* Chicago, 1963. (Essays on many types; incl. contemporary work and historical background.)

11 HANDY, Robert T. *We Witness Together.* New York, 1956. (Thorough discussion of cooperative missions. Bibliog.)

12 HARKNESS, Georgia Elma. *The Church and the Immigrant.* New York, 1921. (Americanizing role of the churches. Bibliog.)

13 HOOKER, Elizabeth R. *Religion in the Highlands; Native Churches and Missionary Enterprises in the Southern Appalachian Area,* 1933.

14 Interdenominational Conference on Work with New Americans, Chicago, 1935. *New Americans Today; Proceedings.* New York, 1936. (Americanization as an aim of home missions.)

15 KING, William Robert. *History of the Home Missions Council, with Introductory Outline History of Home Missions.* New York, 1930.

1 LANDIS, Benson Young, ed. *Uprooted Americans; 5 Pamphlets on Popula-tion Shifts in America Today.* New York, 1940. (Home missions and dis-placed families. Reading lists.)

2 McGUIRE, Frederick A., ed. *Mission to Mankind.* New York, 1963. (Stories of Roman Catholic home missions, including migrant and water-front workers, Navajo Indians, drug addicts.)

3 MOORE, John Milton. *The Challenge of Change, What is Happening to Home Missions.* New York, 1931. (Aim to Christianize all areas of American life. Considered most complete review to date.)

4 MORSE, Hermann Nelson. *These Moving Times; the Home Mission of the Church in the Light of Social Trends and Population Shifts.* Richmond, 1945. (Comprehensive list of readings.)

5 National Lutheran Council. *Christ for the Moving Millions, a Conference on Mobility . . . 1954.* Chicago, 1955. (Mission problems in rapidly shifting populations. Bibliog. notes.)

6 POSEY, Walter Brownlow. *Frontier Mission: a History of Religion West of the Southern Appalachians to 1861.* Lexington, 1966. (Seven dominant denominations, relations to evangelism, sects, Indians, Negroes, slavery, education, social life.)

7 SHOTWELL, Louisa Rossiter. *This Is Your Neighbor.* New York, 1956. (Relation to social problems.)

8 SHRIVER, William Payne. *Missions at the Grass Roots.* New York, 1949. (Relation to social problems. Bibliog.)

9 STEWART, Betty, ed. *New Home Missions Work for Human Rights.* New York, 1952. (Illus.)

6. *Clergy*

10 ADDISON, Daniel Dulaney. *The Clergy in American Life and Letters.* New York and London, 1900. (Contributions and influence; strongly emphasizes 19th-century liberals.)

11 BLIZZARD, Samuel. "The Minister's Dilemma." *Ch Cent,* 73, no. 17 (Apr. 25, 1956), 408–410. (New urban training of clergy to cope with social problems, organization, administration, work services with adults.)

12 COATES, Charles H., and Robert C. KISTLER. "Role Dilemmas of Protestant Clergymen in a Metropolitan Community." *Rev Rel Res,* VI (1965), 147–152. (Administration tending to displace function as pastor; review of literature.)

13 DAVIS, Jerome. "The Minister and Economic Order." *J Educ Socio,* X (1937), 269–279. (Adaptation of leader to economic pattern; minister a pastor, not a social reformer.)

14 ENGEMAN, Jack. *The Catholic Priest, His Training and Ministry; a Picture Story.* New York, 1961. (Valuable to explain a mystery to many Catholics as well as Protestants.)

15 FARBER, Heije. *Pastoral Care and Clinical Training in America; Report of a Three Months Visit.* Arnhem, 1961. (Dutch pastor reviews present state, with reference to historical background of American religion.)

1   FELDMAN, Abraham J. *The American Reform Rabbi: A Profile of a Profession.* New York, 1965. (How the rabbinate meets problems of American society.)

2   FICHTER, Joseph H. *America's Forgotten Priests: What They Are Saying.* New York, 1968.

3   FICHTER, Joseph H. "Catholic Church Professionals." *Ann Am Acad Pol Soc Sci,* 387 (Jan., 1970), 77–85. (Few entrants, many leaving, main losses in specialized ministries; training and work broader and more diversified.)

4   FICHTER, Joseph H. *Priest and People.* New York, 1965. (Sociological study of priest-layman relationships in Roman Catholic Church.)

5   FICHTER, Joseph H. *Religion as an Occupation; a Study in the Sociology of Professions.* Notre Dame, Ind., 1961. (Study of the Roman Catholic clergy as a profession.)†

6   GELBER, Sholome M. *The Failure of the American Rabbi: A Program for the Revitalization of the Rabbinate in America.* New York, 1961. (Social demand for too much business and too little spirituality.)

7   HADDEN, Jeffrey K. *The Gathering Storm in the Churches.* Garden City, N.Y., 1969. (Extensive study of the "new breed" of socially active clergy and their effect in dividing lay opinion.)

8   HADDEN, Jeffrey K. "A Study of the Protestant Ministry of America." *J Sci Stud Rel,* V (1965), 10–23. (Thousands of ministers, covering wide range of belief.)

9   HAGSTROM, Warren O. "The Protestant Clergy as a Profession: Status and Prospects." *Berk Pub Soc Inst,* III (1957), 54–69. (Historic change of minister from spiritual to institutional leader.)

10   ILLICH, Ivan. "The Vanishing Clergyman." *Critic* (June–July, 1967), 18–27. (Argues that the whole concept of the religious life is outmoded.)

11   LUECKE, Richard Henry. "Protestant Clergy: New Forms of Ministry, New Forms of Training." *Ann Am Acad Pol Soc Sci,* 387 (Jan., 1970), 86–95. (Training related to action, continual rapid change, urbanization.)

12   McCOLLOUGH, Charles. *Continuing Education for Clergy and Laity.* Boston, 1969. (Theological institutes, federations of schools, as field training centers for urban work.)

13   MITCHELL, Robert Edward. "Minister-Parishioner Relations." (Colum), 1962. *Univ Mic* (1965), no. 65–7383. *Diss Abs,* XXVI (1965), 1820. (4,000 reports from Protestant ministers, stresses place in community.)

14   MUELLER, Walter Ernest. "Protestant Ministers in Modern American Novels, 1927–1958: the Search for a Role." (Neb), 1961. *Univ Mic* (1961), no. 61–1972. *Diss Abs,* XXI (1961), 3789. ("Lostness" of many clergymen, lack of real influence, uncertain of role.)

15   SMITH, Elwyn Allen. *The Presbyterian Ministry in American Culture; a Study in Changing Concepts, 1700–1900.* Philadelphia, 1962. (History of relation of ministry to the "World," changing concepts of education to deal with secular culture.)

1 VOIGT, Gilbert Paul. "The Protestant Minister in American Fiction." *Luth Q*, XI (1959), 3-13. (Historically important types and attitudes toward them.)

2 WAGONER, Walter D. *The Seminary; Protestant and Catholic.* New York, 1966. (Decline in number of seminarians, closing of schools, cooperation between Roman Catholic and Protestant schools.)

3 WORDEN, James William. "The Portrayal of the Protestant Minister in American Motion Pictures, 1951–1960, and Its Implications for the Church Today." (Bos), 1962. *Univ Mic* (1962), no. 62–4528. *Diss Abs*, XXIII (1962), 1440. (Minister's rôle portrayed as ineffective, declining in influence, less prestigious.)

7. Preaching

4 ATKINS, Gaius Glenn. *Preaching and the Mind of Today.* New York, 1934. (Reflects renewed interest in doctrine.)

5 DAVIS, Ozora S. *Preaching the Social Gospel.* New York and Chicago, 1922. (Prevailing social emphasis before the 1930's.)

6 GRAY, Lloyd J. "A Study of Protestant Preaching in the United States, 1920–1929." *S Bap Sem*, Louisville, Ky., 1946. (Swing from theological dogma toward practical preaching to meet "life situations.")

7 HOYT, Arthur Stephen. *The Pulpit and American Life.* New York, 1921. (Assesses great preachers and influence of the pulpit.)

8 HUDSON, Robert Lofton. "The Sermon as Teaching with Specific Emphasis on Motivation." Peabody Contributions to Education, no. 375. Nashville, 1946. (Based on study of many American sermons.)

9 JONES, Edgar DeWitt. *American Preachers of To-day; Intimate Appraisals of Thirty-two Leaders.* Indianapolis, 1933. (Mostly Protestant; de-emphasis of theology, stress on ethical and social notes.)

10 KENNEDY, Gerald H. "Seventy-Five Years of American Preaching." *Christendom*, VII (1942), 214–225. (Influences that have shaped preaching; its influence.)

11 LEVY, Babette May. *Preaching in the First Half Century of New England History.* New York, 1967. (Favorable view, as expression of rich religious and literary culture, influence on life.)

12 McCANTS, David Arnold. "A Study of the Criticism of Preaching Published in America Between 1865 and 1930." (N W), 1964. *Univ Mic* (1964), no. 64–12,317. *Diss Abs*, XXV (1964), 3745. (Analysis and evaluation of American pulpit; influence in literature, education, social relations, government.)

13 MACARTNEY, Clarence Edward Noble. *Six Kings of the American Pulpit.* Philadelphia, 1942. (George Whitefield, Matthew Simpson, Henry Ward Beecher, Phillips Brooks, T. DeWitt Talmage, William J. Bryan.)

14 MACARTNEY, Clarence Edward Noble. *Sons of Thunder. Pulpit Power of the Past.* New York, 1939. (Peter Cartwright, James Waddel, Gilbert Tennent, Samuel Davies, Eliphalet Nott, Lyman Beecher.)

1   McLEISTER, William, 2nd. "The Use of the Bible in the Sermons of Selected Protestant Preachers in the United States from 1925 to 1950." (Pitts), 1957. *Univ Mic* (1958), no. 24,748. *Diss Abs*, XVIII (1958), 1118. (The new criticism in preaching of 15 outstanding men.)

2   OXNAM, Garfield Bromley. *Preaching in a Revolutionary Age.* New York and Nashville, 1944. (Reflects advanced social and religious liberalism, social melioration.)

3   PARKER, Charles A. "A Study of the Preaching at the Ocean Grove, New Jersey, Camp Meeting, 1870–1900." (La), 1959. *Univ Mic* (1959), no. 59–5524. *Diss Abs*, XX (1960), 2961. (600 sermons, stressing holiness and personal salvation; Fundamentalist, influential.)

4   PARKER, Everett C.; David W. BARRY; and Dallas W. SMYTH. *The Television-radio Audience and Religion.* New York, 1955. (Pervasive influence of preaching as a molder of the "American spirit." Bibliog.)

5   PORTER, Harold Theodore. "Ideas of God Reflected in Published Sermons of 25 American Protestant Preachers Selected as 'Most Influential' in 1924." (Pitts), 1956. *Univ Mic* (1957), no. 19,643. *Diss Abs*, XVII (1957), 179. (Sermons published 1895–1950, incl. wide variety of theological positions.)

6   SMITH, Donald George. "Eighteenth Century American Preaching." (N Bapt Theol Sem.) *Diss Abs*, XVI (1955–1956), index.

7   *The Royalty of the Pulpit; a Survey and Appreciation of the Lyman Beecher Lectures on Preaching Founded at Yale Divinity School.* New York, 1951. (Historical trends in character of American preaching. Bibliog.)

8   THOMPSON, Ernest Trice. *Changing Emphases in American Preaching.* Philadelphia, 1943. (Trends as seen in Bushnell, Beecher, Moody, Gladden, Rauschenbusch.)

9   WEDEL, Theodore Otto. *The Pulpit Rediscovers Theology.* Greenwich, Conn., 1956. (Renewed interest in and understanding of the Bible, shift from liberal, undogmatic preaching. Bibliog.)

8. *Healing Ministry*

10 BEASLEY, Norman. *Mary Baker Eddy.* New York, 1963. (Stresses claim that she revived philosophy of Christian healing.)

11 BISHOP, George Victor. *Faith Healing; God or Fraud?* Los Angeles, 1967. (Skeptical, mainly contemporary, with history of faith healers and cults.)

12 CUNNINGHAM, Raymond Joseph. "Ministry of Healing: The Origins of the Psychotherapeutic Role of the American Churches." (J Hop), 1965. *Univ Mic* (1965), no. 65–10,270. *Diss Abs*, XXVI (1965), 3276. (Complete history, 1870's–1930's; important phases and leaders.)

13 DWYER, W. W. *Spiritual Healing in the United States and Great Britain.* Rev. ed. New York, 1956. (Suggesting widespread popularity.)

1 EPPS, Bryan Crandell. "Religious Healing in the United States, 1940–1960: History and Theology of Selected Trends." (Bos), 1961. *Univ Mic* (1961), no. 61–1096. *Diss Abs*, XXII (1961), 930–931. (Three major movements, vigorous and widespread in Protestant churches.)

2 GLEASON, George. *Horizons for Older People.* New York, 1956. (What should be done, what churches have done.)

3 GLEASON, William Francis. *The Liquid Cross of Skid Row.* Milwaukee, 1966. (Experiences of Roman Catholic priest ministering to alcoholics in Chicago.)

4 GRANT, Fern (Babcock). *Ministries of Mercy.* New York, 1962. (Origins, progress, contemporary status of American churches' caring for dependent, ill, handicapped classes.)†

5 McCANN, Richard Vincent. *The Churches and Mental Health: A Report to the Staff Director, Jack R. Ewalt.* New York, 1962. (Detailed consideration of present ministry, with some history of origins and growth.)

6 MAVES, Paul B., and J. Lennart CEDARLEAF. *Older People and the Church.* New York, Nashville, 1949. (Said to be first comprehensive study relating to Protestant churches; reviews rise of problem, efforts and ways.)

7 MIDDLETON, W. Vernon. *The Arm of Compassion. Methodism's Ministry to the Handicapped.* New York, 1962. (Historical and descriptive.)

8 STUBBLEFIELD, Harold W. *The Church's Ministry in Mental Retardation.* Nashville, 1965. (One of the few works, illus. by case histories; notes on efforts to minister.)

9. Laymen's Ministry

9 CALKINS, Gladys Gilkey. *Follow Those Women; Church Women in the Ecumenical Movement, a History of the Development of United Work Among Women of the Protestant Churches in the United States.* New York, 1961. (Generally neglected story of an interdenominational movement since 1865.)

10 CALLAHAN, Daniel J. *The Mind of the Catholic Layman.* New York, 1963. (Stresses heavily institutional emphasis of American Catholic history.)†

11 CAVERT, Inez M. *Women in American Church Life.* New York, 1949. (Comprehensive interdenominational study.)

12 CLARK, John W. *Religion and the Moral Standards of American Businessmen.* Cincinnati, 1966. (Explores Protestant, Jewish, Roman Catholic influences in formation of ethics, appraisal of actual standards.)

13 DAVIS, Sidney Thomas. "Woman's Work in the Methodist Church." (Pitts), 1963. *Univ Mic* (1964), no. 63–7795. *Diss Abs*, XXV (1964), 1018. (History of organizations to merger, 1939; typical of Protestant women's work.)

1 ENLOW, David R. *Men Aflame; the Story of Christian Business Men's Committee International.* Grand Rapids, 1962. (Since 1930, evangelism among business leaders, revivals, case studies of converts.)

2 GRIMES, Howard. *The Rebirth of the Laity.* New York, 1962. (From theoretical angle, but reviews revival of lay ministry in the U.S.)

3 HARKNESS, Georgia Elma. *The Church and Its Laity.* New York, 1962. (Emergence of idea of priesthood of all believers, description of hopeful movements in U.S.)

4 HARRISON, Paul M. "Church and the Laity Among Protestants." *Ann Am Acad Pol Soc Sci,* CCCXXXII (1960), 37–49. (Increasing attention to role of layman, developing theology.)

5 KANE, John Joseph. "Church and the Laity Among Catholics." *Ann Am Acad Pol Soc Sci,* CCCXXXII (1960), 50–59. (Demands and increase of educated laymen leads to fuller role.)

6 KELLER, James Gregory. *To Light a Candle; the Autobiography of James Keller, Founder of the Christophers.* Garden City, N.Y., 1963. (Founding and development of Roman Catholic lay mission movement.)†

7 LANKFORD, John Errett. "Protestant Stewardship and Benevolence, 1900–1941: A Study in Religious Philanthropy." (Wis), 1962. *Univ Mic* (1962), no. 62–1183. *Diss Abs,* XXII (1962), 3177. (Lay effort to maintain Protestant hegemony in American culture in changing social situation.)

8 LEE, Elizabeth Meredith. *As Among the Methodists; Deaconesses Yesterday, Today, and Tomorrow.* New York, 1963. (Revival of diaconate for women in Protestantism, history and present services in American Methodism.)

9 McCARTHY, Thomas Patrick. *Total Dedication for the Laity; a Guidebook to Secular Institutes.* Boston, 1964. (Virtually a history of rise and activities of Roman Catholic lay mission and service societies in the U.S.)

10 MEYER, Ruth Fritz. *Women on a Mission; the Role of Women in the Church from Bible Times up to and Including a History of the Lutheran Women's Missionary League During Its First Twenty-five Years.* St. Louis, 1967. (Predecessor organizations, detailed account of activities, work in other denominations.)

11 NEILL, Stephen Charles, and Hans-Ruedi WEBER, eds. *The Layman in Christian History.* Philadelphia, 1963. (Chaps. X–XI review American Protestant lay activity since colonial period. Bibliog.)

12 PERRY, John D., Jr. *The Coffee House Ministry.* Richmond, 1966. (Introduction on history of movement and its cause in seeking new lay ministry. Bibliog.)†

13 SALSTRAND, George A. E. *The Story of Stewardship in the United States of America.* Grand Rapids, 1956. (Detailed history of stewardship principle and practice in Protestant denominations since colonial period.)

14 SKLARE, Marshall. "Church and Laity Among Jews." *Ann Am Acad Pol Soc Sci,* CCCXXXII (1960), 61–69. (Congregational programs call for more lay action; marked departure of laity from old ideal norms.)

1 THORMAN, Donald J. *The Emerging Layman; the Role of the Catholic Layman in America.* Garden City, N.Y., 1962. (Increasing spiritual and social awareness since 1945; growing participation in church life; with historical background.)†

2 WARD, Leo Richard. *Catholic Life, U.S.A.; Contemporary Lay Movements.* St. Louis, 1959. (Bibliog.)

3 WEISER, Frederick Sheely. *Love's Response; a Story of Lutheran Deaconesses in America.* Philadelphia, 1962. (Little-appreciated contemporary services, and historical summary 1849–1961.)

10. Industrial Missions

4 EADES, Robert E. *A Study of Management-Sponsored Industrial Chaplaincy Programs in the United States.* S Meth Univ. Dallas, 1961. Typescript, and mic 62–7045.

5 SMITH, Richard Charles. *A Critical Evaluation of Industrial Evangelism in the United States of America.* Geneva, Switzerland, 1959. (Effort to make Christian Gospel relevant to often alienated industrial worker, with refs. to examples in the U.S.; list of American churches with "significant industrial worker outreach.")

11. Ministry to Delinquents and the "Off-Beat"

6 ALLEE, G. Franklin. *Beyond Prison Walls. The Story of Frank Novak, Once a Desperate Criminal and Convict, Now National Prison Chaplain No. 1 by the Grace of God.* Kansas City, Mo., 1960. (Redemptive power of religious conversion, stories of conversions of convicts.)

7 BEASLEY, A. Roy. *In Prison . . . and Visited Me.* As Told to Ewart A. *Autry.* Grand Rapids, 1952. (Experiences of a chaplain; vivid, realistic, turning to, and indifference to, religion.)

8 BONN, John L. *Gates of Dannemora.* Garden City, N.Y., 1951. (Story of Roman Catholic chaplain, somewhat sentimentalized view of prison life, chaplain's duties and contacts.)

9 ERIKSON, Kai T. *Wayward Puritans: a Study in the Sociology of Deviance.* New York, 1966. (Puritan theory of criminal behavior as largely irreversible has influenced American penology.)

10 ESHELMAN, Byron E., and Frank RILEY. *Death Row Chaplain.* Englewood Cliffs, N.J., 1962. (Typical experiences of prison chaplain during many years; religious aspects of prison life.)

11 HOYLES, J. Arthur. *Religion in Prison.* New York, 1955. (Historical survey; incl. U.S. since colonial times.)

12 MATTHEWS, Stanley G. *The Night Pastors.* New York, 1967. (Experiences of 10 ministers with people not usually reached by "respectable" churches.)

1   MUNRO, John Josiah. *Christ in the Tombs, or a Square Deal for the Man in Stripes.* Brooklyn, N.Y., 1917. (Church's part in rehabilitation through conversion and prison reform.)

2   MURPHY, George Lavelle. "The Social Role of the Prison Chaplain." (Pitts), 1956. *Univ Mic* (1957), no. 18,251; *Diss Abs*, XVII (1957), 1142. (With bibliog.)

3   MYERS, C. Kilmer. *Light the Dark Streets.* Greenwich, Conn., 1957. (Personal narrative of Episcopalian missioner striving to bring peace and hope to juvenile gangs.)†

4   ROBERTS, Guy L. *How the Church Can Help Where Delinquency Begins.* Richmond, 1958. (Notes on what churches have been doing in the past two generations. Bibliog.)

5   WEBB, Robert and Muriel. *The Churches and Juvenile Delinquency.* New York, 1957. (Intention of youth work in preventing delinquency.)

6   WILKERSON, David. *The Cross and the Switchblade.* New York, 1963. (Personal narrative of Pentecostal minister's work with gang juveniles in New York.)†

12. Religion and Leisure

7   LEE, Robert. *Religion and Leisure in America. A Study in Four Dimensions.* New York, Nashville, 1964. (Emergence of problem, ways of meeting it in religious sense. Selected bibliog.)†

8   MUELLER, Elwin W., and Giles C. EKOLA, eds. *Missions in the American Outdoors; Concerns of the Church in Leisure-Recreation.* Saint Louis, 1966. (Recent accomplishments of Lutheran churches ministering to visitors in recreation areas; large selected bibliog.)

9   NORDEN, Rudolph F. *The New Leisure.* Saint Louis, 1965. (Growth of leisure in the U.S., discussion of Christian idea of *vocation* as approach to it; bibliog.)

13. Youth Ministry

10   GREELEY, Andrew M. *Strangers in the House: Catholic Youth in America.* New York, 1961. (Social factors that have shaped relations between youth and religion, since 1927.)†

11   HOPKINS, Charles Howard. *History of the Y.M.C.A. in North America.* New York, 1951. (Objective and definitive, based on original sources.)

12   HOPPER, Myron Taggart. *Young People's Work in Protestant Churches in the United States.* Chicago, 1941. (Part of doct. diss., [Chi], with bibliog. notes.)

13   McCLUNG, Charles Harvey. *The Development of the Denominational Youth Program in the Presbyterian Church in the U.S.A., 1881–1954.* (Pitts), 1957. *Univ Mic* (1957), no. 22–855. *Diss Abs*, XVII (1957), 2204–2205. (Bibliog.)

14   SIMS, Mary Sophia Stevens. *The Natural History of a Social Institution—the Young Women's Christian Association.* New York, 1936. (Semi-official, objective, scientific, but not sociologically deep.)

1 STRACHAN, Malcolm, and Alvord M. BEARDSLEE, eds. *The Christian Faith and Youth Today.* Greenwich, 1957. (Thorough study, with bibliog.)

2 TODD, Floyd, and Pauline. *Camping for Christian Youth; a Guide to Methods and Principles for Evangelical Camps.* New York, 1963. Rev. ed., 1968. (Origin and history of religious camp movement in the U.S.)†

3 ZALD, Mayer N., and Patricia DENTON. "From Evangelism to General Service: The Transformation of the YMCA." *Admin Sci Q*, VIII (1963), 214–234. (Typical example of shift in religious emphasis to social work.)

XVIII. Religion and Education

1. Religious Education and Sunday Schools

4 BROWN, Marianna C. *Sunday-School Movements in America.* New York, 1901. (Still authoritative, very complete, with critical comment. Bibliog.)

5 CULLY, Kendig Brubaker. *The Search for a Christian Education Since 1940.* Philadelphia, 1965. (Historical treatment of competing philosophies and their influence, especially in the U.S.)

6 EAKIN, Mildred Olivia Moody and Frank. *The Sunday School Fights Prejudice.* New York, 1953. (Shift of stress toward democratic, tolerant citizenship.)

7 EAVEY, Charles Benton. *History of Christian Education.* Chicago, 1964. (Largely on the U.S.; incl. wide variety of organizations and discussion of trends.)

8 FERGUSSON, E. Morris. *Historic Chapters in Christian Education in America, A Brief History of the American Sunday School Movement and the Rise of the Modern Church School.* New York, 1935. (Invaluable for study of "Christian nurture.")

9 FLEMING, Sandford. *Children and Puritanism.* New Haven, 1933. (Didactic view in early American religious education.)

10 HUNT, Rolfe Lanier. "Religion and Education." *Ann Am Acad Pol Soc Sci*, CCCXXXII (1960), 89–100. (Growth of institutions, efforts to coordinate with mass media.)

11 LANKARD, Frank Glenn. *A History of the American Sunday School Curriculum.* New York and Cincinnati, 1927. Authoritative and definitive. (Bibliog.)

12 LITTLE, Lawrence Calvin. *Researches in Personality, Character and Religious Education; a Bibliography of American Doctoral Dissertations, 1885–1959.* Pittsburgh, 1962. (6,300 entries, many on religion, subject index.)†

13 MYERS, A. J. W. *Horace Bushnell and Religious Education.* Boston, 1937. (Shift from didactic and revivalist view to social Christian nurture.)

1   POEHLER, Willy August. *Religious Education Through the Ages.* St. Paul, 1966. (Brief sketch of development of religious education in the U.S., with bibliog.)

2   RICE, Edwin Wilbur. *The Sunday-School Movement, 1780–1917, and the American Sunday-School Union, 1817–1917.* Philadelphia, 1917. (The most complete work on the subject to its time.)

3   SQUIRES, Walter Albion. *Educational Movements of Today . . . Their Significance for Morality and Religion.* Philadelphia, 1930. (Trends of religious education in church and public schools.)

4   TUTTLE, Harold Saxe. *Character Education by State and Church.* New York and Cincinnati, 1930. (Reaction toward cooperation. Bibliog.)

2. *Religion and Public Schools*

5   American Association of School Administrators. Commission on Religion in the Public Schools. *Religion in the Public Schools.* New York, 1964. (Brief review of the problem, legal cases, adjustment of schools to multifaith community.)†

6   BEGGS, David W., III, and R. Bruce McQUIGG, eds. *America's Schools and Churches, Partners in Conflict.* Bloomington, Ind., 1965. (Essays summarize historical and legal background, religious viewpoints, suggestions for viable relationships. Bibliog.)

7   BOLES, Donald E. *The Bible, Religion, and the Public Schools.* 3rd ed. Ames, Iowa, 1965. (Complete historical review from colonial times, including constitutional provisions, statutes, court decisions, attitudes.)†

8   BRAITERMAN, Marvin. *Religion and the Public Schools.* New York, 1958. (Problem reviewed from Jewish standpoint, background of First Amendment and its application.)

9   BRICKMAN, William W., and Stanley LEHRER, eds. *Religion, Government, and Education.* New York, 1961. (Detailed record of church-state-school controversy, citing laws, court decisions, opinions, practices; chronology, selected documents.)

10   DIERENFIELD, Richard B. *Religion in American Public Schools.* Washington, 1962. (Reviews history, applicable laws, court decisions, various practices.)

11   DUNN, William Kailer. *What Happened to Religious Education? The Decline of Religious Teaching in the Public Elementary School, 1776–1861.* Baltimore, 1958. (Long-dominant secularizing trend. Bibliog.)

12   GRIFFITHS, William E. *Religion, the Courts, and the Public Schools. A Century of Litigation.* Cincinnati, 1966. (Commentary, with historical background, on decisions involving religion and public schools, refs. to cases and selected bibliog.)

13   LITTLE, Lawrence Calvin. *Religion and Public Education: A Bibliography.* Pittsburgh, 1966. (Incl. selected U.S. Supreme Court cases; 3,200 items.)

1 MITCHELL, Fredric. "The Supreme Court of the United States on Religion and Education." (Colum), 1959. *Univ Mic* (1960), no. 60–1153. *Diss Abs* (1960), 4001–4002. (Studies 11 principal cases, 1844–1948, moving social forces, opinions of scholars.)

2 MUIR, William K., Jr. *Prayer in the Public Schools. Law and Attitude Change.* Chicago, 1967. (Interviews with 28 public school officials, revealing attitudes toward "schoolhouse religion.")

3 STOKES, Anson Phelps. *Church and State in the United States.* New York, 1950. (Vol. II has comprehensive survey of religious aspects of public education problems.)

3. Religion in Higher Education

4 BUTLER, Richard. *God on the Secular Campus.* Garden City, N.Y., 1963. (History of religion on campus; experiences of students, chaplains, administrators.)

5 EARNSHAW, George L., et al., eds. *The Campus Ministry.* Valley Forge, Pa., 1964. ("A Brief History of Student Christian Movements" since 1690's, other scattered historical refs.)

6 GODBOLD, Albea. *The Church College of the Old South.* Durham, N.C., 1944. (Religious coloring of early higher education. Bibliog.)

7 HINTZ, Howard W. *Religion and Public Higher Education.* Brooklyn College, 1955. (Brief, readable account of historic and contemporary problem; good selected bibliog.)

8 HOLBROOK, Clyde A. *Religion, a Humanistic Field.* Englewood Cliffs, 1963. (History and quality of instruction and writing on religion in American colleges and universities.)

9 JONES, Lawrence Neale. "The Inter-Varsity Christian Fellowship in the United States: A Study of Its History, Theology, and Relations with Other Groups." (Yale), 1961. *Univ Mic* (1964), no. 64–9660. *Diss Abs*, XXV (1964), 2079–2080. (History of an effort, since 1939–1940, to promote conservative evangelicalism on campuses.)

10 KEMP, Charles F. *Counseling with College Students.* Englewood Cliffs, N.J., 1964. (Refs. to history of student ministry and counseling. Bibliog.)†

11 LANG, Brother Martin A. "Religion in the Undergraduate Curriculum of the American State University: An Historical Study." (Cath), 1964. *Univ Mic* (1965), no. 65–5558. *Diss Abs*, XXVI (1965), 1195. (Evolution of religion in curriculum from origin to present.)

12 MICHAELSEN, Robert. *The Study of Religion in American Universities.* New Haven, 1965. (Case studies in ten universities, mostly state, reviewing history and character of programs, discussing place of religion in the curriculum.)

1 PETERSON, Harry Donl. "The Role of Religion at Selected State Colleges and Universities in the United States." (Wash), 1965. *Univ Mic* (1965), no. 65–7708. *Diss Abs*, XXVI (1965), 206. (200 largest institutions, attitude generally favorable to religious activity and study.)

2 PLATT, Robert Martin. "Religion in State-Supported Colleges and Universities." (Texas Tech Col), 1963. *Univ Mic* (1963), no. 63–7389. *Diss Abs*, XXIV (1963), 1488. ("Extensive religious influences are present on most state university campuses.")

3 ROSSMAN, Parker. "Church Student Work Since 1938." (Yale Div Sch), 1953. (Full review of 2,971 religious groups on campuses.)

4 SHEDD, Clarence Prouty. *The Church Follows Its Students*. New Haven, 1938.) (Thorough, story of student chaplain movement, begun by pioneer university pastors.)

5 SHEDD, Clarence Prouty. *Two Centuries of Student Christian Movements, Their Origin and Intercollegiate Life*. New York, 1934. (Standard account; incl. the U.S., 1700–1900.)

6 SMITH, Seymour A. *The American College Chaplaincy*. New York, 1954. (History of worship, teaching, counseling functions.)

7 UNDERWOOD, Kenneth Wilson. *The Church, the University, and Social Policy*. 2 vols. Middletown, Conn., 1969. (Study of campus ministries, based on a national survey of six major Protestant denominations; involvement in civil rights movement.)

8 WALTER, Erich A., ed. *Religion and the State University*. Ann Arbor, 1958. (Campus religion in a pluralistic society, religious centers.)†

XIX. Theology and Religious Philosophy

1. General Works

9 AHLSTROM, Sydney E. "Theology and the Present-Day Revival." *Ann Am Acad Pol Soc Sci*, CCCXXXII (1960), 20–36. (Locus of religious thought now in the U.S., reinvigorated theology relevant to present life.)

10 AHLSTROM, Sydney E., comp. *Theology in America; the Major Protestant Voices from Puritanism to Neo-Orthodoxy*. Indianapolis, 1967. (History of doctrinal theology and collection of Protestant authors. Bibliog.)

11 BEARDSLEE, William A., ed. *America and the Future of Theology*. Philadelphia, 1967. (See, particularly, Thomas J. J. Altizer, "Apocalypse." Essays by 15 authors, predominantly Protestant, show future lying in deeper interaction with contemporary world.)†

12 BLAU, Joseph Leon. *Men and Movements in American Philosophy*. New York, 1952. (Development of ideas and systems, including religious ones, with bibliog.)

1 CALDECOTT, Alfred. *The Philosophy of Religion in England and America.* London, 1901. (Variety of American theistic systems around 1900; 13 schools discussed, with refs. to more important writings.)

2 *Doctoral Dissertations in the Field of Religion, 1940–1952.* New York, 1954. Supplement to *Review of Religion*, XVIII (1954). (500 theses summarized; many on American theology.)

3 FOERSTER, Norman, ed. *Humanism and America; Essays on the Outlook of Modern Civilisation.* Port Washington, N.Y., 1967. (Reviews humanist impact upon American thought and life, incl. religious ideas.)

4 GIBSON, Raymond E. *God, Man and Time; Human Destiny in American Theology.* Philadelphia, 1966. (History largely of the American theology of Man. Bibliog. refs. in notes.)

5 GRANFIELD, Patrick. *Theologians at Work.* New York, 1967. (Review of modern schools of thought, incl. American, in interviews.)

6 JOHNSON, Frederick Ernest. *Patterns of Faith in America Today.* New York, 1958. (Essays on major religious traditions, chiefly from theological viewpoint.)†

7 MARTIN, James Alfred. *Empirical Philosophies of Religion, with Special Reference to Boodin, Brightman, Hocking, Macintosh and Wieman.* New York, 1947. (Review of modern empiricism in America, with bibliog.)

8 METCALF, George Reuben. "American Religious Philosophy and the Pastoral Letters of the House of Bishops." *Hist Mag P E Ch*, XXVII (1958), 10–84. (Bibliog. arranged according to representative men and movements.)

9 MONDALE, R. Lester. "Henry David Thoreau and the Naturalizing of Religion." *Unity*, CXXXVII (1951), 14–17. (Thoreau as a pioneer naturalistic philosopher.)

10 NOVAK, Michael. "The New Relativism in American Theology." Donald R. Cutler, ed., *The Religious Situation: 1968.* Boston, 1968, pp. 197–253. (With refs., and commentary by other writers.)

11 O'BRIEN, Elmer, ed. *Theology in Transition; a Bibliographical Evaluation of the "Decisive Decade," 1954–1964.* New York, 1965. (Bibliog.)

12 PAUCK, Wilhelm. "Theology in the Life of Contemporary American Protestantism," in Walter Leibrecht, ed., *Religion and Culture: Essays in Honor of Paul Tillich.* New York, 1959.

13 PEERMAN, Dean G., and Martin E. MARTY, eds. *A Handbook of Christian Theologians.* Cleveland, 1965. (Brief biographies, and critical reviews of theologies of five Americans.)†

14 RICHARDSON, Herbert W. *Toward an American Theology.* New York, 1967. (Decisive engagement between Christian faith and "sociotechnic" culture will be effected by ecumenically Christian American theology.)†

15 ROTH, Robert J. *American Religious Philosophy.* New York, 1967. (Clear estimate of James, Peirce, Dewey, Whitehead, and Royce; history of little appreciated American gifts to religious thought.)†

1 SCHNEIDER, Herbert Wallace. *A History of American Philosophy.* 2nd ed. New York, 1963. (Incl. various aspects of theology and religious philosophy.)†

2 SMITH, Hilrie Shelton. *Changing Conceptions of Original Sin; a Study in American Theology Since 1750.* New York, 1955.

3 SOPER, David Wesley. *Major Voices in American Theology.* 2 vols. Philadelphia, 1953-1955. (Vol. I, "Six Contemporary Leaders." Vol. II, "Men Who Shape Belief.")

4 *Spectrum of Protestant Beliefs.* Ed. by Robert Campbell. Milwaukee, 1968. ("Statements illustrating the religious, moral, and political attitudes of American Protestantism.")

5 THOMAS, George F. "New Forms for Old Faith." *Changing Patterns in American Civilization.* Ed. by Dixon Wecter et al. Philadelphia, 1949. (American theological scene at close of World War II.)

6 WIEMAN, Henry Nelson, and Bernard Eugene MELAND. *American Philosophies of Religion.* Chicago and New York, 1936. (Interpretation of contemporary types, for academic people, with bibliog.)

7 WILLIAMS, Daniel Day. *What Present-Day Theologians Are Thinking.* 3rd ed. rev. New York, 1967. (Prominent theologians and American religious thought especially since the 1930's, with bibliog.)†

2. New England Theology

8 BUCKHAM, John Wright. "The New England Theologians." *Am J Theol,* XXIV (1920), 19-29. (Review of doctrines, and of "disinterested benevolence." Bibliog.)

9 DeJONG, Peter Ymen. *The Convenant Idea in New England Theology, 1620-1847.* Grand Rapids, 1945. (Abbreviated doct. diss., Hart Theol Sem; with bibliog.)

10 FOSTER, Frank Hugh. *A Genetic History of the New England Theology.* Chicago, 1907. (Survey from Jonathan Edwards to Edwards A. Park. Stresses influence of Yale.)

11 GORDON, George Angier. *Humanism in New England Theology.* Boston and New York, 1920. (New England divinity as an enduring type of humanism.)

12 HAROUTUNIAN, Joseph G. *Piety Versus Moralism: the Passing of the New England Theology.* New York, 1932. (Period 1750-1850, struggle between God-centered and Man-centered salvation.)

13 MILLER, Perry. *Orthodoxy in Massachusetts, 1630-1650, A Genetic Study.* Cambridge, Mass., 1933. (Discusses early covenant stage of New England theology.)

14 ROSENFELD, William. "The Divided Burden: Common Elements in the Search for a Religious Synthesis in the Works of Theodore Parker, Horace Bushnell, Nathaniel Hawthorne, and Herman Melville." (Minn), 1961. *Univ Mic* (1962), no. 62-1843. *Diss Abs,* XXII (1962), 4019. (Effort to use Puritan religious past to guide a new age.)

1 WILCOX, William George. "New England Covenant Theology: Its English Precursors and Early American Exponents." (Duke), 1959. *Univ Mic* (1960), no. 60–1257. *Diss Abs*, XX (1960), 4195. (Close working relation between theoretically separated church and state, important in future U.S.)

3. *Jonathan Edwards and His Followers*

2 AHLSTROM, Sydney E. "The Scottish Philosophy and American Theology." *Church Hist*, XXIV (1955), 257–272. (A realistic philosophy that helped to modify Calvinism.)

3 DAVIDSON, Edward Hutchings. *Jonathan Edwards: the Narrative of a Puritan Mind.* Cambridge, Mass., 1968. (Succinct review of life and theology, fixing his place in American thought.)†

4 EDWARDS, Jonathan. *Representative Selections, with Introduction, Bibliography, and Notes.* Ed. by Clarence H. Faust and Thomas H. Johnson. Rev. ed. New York, 1962. (Introduction is essential to understanding him.)†

5 ELWOOD, Douglas J. *The Philosophical Theology of Jonathan Edwards.* New York, 1960. (Full bibliog. of writings; principal MSS; refs. to him.)

6 FOSTER, Frank Hugh. *The Life of Edwards Amasa Park . . . Abbot Professor, Andover Theological Seminary.* New York, 1936. (Last of Andover triumvirate, lived to see liberalism triumphant in many seminaries.)

7 HAROUTUNIAN, Joseph G. "Jonathan Edwards, Theologian of the Great Commandment." *Theol To*, I (1944), 361–377. (Most understanding and sympathetic comment by a modern theologian.)

8 JAMES, Walter Thomas. "The Philosophy of Noah Porter." (Colum), 1951. *Univ Mic* (1951), no. 2823. *Diss Abs*, XI, 1064–1065. (Effort to reformulate "Yale Orthodoxy" to combat modern philosophies.)

9 MEAD, Sidney Earl. *Nathaniel William Taylor, 1786–1858: A Connecticut Liberal.* Hamden, Conn., 1967. (Influential in transition from Calvinism to "Liberal Orthodoxy." Bibliog.)

10 MILLER, Perry. *Jonathan Edwards.* New York, 1949. (Significance of his thought for 20th-century America. Note on sources.)†

11 MORRIS, William S. "The Reappraisal of Edwards." *N Eng Q*, XXX (1957), 515–525. (Comment on literature about him, various interpretations.)

12 PARK, Edwards Amasa. *The Life and Character of Leonard Woods.* Andover, Mass., 1880. (Symbol of a group between "Tylerites" and "Taylorites.")

13 SCHNEIDER, Herbert Wallace. *The Puritan Mind.* Ann Arbor, Mich., 1958. (Best general account of liberalization of New England Calvinism.)†

14 WILLIAMS, Daniel Day. *The Andover Liberals: a Study of American Theology.* New York, 1941. (A group of modified Calvinists at the Andover seminary. Bibliog.)

4. Presbyterian Theology

1 ALEXANDER, James Waddel. *The Life of Archibald Alexander, D.D., First Professor in the Theological Seminary, at Princeton, New Jersey.* New York, 1854. (His influence on "Princeton Theology," by his Biblicism.)

2 BROWN, William Adams. "Changes in the Theology of American Presbyterianism." *Am J Theol,* X (1906), 387–411. (Liberal modifications, trend to catholicity. Bibliog. in footnotes.)

3 DANHOF, Ralph J. *Charles Hodge as a Dogmatician.* . . . Goes, Netherlands, 1930. (Regards him as America's "greatest theologian." Bibliog. of writings.)

4 HODGE, Archibald Alexander. *The Life of Charles Hodge . . . Professor in the Theological Seminary, Princeton, N.J.* New York, 1880. (Estimates widespread influence of this Nestor of Calvinism.)

5 HOOGSTRA, Jacob Tunis, ed. *American Calvinism; a Survey.* Grand Rapids, 1957. (Papers and discussions, Calvinist Conference, Grand Rapids, 1956.)

6 LOETSCHER, Lefferts A. *The Broadening Church: A Study of Theological Issues in the Presbyterian Church Since 1869.* Philadelphia, 1954. (Modification of theology, away from Princeton orthodoxy.)

5. Mercersburg Reformed Theology

7 APPEL, Theodore. *The Life and Work of John Williamson Nevin.* Philadelphia, Lancaster, 1889. (Estimate of Reformed "ritualist," sacramentalist and theologian.)

8 BINKLEY, Luther John. *The Mercersburg Theology.* Lancaster? Pa., 1953. (Most systematic study of Nevin and Schaff.)

9 BRENNER, Scott Francis. "Nevin and the Mercersburg Theology." *Theol To,* XII (1955), 43–56. (Excellent brief review, likeness to Anglican Oxford Movement. Bibliog.)

10 HARBAUGH, Linn. *Life of the Rev. Henry Harbaugh.* Philadelphia, 1900. (A leader of confessional and doctrinal phase. Bibliog. of works.)

11 NICHOLS, James Hastings, ed. *The Mercersburg Theology.* New York, 1966. (Selected writings of Nevin and Schaff, who promoted Protestant revival of catholic views.)

12 NICHOLS, James Hastings. *Romanticism in American Theology. Nevin and Schaff at Mercersburg.* Chicago, 1961. (Pioneers in theological reinterpretations stimulated by German idealistic philosophy, new theories of historical development.)

13 RICHARDS, George Warren. *History of the Theological Seminary of the Reformed Church in the United States.* . . . Lancaster, Pa., 1952. (Valuable comments on leaders of Mercersburg movement.)

6. Anti-Calvinist Reaction. Arminianism

1 *Free Baptist Cyclopedia*, 1889. (Sections on free-will or Arminian Baptist theology and doctrines.)

2 CHANNING, William Ellery. *Unitarian Christianity; a Discourse on some of the Distinguishing Opinions of Unitarians, Delivered at Baltimore in 1819.* Boston, 1919. (Manifesto of early liberal Anti-Calvinist movement. See also: "The Moral Argument Against Calvinism," *Unitarian Christianity and Other Essays.* Ed. by Irving H. Bartlett. New York, 1957.)†

3 CHILES, Robert Eugene. "Theological Transition in American Methodism." (Colo), 1964. *Univ Mic* (1964), no. 64–9866. *Diss Abs*, XXV (1964), 3717. (Development of Arminian thought since 1790, changes in basic doctrines.)

4 CHRISTIE, Francis Albert. "The Beginnings of Arminianism in New England." *Pap Am Soc Ch Hist*, 2nd ser., III (1912), 153–172. (Theological and philosophical background of Arminian anti-Calvinist movement.)

5 CHRISTIE, Francis Albert. "Unitarianism." *Am J Theol*, XXI (1917), 554–570. (General development of American Unitarian theology.)

6 DIRKS, John Edwards. *The Critical Theology of Theodore Parker.* New York, 1948. (Advance of Unitarian theology toward radical liberalism. Bibliog.)

7 EAMES, Samuel Morris. *The Philosophy of Alexander Campbell . . . A Comprehensive Bibliography of Alexander Campbell's Writings.* Bethany, W. Va., 1966. (Contribution to Anti-Calvinist liberal theology and American ecumenical movement.)

8 SCHNEIDER, Herbert Wallace. "The Intellectual Background of William Ellery Channing." *Church Hist*, VII (1938), 3–23. (Derivation of liberal theological and philosophical ideas.)

9 SCOTT, Leland H. "Methodist Theology in America in the Nineteenth Century." Doct. diss. (Yale), partly pub. in *Rel Life*, XXV (1955–1956), 87–98. (The nearest approach to a general history of Methodist Arminian theology.)

10 THAYER, Thomas Baldwin. *Theology of Universalism: Being an Exposition of Its Doctrines and Teachings.* Boston, 1891. (Modern exposition of Universalism as a system.)

11 WEST, Robert Frederick. *Alexander Campbell and Natural Religion.* New Haven, 1948. (Tension between natural theology and orthodox Christianity. Bibliog.)

12 WRIGHT, Conrad. *The Beginnings of Unitarianism in America.* Boston, 1955. (Comprehensive research on origins of American Unitarian thought.)†

7. Anglican Theology

1 ANDREWS, William Given. "The Parentage of American High Church-manship." *P E Rev*, XII (1899), 196–221. (Traces early American Anglo-Catholic theology to 17th-century English divines.)

2 BRATTON, Theodore DuBose. *An Apostle of Reality; the Life and Thought of the Reverend William Porcher DuBose*. London and New York, 1936. (Summarizes theology of a modern American liberal Anglican.)

3 CHORLEY, Edward Clowes. *Men and Movements in the Episcopal Church*. New York, 1946. (Notes on Anglo-Catholic, Evangelical, and Broad Church theologies.)

4 DeMILLE, George Edmed. *The Catholic Movement in the American Episcopal Church*. Philadelphia, 1941. (Detailed, scholarly remarks on rise of Anglo-Catholic theology. Bibliog.)

5 GOODWIN, Gerald Joseph. "The Anglican Middle Way in Early Eighteenth-Century America: Anglican Religious Thought in the American Colonies, 1702–1750." (Wis), 1965. *Univ Mic* (1965), no. 65–5125. *Diss Abs*, XXV (1965), 6568–6569. (Defense of reason; spiritual value of good moral conduct; and intellectual leaven.)

6 HARDY, Edward Rochie, Jr. "The Significance of Seabury." *Am Ch Mo*, XXXVII (1935), 26–40. (Remarks on his Anglo-Catholic theology.)

7 HORNBERGER, Theodore. "Samuel Johnson of Yale and King's College, a Note on the Relation of Science and Religion in Provincial America." *N Eng Q*, VIII (1935), 378–397. (Philosophical and theological position of colonial "High Church" Anglicans.)

8 MARSHALL, John Sedberry. *The Word Made Flesh: the Theology of William Porcher DuBose*. Sewanee, Tenn., 1949. (Stresses incarnational aspect of his theology.)

9 METCALF, George Reuben. "American Religious Philosophy and the Pastoral Letters of the House of Bishops." *Hist Mag P E Ch*, XXVII (1958), Chap. II, "Types of Religious Philosophy in the Pastoral Letters, 1808–1953."

10 SCHNEIDER, Herbert Wallace, and Carol SCHNEIDER, eds. *Samuel Johnson, President of King's College, His Career and Writings*. 4 vols. New York, 1929. (Excellent, scholarly study of Johnson as a theologian is included.)

11 STOWE, Walter Herbert. *The Life and Letters of Bishop William White*. New York and Milwaukee, 1937. (Valuable notes on his theology.)

12 TEMPLE, Sydney Absalom. *The Common Sense Theology of Bishop White: Selected Essays . . . with an Introductory Survey of His Theological Position*. New York, 1946. (Emphasizes his antidualist position. Bibliog.)

8. Lutheran Theology

1 ANSTADT, Peter. *Life and Times of Rev. S. S. Schmucker.* York, Pa., 1896. (Summarizes thought of theologian who leaned to popular American Protestantism. Bibliog. of writings.)

2 DALLMANN, William; W. H. T. DAU; and Theodore E. ENGELDER, eds. *Walther and the Church.* St. Louis, Mo., 1938. (Influence as conservator of orthodox Lutheranism.)

3 FERM, Vergilius Ture Anselm. *The Crisis in American Lutheran Theology, A Study of the Issue Between American Lutheranism and Old Lutheranism.* Grand Rapids, 1927. (Many quotations from minutes and periodicals. Detailed bibliog.)

4 POLACK, William Gustave. *The Story of C. F. W. Walther.* Rev. ed. St. Louis, 1947. (Stresses Biblical and doctrinal character of his thought.)

5 SPAETH, Adolph. *Charles Porterfield Krauth.* 2 vols. New York, 1898. (Best appreciation of American Lutheranism's greatest conservative theologian.)

9. Horace Bushnell, Herald of Liberalism

6 ADAMSON, William R. *Bushnell Rediscovered.* Philadelphia, 1966. (Importance in adjustment of theology to contemporary conditions.)†

7 BACON, Benjamin Wisner. *Theodore Thornton Munger, New England Minister.* New Haven, 1913. (Influence of Bushnell, Munger's influence on liberalism. Bibliog. of selected writings.)

8 BUSHNELL, Horace. *Horace Bushnell; Twelve Selections.* Ed. by H. Shelton Smith. New York, 1965. (Principal themes with editorial notes, valuable introduction on background of his thought; selected bibliog.)

9 CROSS, Barbara M. *Horace Bushnell: Minister to a Changing America.* Chicago, 1958. (Bushnell as mediator of liberal theology to the people. Bibliog.)

10. Modern Liberalism

10 AMES, Edward Scribner. *Beyond Theology. The Autobiography of Edward Scriber Ames.* Ed. by Van Meter Ames. Chicago, 1959. (Entertaining "life and times" of a leader in the development of liberal religion, University of Chicago.)

11 AVERILL, Lloyd James. *American Theology in the Liberal Tradition.* Philadelphia, 1967. (Triumph of liberalism, 1879–1918, decline after World War I, recent revival, estimates of leaders.)

1 BROWN, Jerry Wayne. *The Rise of Biblical Criticism in America, 1800–1870; the New England Scholars.* Middletown, Conn., 1969. (Background of the growing liberalizing of theology.)

2 BUCKHAM, John Wright. *Progressive Religious Thought in America; a Survey of the Enlarging Pilgrim Faith.* Boston and New York, 1919. (Liberal Congregational theologians in the late 19th century.)

3 COCHRAN, Bernard Harvey. "William Newton Clarke: Exponent of the New Theology." (Duke), 1962. *Univ Mic* (1963), no. 63–865. *Diss Abs,* XXIII (1963), 3512. (Importance as systematizer and popularizer of liberalism, Social Gospel, Christian unity.)

4 COFFIN, Henry Sloane. *Religion Yesterday and Today.* Nashville, 1940. (Popular essays reveal adjustment of American Protestant thought to evolutionary theory, Biblical criticism, social gospel.)

5 FERM, Vergilius Ture Anselm, ed. *Contemporary American Theology; Theological Autobiographies.* 2 vols. New York, 1932–1933. (Stresses growth of scientific liberal temper and anti-dogmatism.)

6 HUTCHISON, William R., ed. *American Protestant Thought: The Liberal Era.* New York, 1968. (Anthology of liberal religious writing, with general introduction and selected bibliography.)†

7 JONES, Gerald Harvey. *George A. Gordon and the New England Theology.* Boston, 1942. (Brief review of contribution to liberal theology; abstract of thesis.)

8 KELLEY, Alden Drew. "The Chicago School of Theology." *Theology,* LV (1952), 19–24. (Review of radical, scientifically oriented type of liberalism.)

9 PATTON, Carl S. "The American Theological Scene: Fifty Years in Retrospect." *J Rel,* XVI (1936), 445–462. (Orthodoxy changing into modern liberal philosophy of religion, influence of evolutionary concept.)

10 SMITH, Kenneth Lee. "Shailer Mathews: Theologian of Social Process." (Duke), 1959. *Univ Mic* (1960), no. 60–272. *Diss Abs* (1960), 3870–3871. (Pioneer of Protestant Modernism, advocate of Christianizing social order.)

11 WEAVER, Samuel Robert. "The Theology and Times of Harry Emerson Fosdick." (Princeton Theol Sem), 1961. *Univ Mic* (1961), no. 61–5448. *Diss Abs,* XXII (1962), 3759. (Epitome of strength and weakness of early 20th-century Protestant liberalism.)

11. Reaction Against Liberalism: Neo-Orthodoxy

12 AHLSTROM, Sydney E. "Continental Influence on American Christian Thought Since World War I." *Church Hist,* XXVII (1958), 256–272. (Four phases of influence upon "post-liberal" thinking.)

13 FUSE, T. M. "Religions, Society and Accommodation: Some Remarks on Neo-Orthodoxy in American Protestantism." *Soc Com,* XII (1965), 345–358. (Conflict between universalistic religion and particular interests, Neo-Orthodoxy's accommodative compromises.)

1 HAMMAR, George. *Christian Realism in Contemporary American Theology.* Uppsala, Sweden, 1940. (Best analysis of emergence of Neo-Orthodoxy in America.)

2 HARLOW, Victor Emmanuel. *Bibliography and Genetic Study of American Realism.* Oklahoma City, 1931. (Sources and character of American realistic theology.)

3 PITTENGER, W. Norman. "Changing Emphases in American Theology." *Rel Life,* XII (1943), 412–420. (Shift from liberalism to conservatism since 1920's.)

4 SOPER, David Wesley. *Major Voices in American Theology; Six Contemporary Leaders.* Philadelphia, 1953. (Reviews critics of liberalism.)

5 WILLIAMS, Daniel Day. *What Present-Day Theologians Are Thinking.* New York, 1959. (Incl. general survey of American Neo-Orthodoxy.)†

12. The Niebuhrs and Tillich

6 AHLSTROM, Sydney E. "H. Richard Niebuhr's Place in American Thought." *Chr and Crisis,* 23, no. 20 (Nov. 25, 1963), 213–217. (His effort, 1930–1960, to educate American theology toward a realistic stance, away from religious imperialism.)

7 BINGHAM, June. *Courage to Change; an Introduction to the Life and Thought of Reinhold Niebuhr.* New York, 1961. (Intimate, appreciative portrait and estimate, many quotations; bibliog. of writings.)

8 CARNELL, Edward John. *The Theology of Reinhold Niebuhr.* Grand Rapids, 1951. (Summary of theological position.)†

9 DAVIES, David R. *Reinhold Niebuhr: Prophet from America.* New York, 1948. (Niebuhr's movement from liberalism to Neo-Orthodoxy.)

10 HARLAND, Gordon. *The Thought of Reinhold Niebuhr.* New York, 1960. (His thought against background of major events; views on contemporary questions.)

11 HOFMANN, Hans. *The Theology of Reinhold Niebuhr.* Trans. by Louise Pettibone Smith. New York, 1956. (Summary of his theological position.)

12 KEGLEY, Charles W., and Robert W. BRETALL, eds. *Reinhold Niebuhr, His Religious, Social and Political Thought.* New York, 1956. (Essays in appreciation and criticism, with response by him.)†

13 KEGLEY, Charles W., and Robert W. BRETALL, eds. *The Theology of Paul Tillich.* New York, 1952. (Excellent analysis and critique.)†

14 LANDON, Harold R., ed. *Reinhold Niebuhr: a Prophetic Voice in Our Time; Essays in Tribute,* by Paul Tillich, John C. Bennett and Hans J. Morgenthau. Greenwich, Conn., 1962. (Influence as critic and counselor in social, ethical, political matters.)†

1 RAMSEY, Paul, ed. *Faith and Ethics: The Theology of H. Richard Niebuhr.* New York, 1957. (Essays by Hans Frei on his theological background and thought.)

2 ROBERTSON, Duncan. *Reinhold Niebuhr's Works; a Bibliography.* Berea, Ky., 1954.

3 THELEN, Mary Frances. *Man as Sinner in Contemporary American Realistic Theology.* New York, 1946. (Examines doctrine of man of Reinhold Niebuhr. Bibliog.)

4 THOMAS, John Heywood. *Paul Tillich.* Richmond, 1966. (Succinct appreciation of his thought, its historical significance.)†

13. "Death of God" Theology

5 ALTIZER, Thomas J. J., and William HAMILTON. *Radical Theology and the Death of God.* Indianapolis, 1966. (With a bibliography of the movement.)

6 BALL, Virginia. *The Godless Christians.* Atlanta, 1966. (Compendium of American "Death of God," notes on philosophical background, biographical sketches of principals in the debate.)

7 BENT, Charles N. *The Death-of-God Movement; a Study of Gabriel Vahanian, William Hamilton, Paul Van Buren and Thomas J. J. Altizer.* Westminster, Md., 1967. (Bibliog. refs.)†

8 OGLETREE, Thomas W. *The "Death of God" Controversy.* London, 1966. ("Christian atheism" of three American theologians, with notes on historical setting and development.)†

XX. Science and Religion— Evolution

1. General History

9 ALLEN, Leslie Henri, ed. *Bryan and Darrow at Dayton; the Records and Documents of the "Bible-evolution Trial."* New York, 1967. (Important; cuts through jungle of accounts and gets the record straight.)

10 BROWN, Ira V. "Lyman Abbott: Christian Evolutionist." *N Eng Q*, XXIII (1950), 218–231. ("Reconciliation" of evolution and religion, and results.)

11 FOSTER, Frank Hugh. *The Modern Movement in American Theology; Sketches in the History of American Protestant Thought from the Civil War to the World War.* New York, 1939. (Chap. III, "The Reception of Evolution by Theologians.")

12 GINGER, Ray. *Six Days or Forever?* Boston, 1958. (Scopes trial and its importance to religion, science, civil liberty.)

13 GREENE, John C. *Darwin and the Modern World View.* Baton Rouge, 1961. (History of religion and evolution controversy, numerous refs. to American thinkers, quotations from their works.)†

1   HIBBEN, Paxton. *Henry Ward Beecher: an American Portrait.* New York, 1927. (His role in popularizing evolution.)

2   HOFSTADTER, Richard. *Social Darwinism in American Thought.* Rev. ed. New York, 1959. (Darwinism's challenge to religious ideas and theology.)†

3   KENNEDY, Gail, ed. *Evolution and Religion. The Conflict Between Science and Theology in Modern America.* Boston, 1957. (Selected readings, reaction of American minds to religious challenge of evolution.)†

4   LOEWENBERG, Bert James. "Darwinism Comes to America, 1859–1900." *Miss Val Hist Rev,* XXVIII (1941), 339–368. (Reaction of various schools of thought and preachers.)

5   MORRISON, John Lee. "A History of American Catholic Opinion on the Theory of Evolution, 1859–1950." (Mo). *Univ Mic* (1951), no. 2894; *Diss Abs,* XI (1951), 1007–1008. (Division of opinion, with increasing toleration.)

6   OSBORN, Henry Fairfield. *Evolution and Religion in Education; Polemics of the Fundamentalist Controversy of 1922 to 1926.* New York, 1926. (Valuable especially for bibliog. of the controversy.)

7   PANNILL, H. Burnell. *The Religious Faith of John Fiske.* Durham, N.C., 1957. (Evaluation of a popular exponent of evolutionary theism.)

8   PERSONS, Stow. "Evolution and Theology in America." In his *Evolutionary Thought in America.* New Haven, 1950. (Efforts of American religious thinkers to reconcile theology with evolution.)

9   ROBERTS, Windsor Hall. *The Reaction of American Protestant Churches to the Darwinian Philosophy, 1860–1900.* Chicago, 1938. (Reviews intellectual contest in five Northern Protestant churches, with bibliog. footnotes. Summary of doct. diss. [Chi].)

10 SCHNEIDER, Herbert Wallace. "The Influence of Darwin and Spencer on American Philosophical Theology." *J Hist Ideas,* VI (1945), 3–18. (Summarizes four philosophical attitudes toward evolutionism.)

11 SHIPLEY, Maynard. *The War on Modern Science. A Short History of the Fundamentalist Attacks on Evolution and Modernism.* New York, 1927. (Review of the past five years, from philosophical viewpoint, scoring religious obscurantism and defending freedom of teaching.)

12 WHITE, Edward A. *Science and Religion in American Thought: The Impact of Naturalism.* Stanford, Calif., 1952. (Relation of science to religion as viewed by six leading thinkers, chapter on Fundamentalist-Modernist controversy.)

13 WILLIAMS, Wayne C. *William Jennings Bryan.* New York, 1936. (Sympathetic account of Bryan's presentation of Fundamentalist view at the "monkey trial.")

2. Fundamentalism

1 COLE, Stewart Grant. *The History of Fundamentalism.* New York, 1931. (First scholarly critique, especially exploring social and theological background. Bibliog.)

2 FURNISS, Norman F. *The Fundamentalist Controversy, 1918–1931.* Hamden, Conn., 1963. (Fundamentalist attitude part of a defense of traditional American ways.)

3 GATEWOOD, Willard B., Jr., ed. *Controversy in the Twenties: Fundamentalism, Modernism, and Evolution.* Nashville, 1969. (Source book of polemical literature, with long introduction; not creditable to either side.)

4 GOEN, C. C. "Fundamentalism in America." *S W J Theol,* II (1959), 52–62. (Basic ideological conflict against romanticized humanism in modern theology and denial of Biblical supernaturalism.)

5 PERRY, Everett L. "Socio-Economic Factors and American Fundamentalism." *Rev Rel Res,* I (1959), 57–61. (Rise of Fundamentalism in northern industrial metropolis; similarity to nationalistic, nativist and language revivals.)

6 SAGER, Allan H. "The Fundamentalist-Modernist Controversy, 1918–1930, in the History of American Public Address." (N W), 1963. *Univ Mic* (1964), no. 64–5864. *Diss Abs,* XXV (1964), 699–700. (Leading spokesmen and their audiences, analysis and interpretation of ideas.)

7 SANDEEN, Ernest R. *The Origins of Fundamentalism. Toward a Historical Understanding.* Philadelphia, 1968. (Fundamentalism as a genuinely conservative religious movement from about 1875, not a product of the evolution controversy.)†

8 STONEHOUSE, Ned B. *J. Gresham Machen, A Biographical Memoir.* Grand Rapids, 1955. (Documented account of epic conflict in Princeton Seminary.)

9 STROMAN, John Albert. "The American Council of Christian Churches: A Study of Its Origin, Leaders and Characteristic Positions." (Bos), 1966. *Univ Mic* (1967), no. 67–277; *Diss Abs* XXVII (1967), 2608A–2609A. (General history and statement of purpose of a Fundamentalist counterpart to the "liberal" National Council of Churches.)

10 WHITE, Edward A. "Fundamentalism Versus Modernism, 1920–1930." *Pac Spec,* V (1951), 112–120. (Regional, economic, class, theological aspects.)

3. Intellectuals and Religion

11 Conference on Science, Philosophy and Religion, in Their Relation to the Democratic Way of Life. *Science, Philosophy and Religion, A Symposium, 1940–1955.* 15 vols. New York, 1941–1956. (Essays reveal impact of religious dilemmas upon intellectuals.)

1 LEUBA, James H. "Religious Beliefs of American Scientists." *Har Mag*, CLXIX (1934), 291–300. (Decline of belief in supernaturalism. God as influenced by worship, immortality.)

2 LONG, Edward LeRoy, Jr. *Religious Beliefs of American Scientists.* Philadelphia, 1952. (Systematic study of types of religious philosophy.)

3 MAYER, Ronald Wesley. "Religious Attitudes of Scientists." (Ohio State), 1959. *Univ Mic* (1959), no. 59–5921. *Diss Abs*, XX (1959), 2412–2413. (American scientists vary widely respecting God and immortality.)

4 NEDERHOOD, Joel H. *The Church's Mission to the Educated American.* Grand Rapids, 1960. (Revitalization by effort to understand mind of the educated, shaped by reading and social forces.)

5 *Religion and the Intellectuals; a Symposium with James Agee and Others.* New York, 1950. First published in *Partisan Rev*, XVII (1950), no. 2–5. (Collection of opinions, with responses, interesting insights.)

XXI. Art and Religion

1. Liturgy and Worship

6 BLUHM, David Rodney. "Trends of Worship Reflected in the Three Editions of the Book of Common Worship of the Presbyterian Church in the United States of America." (Pitts), 1956. *Univ Mic* no. 19–614. *Diss Abs*, XVII (1957), 178. (Increasing concern for liturgy, influences of Neo-Orthodoxy and ecumenical movement.)

7 BRENNER, Scott Francis. *The Way of Worship, a Study in Ecumenical Recovery.* New York, 1944. (Liturgical movement centering in Reformed Mercersburg Seminary, truly American development. Bibliog.)

8 COIT, Stanton. *The Soul of America; a Constructive Essay in the Sociology of Religion.* New York, 1914. (Liberal view of worship as expression of American spirit.)

9 DUNKELBERGER, Harold Aberley. "Symbols in the Service: A Study of Symbolic Functions of Liturgy in American Lutheranism." (Colum), 1950. *Univ Mic* (1950), no. 2106; *Diss Abs*, XI (1951), 182–183. (Value of symbolism in worship, its loss in Protestant emphasis upon verbalism.)

10 ELLARD, Gerald. *The Dialog Mass, A Book for Priests and Teachers of Religion.* New York, 1942. (Notes on progress of reform in dioceses, especially in Middle West.)

11 ELLARD, Gerald. *Men at Work at Worship; America Joins the Liturgical Movement.* New York, 1940. (For the layman, in popular lecture style, with illus. and bibliog.)

12 GIGUERE, Robert Joseph. *The Social Value of Public Worship According to Thomistic Principles.* Washington, 1950. (Reviews present trends in American liturgy, after long decline of genuine worship. Bibliog.)

1 HYLAN, John Perham. *Public Worship; a Study in the Psychology of Religion*. Chicago and London, 1901. (Classic on place of worship in American life, based on case studies, with bibliog.)

2 JONES, Ilion Tingnal. *A Historical Approach to Evangelical Worship*. Nashville, 1954. (Criticizes Protestant trend towards liturgy as stressing priestly rather than prophetic religion.)

3 MARX, Paul B. *Virgil Michel and the Liturgical Movement*. Collegeville, Minn., 1957. (General survey in Roman Catholic Church in the U.S., with bibliog. and bibliog. essay.)

4 MELTON, Julius. *Presbyterian Worship in America: Changing Patterns Since 1787*. Richmond, Va., 1967. (Worship shaped by American culture more than by Calvinistic theology; no one tradition dominant.)

5 NICHOLS, James Hastings. *Corporate Worship in the Reformed Tradition*. Philadelphia, 1968. (Solid account of development of European and American Protestant worship; influences of Pietism, Evangelicalism, Roman Catholic worship.)

6 PHIFER, Kenneth G. *A Protestant Case for Liturgical Renewal*. Philadelphia, 1965. (History of American Protestant worship, efforts to make it more appealing and significant, without losing prophetic ministry.)

7 SHEPHERD, Massey Hamilton. *The Liturgical Movement and the Prayer Book*. Evanston, Ill., 1946. (Influence of movement, philosophical and theological background, revival of central position of Eucharist.)

8 SUTER, John Wallace, and George Julius CLEAVELAND. *The American Book of Common Prayer; its Origin and Development*. New York, 1949. (Character and influence, contemporary value.)

9 TAYLOR, Michael J. *The Protestant Liturgical Renewal; a Catholic Viewpoint*. Westminster, Md., 1963. (Surveys history in Europe and America, with large bibliog.)

10 WALKER, Williston. "The Genesis of the Present Customary Form of Public Worship in the Reformed Non-prelatical Churches of America." *Pap Am Soc Ch Hist*, 2nd ser., I (1913), 79–91. (Excellent background for understanding Anglo-American Protestant worship.)

2. Music. General Histories

11 BUSZIN, Walter E.; Theodore M. FINNEY; and Donald M. McCORKLE, eds. *A Bibliography on Music and the Church*. New York, 1958. (Very comprehensive; indispensable.)

12 COVEY, Cyclone. "Religion and Music in Colonial America." (Stan), 1949. Ref. in *Doctoral Dissertations in Musicology*. Denton, Tex., 1952, p. 40. (Incl. detailed, scholarly study of church music.)

13 CRAWFORD, Richard A. *Andrew Law, American Psalmodist*. Evanston, Ill., 1968. (Scholarly biography of post-Revolutionary reformer of psalmody, who compiled tune books and established singing schools.)

1 DAVISON, Archibald Thompson. *Protestant Church Music in America.* Boston, 1933. (General survey and criticism of taste and practice, with illus. and music.)

2 ELLINWOOD, Leonard Webster. *English Influences in American Church Music.* Taunton? Eng., 1954. (Incl. notes on early organs and English musicians; influence of Oxford Movement in improvement.)

3 ELLINWOOD, Leonard Webster. *The History of American Church Music.* New York, 1953. (Best modern authority, with notes, bibliog., music, biographies, ports.)

4 GLASS, Henry Alexander. *The Story of the Psalters; a History of the Metrical Versions of Great Britain and America from 1549 to 1885.* London, 1888. (Chronological treatment, with full notes.)

5 HARTLEY, Kenneth R. *Bibliography of Theses and Dissertations in Sacred Music.* Detroit, 1967.

6 HOOPER, William L. *Church Music in Transition.* Nashville, 1963. (Illus., bibliogs.)

7 HOWARD, John Tasker. *Our American Music: Three Hundred Years of It.* 4th ed. rev. New York, 1946. (A classic, with bibliog. incl. religious music.)

8 MacDOUGALL, Hamilton Crawford. *Early New England Psalmody; an Historical Appreciation, 1620–1820.* Brattleboro, Vt., 1940. (With illus. and music; rescues subject from ignorance and ridicule.)

9 MAURER, Sister Hermana. "The Musical Life of Colonial America in the Eighteenth Century." (Ohio State), 1950. Ref. in *Doctoral Dissertations in Musicology.* Denton, Tex., 1952, p. 40.

10 METCALF, Frank Johnson. *American Writers and Compilers of Sacred Music.* New York, 1967. (Most thorough work to date; about 90 composers; notes on revivalist composers, camp-meeting music.)

11 NININGER, Ruth. *Church Music Comes of Age.* New York, 1957. (Especially on Protestant music.)

12 OSBECK, Kenneth W. *The Ministry of Music.* Grand Rapids, 1961. (Especially Protestant music. Illus., bibliog.)

13 PATRICK, Millar. *The Story of the Church's Song.* Rev. for American use by James Rawlings Sydnor. Richmond, 1962.

14 PRATT, Waldo Selden. *American Music and Musicians.* Philadelphia, 1920. (Highly valuable refs. to church music; bibliogs. of hymnbooks and tunebooks.)

15 SCHOLES, Percy Alfred. *The Puritans and Music in England and New England.* . . . London and Oxford, 1934. (Distinctive gifts of Puritans to religious music.)

3. Music of Groups

16 ALFORD, Delton L. *Music in the Pentecostal Church.* Cleveland, Tenn., 1967. (Bibliog.)

1 ANDREWS, Edward Deming. *The Gift to be Simple; Songs, Dances and Rituals of the American Shakers.* New York, 1940. (Music and rituals as expressions of true folk art.)†

2 COOK, Harold. "Shaker Music: a Manifestation of American Folk Culture." (W Res), 1947. Ref. in *Doctoral Dissertations in Musicology.* Denton, Tex., 1952, p. 50. (Its character as a communal influence.)

3 DaSILVA, Owen, ed. *Mission Music of California, A Collection of Old California Hymns and Masses.* Los Angeles, 1941. (Style of mission music, list of padre musicians, large bibliog.)

4 *The Development of Lutheran Hymnody in America.* N.p. 1967. (Facsim.)

5 GRIDER, Rufus A. *Historical Notes on Music in Bethlehem, Pa. (From 1741–1871).* Winston-Salem, N.C., 1957. (Repr. from original ed. of 1873.)

6 HOELTY-NICKEL, Theodore, ed. *The Musical Heritage of the Church.* Valparaiso, Ind., 1946? (Effort to improve Lutheran music during liturgical movement.)

7 HORN, Henry E. *O Sing unto the Lord; Music in the Lutheran Church.* Philadelphia, 1966. (Reviews contemporary ideals and practices.)†

8 HUME, Paul. *Catholic Church Music.* New York, 1956. (Criticizes current practices and suggests reforms; bibliog. of recordings.)

9 JACKSON, George Pullen. "The Strange Music of the Old Order Amish." *Music Q,* XXXI (1945), 275–288. (Musical tradition since Reformation, discussion of music books.)

10 JOAN of Arc, Sister. *Catholic Music and Musicians in Texas.* San Antonio, 1936. (Incl. examples of mission music.)

11 McCORKLE, Donald M. "The Moravian Contribution to American Music." *Mus Lib Assn Notes,* 2nd ser., XIII (1956), 597–606. (By an authority, on the period 1740–1840.)

12 National Society of the Colonial Dames of America, Pennsylvania Branch. *Church Music and Musical Life in Pennsylvania in the Eighteenth Century.* 3 vols. in 4. Philadelphia, 1926–1947. (Most scholarly and authoritative work, stresses religious music, especially "Pennsylvania Dutch.")

13 NEMMERS, Erwin Esser. *Twenty Centuries of Catholic Church Music.* Milwaukee, 1949. (Incl. America, with illus., music, bibliogs., glossary of musical terms.)

14 PURDY, William Earl. "Music in Mormon Culture, 1830–1876." (N W), 1960. *Univ Mic* (1960), no. 60–6576. *Diss Abs,* XXI (1961), 3116. (Music employed as means to group unity and purposes.)

15 SACHSE, Julius Friedrich. *The Music of the Ephrata Cloister.* Lancaster, Pa., 1903. (Based largely on original score and tune books of German Seventh-Day Baptist brethren.)

16 SCHALK, Carl. *The Roots of Hymnody in the Lutheran Church, Missouri Synod.* St. Louis, 1965. (Bibliog., facsims, music.)

1   STEVENSON, Robert Munsell. *Protestant Church Music in America; a Short Survey of Men and Movements from 1564 to the Present.* New York, 1966. (Bibliog., music.)

2   SWAN, Howard. *Music in the Southwest, 1825–1850.* San Marino, Calif., 1952. (Illus. and bibliog. Four chapters on Mormon music; its importance in communal life.)

3   WALTERS, Raymond. *The Bethlehem Bach Choir; a History and a Critical Compendium.* Boston and New York, 1932. (Nationally famous choir, culmination of over 200 years of cultivation.)

4   WERNER, Eric. *In the Choir Loft; a Manual for Organists and Choir Directors in American Synagogues.* New York, 1957. (Chapter on development of American synagogue music, trends, influences, personal contributions. Music and bibliog.)

5   WEST, Edward N. "History and Development of Music in the American Church." *Hist Mag P E Church,* XIV (1945), 15–37. (Summarizes contributions of Episcopal Church to 1940, with refs.)

6   WOLF, Edward Christopher. "Lutheran Church Music in America During the Eighteenth and Early Nineteenth Centuries." (Ill), 1960. *Univ Mic* (1961), no. 61–218. *Diss Abs,* XXI (1961), 3118–3119. (Careful cultivation; probably had important effect upon early American attitude toward church music.)

4. Hymns

7   BENSON, Louis FitzGerald. *The English Hymn: Its Development and Use in Worship.* Richmond, 1962. (Unrivaled standard history, with many refs. to America; special section on hymns of Social Gospel.)

8   BREED, David Riddle. *The History and Use of Hymns and Hymn-Tunes.* 8th ed. New York and Chicago, 1934. (Incl. American writers, stresses work of Lowell Mason.)

9   BUCHANAN, Annabel (Morris), ed. *Folk Hymns of America.* New York, 1938. (Bibliog.)

10 DAVES, Michael. *Famous Hymns and Their Writers.* Westwood, N.J., 1962. (Popular thumbnail biographies, with circumstances of composition; incl. American authors.)

11 EMURIAN, Ernest K. *Sing the Wondrous Story.* Natick, Mass., 1963. (Popular sketches of 18 authors, incl. 16 Americans.)

12 FOOTE, Henry Wilder. *Three Centuries of American Hymnody.* Hamden, Conn., 1968. (Indispensable, standard work, relating hymnody to religious development. Bibliog.)

13 GOODENOUGH, Caroline Louisa (Leonard). *High Lights on Hymnists and Their Hymns.* New Bedford, Mass., 1931. (Much information on American hymn-writers, indexes of authors and first lines.)

14 HALL, James William. "The Tune-Book in American Culture: 1800–1820." (Penn), 1967. *Univ Mic* (1967), no. 67–12,749. *Diss Abs,* XXVIII (1967), 1743A–1744A. (Religious folk music as cultural influence, psalm and hymn tunes.)

1 HEWITT, Theodore B. "German Hymns in American Hymnals." *Ger Q,* XXI (1948), 37–50. (Large German pietist influence, with lists of German hymn-writers and translators into English.)

2 McALL, Reginald Ley. "The Hymn Festival Movement in America." *Pap Hymn Soc Am,* XVI (1951). (Stresses ecumenicity, penetration of religion into people's lives thru music.)

3 MASON, Henry Lowell. "Lowell Mason, An Appreciation of His Life and Work." *Pap Hymn Soc Am,* VIII (1941). (On his work in making hymns part of American everyday life.)

4 NOYES, Morgan Phelps. "Louis F. Benson, Hymnologist." *Pap Hymn Soc Am,* XIX (1955). (Estimate of America's foremost hymnologist. Bibliog. in footnotes.)

5 PRICE, Carl Fowler. *One Hundred and One Hymn Stories.* New York, 1962. (By first president of Hymn Society of America; incl. American writers and hymns.)†

6 Protestant Episcopal Church. Joint Commission on Revision of the Hymnal. *The Hymnal 1940 Companion.* New York, 1940. (One of the best studies of hymnody, based on researches by Rev. Dr. Leonard W. Ellinwood.)

7 RICHARDSON, Alice Marion. *Index to Stories of Hymns; an Analytical Catalog of Twelve Much-used Books.* Yardley, Pa., 1929. (Introduction to knowledge of part of hymns in religious living.)

8 STEVENSON, Arthur Linwood. *The Story of Southern Hymnology.* Salem, Roanoke, Va., 1931. (Incl. gospel hymns and singing schools. Bibliog.)

9 WHITTEMORE, Mildred C. *Hymn Writers of the Christian Church.* Boston, 1963. (Popular thumbnail biographies of 180, nearly half American, with ports and over 300 hymns.)

5. Gospel Songs

10 ASBURY, Samuel E., and H. E. MEYER. "Old-Time White Camp Meeting Spirituals." *Pub Tex Folk Soc,* X (1932), 169–185. (With music. One of the best studies.)

11 HALL, Jacob Henry. *Biography of Gospel Song and Hymn Writers.* New York and Chicago, 1914. (Incl. 76 men and women, beginning with Lowell Mason; ports.)

12 JACKSON, George Pullen, ed. *Spiritual Folk-Songs of Early America. . . .* New York, 1964. (By the greatest authority in study and interpretation of the "white spiritual." Bibliog.)†

13 JACKSON, George Pullen. *The Story of the Sacred Harp, 1844–1944, a Book of Religious Folk Song as an American Institution.* Nashville, 1944. (Influence of famous collection of psalm and hymn tunes as shaper of religious thought.)

14 JACKSON, George Pullen. *White and Negro Spirituals, Their Life Span and Kinship.* New York, 1944. (Thorough study of white-spiritual origin of Negro religious folk song.)

1 KERR, Phillip Stanley. *Music in Evangelism and Stories of Famous Christian Songs.* 4th ed. Glendale, Calif., 1954. (Origins in lives of ordinary people, incl. many Americans.)

2 LOVELACE, Austin C. "Early Sacred Folk Music in America." *Hymn,* III (1952), 11–14, 56–63. (Excellent brief review of background and development of gospel hymns. Bibliog.)

3 RODEHEAVER, Homer Alan. *Hymnal Handbook for Standard Hymns and Gospel Songs.* Chicago and Philadelphia, 1931. (Discusses origins of gospel hymns in popular religion, influence upon lives.)

4 SANKEY, Ira David. *Sankey's Story of the Gospel Hymns and of Sacred Songs and Solos.* Philadelphia and Toronto, 1907. (Popular, by internationally famous singer, companion of the evangelist, Dwight L. Moody.)

5 SANVILLE, George Washington. *Forty Gospel Hymn Stories.* Winona Lake, Ind., 1943. (Popular; human-interest aspect of hymns, popular appeal, spiritual origins.)

6. *Negro Spirituals*

6 BELAFONTE, Harold, comp. *Songs Belafonte Sings.* New York, 1962. (Illus. Commentary on each song.)

7 BUTCHER, Margaret Just. *The Negro in American Culture.* New York, 1956. (Chaps. II, III and V discuss religiosity, Biblicism, artistry, emotions of spirituals.)

8 DuBOIS, William Edward Burghardt. *The Souls of Black Folk; Essays and Sketches.* 16th ed. Chicago, 1929. (Contains a famous interpretive chapter on the spirituals.)†

9 FISHER, Miles Mark. *Negro Slave Songs in the United States.* Ithaca, N.Y., 1953. (One of the most extensive studies, with bibliog. and texts.)

10 FRIEDEL, L. M. *The Bible and the Negro Spirituals.* N.p., 1947. (One of the few Roman Catholic works on spirituals; suggests retention in Catholic worship.)

11 HAYES, Roland. *My Songs; Aframerican Religious Folk Songs Arranged and Interpreted.* Boston, 1948. (Spirituals a fusion of American religious experiences and native African musical gifts.)

12 HAYWOOD, Charles. *A Bibliography of North American Folklore and Folksong.* New York, 1951. (Excellent section on Negro spirituals, incl. recordings.)

13 JOHNSON, James Weldon. *The Book of American Negro Spirituals.* New York, 1933. (By a Negro musician and collector of songs, with critical notes; musical arrangement by J. Rosamond Johnson.)

14 KREHBIEL, Henry Edward. *Afro-American Folk Songs; a Study in Racial and National Music.* New York and London, 1962. (Important for adequate musical analysis and interpretation.)

1   ODUM, Howard W., and Guy B. JOHNSON. *The Negro and His Songs; a Study of Typical Negro Songs in the South.* Chapel Hill, N.C., 1925. (Two chaps on spirituals, with many texts; select bibliog. of songs.)

2   THURMAN, Howard. *Deep River: Reflections on the Religious Insight of Certain of the Negro Spirituals.* Rev. and enl. ed. New York, 1955. (Spirituals helped Negro attain courage, self-respect, emotional security.)

3   WORK, John Wesley, ed. *American Negro Songs and Spirituals.* New York, 1940. (Large collection, with bibliog., notes, index of titles.)

7. Architecture

A. General

4   BRODERICK, Robert Carlton. *Historic Churches of the United States.* New York, 1958. (Drawings by Virginia Broderick; remarkable churches, by states.)

5   EMBURY, Aymar, II. *Early American Churches.* Garden City, N.Y., 1914. (Classic by a well-known architect, illus., brief historical sketches.)

6   HASKIN, Frederic Jennings. *Historic Churches in the United States.* Washington, 1938. (Survey of various types, with brief historical notes.)

7   Historic American Buildings Survey, National Park Service. *Catalog of the Measured Drawings and Photographs of the Survey in the Library of Congress.* Washington, 1951. (Hundreds of buildings, incl. churches, indexed, with photos and notes. Indispensable.)

8   HOLLIS, Daniel Walker. *Look to the Rock: One Hundred Ante-bellum Presbyterian Churches of the South.* Richmond, 1961. (Illus. Photos by Carl Julien.)

9   MAASS, John. *The Gingerbread Age; a View of Victorian America.* New York, 1957. (Photos of churches of various styles; bibliog.)

10   MORRISON, Hugh Sinclair. *Early American Architecture from the First Colonial Settlements to the National Period.* New York, 1952. (Extensive coverage of churches and meetinghouses, with ref. notes, index of sources of illus. Bibliogs.)

11   RINES, Edward Francis. *Old Historic Churches of America; Their Romantic History and Their Traditions.* New York, 1936. (Based upon vast research, with bibliog., photos, chronological list, historical sketches.)

12   ROSE, Harold Wickliffe. *The Colonial Houses of Worship in America: Built in the English Colonies Before the Republic, 1607–1789, and Still Standing.* New York, 1964. (Illus., maps, bibliog.)

13   SELLERS, Mrs. Hazel Crowson. *Old South Carolina Churches.* Columbia, S.C., 1941. (Illus.)

1 UPJOHN, Hobart Brown. *Churches in Eight American Colonies Differing in Elements of Design.* New York, 1929. (Covers period 1736–1835, with measured drawings.)

2 VANDERBILT, Paul, comp. *Guide to the Special Collections of Prints & Photographs in the Library of Congress.* Washington, 1955. (Lists collections containing illus. of many American churches.)

B. Spanish Catholic Tradition

3 BROOKS, Charles Mattoon, Jr. *Texas Missions; Their Romance and Architecture.* Dallas, 1936. (Pictures of contemporary state, and as if re-constructed, architectural sketches. Bibliog.)

4 HEWITT, Edgar Lee, and Reginald G. FISHER. *Mission Monuments of New Mexico.* Alburquerque, 1943. (Illus., selected bibliog.)

5 KUBLER, George. *The Religious Architecture of New Mexico in the Colonial Period and Since the American Occupation.* Chicago, 1962. Reprod. of 1940 ed. (First study of churches as buildings, with illus., maps, plans, bibliog.)

6 McCALEB, Walter Flavius. *The Spanish Missions of Texas.* Rev. ed. San Antonio, 1961. (Notes on buildings, photos, illus. of details. Bibliog.)

7 NEWCOMB, Rexford. *The Franciscan Mission Architecture of Alta California.* New York, 1916. (Lavish, complete study, with plans, detail drawings, views, photos of models.)

8 NEWCOMB, Rexford. *Spanish-Colonial Architecture in the United States.* New York, 1937. (Many photos and drawings; historic and artistic backgrounds, contemporary work.)

9 PRINCE, LeBaron Bradford. *Spanish Mission Churches of New Mexico.* Cedar Rapids, Iowa, 1915. (First comprehensive account. Photos.)

C. New England Meeting House

10 BELLOWS, Robert Peabody. *An Architectural Monograph: Country Meeting Houses along the Massachusetts-New Hampshire Line.* New York, 1925. (Richly illus., showing wooden country meeting house of early 1800's at its best.)

11 DEXTER, Henry Martyn. *Meeting-houses: Considered Historically and Suggestively.* Boston, 1859. (American Culture Series, 28:3. Microfilm 01291, 1956. Illus., plans.)

12 DONNELLY, Marian Card. *The New England Meeting Houses of the Seventeenth Century.* Middletown, Conn., 1968. (Carefully documented, model reference book, more concerned with architecture *per se* than with its origin in religious belief.)

13 GARVAN, Anthony. "The New England Plain Style." *Comp Stud Soc Hist,* III (1960), 106–122. (Evolution of New England meeting-house; Puritan influence in art and architecture.)

1 KELLEY, John Frederick. *Early Connecticut Meeting Houses.* 2 vols. New York, 1948. (A classic, by a professional architect, with illus., map, plans, bibliog.)

2 LATHROP, Elise L. *Old New England Churches.* Rutland, Vt., 1963. (Illus.; special attention to Boston and Massachusetts. Large bibliog.)

3 Maine Writers Research Club. *Historic Churches and Homes of Maine,* . . . *with Photographic Illustrations.* Portland, 1937. (Competent study of old village churches.)

4 MARLOWE George Francis. *Churches of Old New England, Their Architecture and Their Architects, Their Pastors and Their People.* New York, 1947. (Popular guidebook, stressing cultural medium of buildings, beauty of Puritan architecture, lives of people.)

5 SINNOTT, Edmund Ware. *Meetinghouse & Church in Early New England.* Jerauld A. Manter, photographic collaborator. New York, 1963. (Illus., bibliog.)

6 SPEARE, Eva Augusta (Clough). *Colonial Meeting-houses of New Hampshire Compared with Their Contemporaries in New England.* Littleton, N.H., 1938. (List of buildings, illus., bibliog. Discusses different types of popular style.)

7 SWARTOUT, Egerton. *An Architectural Monograph: Some Old Time Churches of Vermont.* New York, 1927. (Period 1780–1840. Analyzes a group, with photos and drawings.)

8 WEDDA, John. *New England Worships; 100 Drawings of Churches and Temples with Accompanying Text.* New York, 1965. (Styles from colonial to contemporary modern, with historical notes and introductory essay.)

9 WINSLOW, Ola Elizabeth. *Meetinghouse Hill: 1630–1783.* New York, 1952. (Discusses the structure, and social life it symbolizes.)

D. *Anglican Gothic Tradition*

10 BROCK, Henry Irving. *Colonial Churches in Virginia.* Richmond, 1930. (Essay for each church; photos.)

11 CLARKE, Basil F. L. *Anglican Cathedrals Outside the British Isles.* London, 1958. (Incl. American cathedrals; illustrates triumph of Gothicism.)

12 CRAM, Ralph Adams, ed. *American Church Building of Today.* New York, 1929. (Recently erected churches predominantly Gothic; surveys church architecture since about 1885.)

13 DORSEY, Stephen Palmer. *Early English Churches in America, 1607–1807.* New York, 1952. (Anglican churches. Illus., map, bibliog.)

14 MASON, George Carrington. *Colonial Churches of Tidewater Virginia.* Richmond, 1945. (Fifty ancient brick churches, with maps, plans, bibliog. footnotes; impressions of society.)

1 RAWLINGS, James Scott. *Virginia's Colonial Churches, an Architectural Guide; Together with Their Surviving Books, Silver & Furnishings.* Richmond, 1963. (Col. illus., map, diags, bibliog.)

2 STANTON, Phoebe B. *The Gothic Revival & American Church Architecture: An Episode in Taste, 1840–1856.* Baltimore, 1968. (Excellent, exhaustively researched, better on architecture itself than on its ecclesiological background.)

3 VOGT, Von Ogden. *Art and Religion.* Rev. ed. Boston, 1960. (Influence of Ralph Adams Cram and Anglo-Catholicism upon American church architecture.)

E. Middle Colony Tradition

4 BRUMBAUGH, G. Edwin. "Colonial Architecture of the Pennsylvania Germans." *Proc Penna Ger Soc,* XLI (1931), 1–60. (Discusses European origins, building methods, special essay on church building.)

5 HAYES, John Russell. *Old Quaker Meeting-Houses.* 2nd ed., rev. and enl. Philadelphia, 1911. (Discourse on the plain type; 166 illus.)

6 WALLACE, Philip B., and William Allen DUNN. *Colonial Churches and Meeting Houses, Pennsylvania, New Jersey and Delaware.* New York, 1931. (Measured drawings, handsome photos, illus. denominational styles.)

F. Synagogues

7 HOLISHER, Desider. *The Synagogue and Its People.* New York, 1955. (Portrays classic pattern and new designs; synagogue as community center.)

8 Jewish Theological Seminary of America. Jewish Museum. *Recent American Synagogue Architecture.* [Exhibition organized by Richard Meier.] New York, 1963. (Illus., facsim., plans, bibliog. Incl. brief essays on synagogue architecture.)

9 KAMPF, Avram. *Contemporary Synagogue Art; Developments in the United States, 1945–1965.* New York, 1966. (Illus., bibliog.)

10 WISCHNITZER, Rachel (Bernstein). *Synagogue Architecture in the United States; History and Interpretation.* Philadelphia, 1955. (All styles, with illus. and bibliogs.; growing idea of community centers.)

XXII. Religion in Literature

1. Bibliography

11 BLANCK, Jacob Nathaniel. *Bibliography of American Literature.* 5 vols. New Haven, 1955–[68.] (To Henry Wadsworth Longfellow. Basic source on works with refs. to religious and theological influence.)

1 COPE, Jackson; Otis B. DAVIS; Samuel HENDERSON; Elizabeth A. LARSON; and Joseph SMEALE. "Addenda to 'Articles on American Literature Appearing in Current Periodicals, 1920–1945.'" *Am Lit*, XXII (1950), 61–74. N.B. Consult the section, "Articles on American Literature Appearing in Current Periodicals," in *American Literature*, 1945– .

2 GOHDES, Clarence Louis Frank. *Bibliographical Guide to the Study of the Literature of the U.S.A.* 2nd ed., rev. and enl. Durham, N.C., 1963.

3 GOHDES, Clarence Louis Frank. *Literature and Theater of the States and Regions of the U.S.A.; an Historical Bibliography.* Durham, N.C., 1967.

4 JONES, Howard Mumford, and Richard M. LUDWIG. *Guide to American Literature and Its Backgrounds since 1890.* 3rd ed., rev. and enl. Cambridge, Mass., 1964. (Refs. to religious history, especially in Part II.)†

5 LEARY, Lewis Gaston, ed. *Articles on American Literature, 1900–1950.* Durham, N.C., 1954. (Section on religion, 85 entries; other refs. to religious influences.)

6 LEISY, Ernest E., and Jay Broadus HUBBELL, comps. "Doctoral Dissertations in American Literature." *Am Lit*, IV (1933), 419–465. (Also a reprint. Considerable number of entries on relation of religion to American literature. Cont. 1933–1948, XX (1948), 169–229, comp. by Lewis Leary.) N.B. Consult the section, "Research in Progress," in *American Literature*, 1948– .

7 MARSHALL, Thomas F. An Analytical Index to *"American Literature,"* vols. I–XX (Mar. 1929–Jan. 1949). Durham, N.C., 1954. (Author-subject and book review indexes.)

8 *Twayne's United States Authors Series.* (Catalogued by authors of the volumes; see also subject headings for authors. Over 100 published, 1968. Most of the vols. have comment on authors' religious views, and some have extensive discussion.)

9 WILDER, Amos Niven. "Bibliography." *Bull Har Univ Div Sch*, "Annual Lectures and Book Reviews," XXI (1955–1956), 151–159. (Many writings, 1923–1955, on relations among theology, religion and literature.)

10 WILDER, Amos Niven. "Bibliography on Theology and Modern Literature." *Bull Bost Gen Theol Lib*, XLIX (1957), 4–8.

11 WOODRESS, James Leslie. *Dissertations in American Literature, 1891–1955.* Durham, N.C., 1957. (Many refs. to religion and literature.)

12 WOODRESS, James Leslie. *Dissertations in American Literature, 1956–1961.* Durham, N.C., 1962.

2. General Works

13 BROOKS, Cleanth. *The Hidden God; Studies in Hemingway, Faulkner, Yeats, Eliot, and Warren.* New Haven, 1963.†

14 CAMPBELL, Harry M. "Notes on Religion in the Southern Renascence." *Shenandoah*, VI (1955), 10–18. (Analyzes Southern "liberal" writers' attitudes.)

1 CLARK, Harry Hayden, ed. *Transitions in American Literary History.* Durham, N.C., 1967. (Valuable bibliog. footnotes on religious influences, and refs. to Biblical and theological ones.)

2 GARDINER, Charles, ed. *American Classics Reconsidered; a Christian Appraisal.* New York, 1958. (Symposium by Roman Catholic scholars, on representative 19th-century authors. Bibliog.)

3 GLICKSBERG, Charles Irving. *Literature and Religion, a Study in Conflict.* Dallas, 1960. (American authors try to be religious with new words and concepts. Large bibliog.)

4 GLICKSBERG, Charles Irving. *Modern Literature and the Death of God.* The Hague, 1966. (Points out, with refs. to American authors, the problem of perceiving meaning and morality in a world of unfaith.)

5 HUBBELL, Jay Broadus. *The South in American Literature, 1607–1900.* Durham, N.C., 1954. (Many passages on religious influences.)

6 JONES, Howard Mumford. *Belief and Disbelief in American Literature.* Chicago, 1967. (Lectures. Bibliog. footnotes.)

7 JULIAN, Constance. *Shadows Over English Literature.* New York, Milwaukee, Chicago, 1944. (New England 19th-century writers tragically missed real Christian faith; so for modern agnostics.)

8 KELLER, Isaac Clayton. *Literature and Religion.* Rindge, N. H., 1956. (Essays on 19th-century American literature.)

9 LUCCOCK, Halford Edward. *American Mirror; Social, Ethical and Religious Aspects of American Literature, 1930–1940.* New York, 1940. (Quest for religious and spiritual certainty during the Depression. Bibliog.)

10 LUCCOCK, Halford Edward. *Contemporary American Literature and Religion.* Chicago and New York, 1934. (Creative literature since World War I; intermediary between church and world. Bibliogs.)

11 MAYS, Benjamin Elijah. *The Negro's God as Reflected in His Literature.* New York, 1968. (Brilliant study of Negro religious ideology, 1760– , in "mass" and "classical" literature, growing from social situation.)†

12 MIMS, Edwin. *Great Writers as Interpreters of Religion.* New York, Nashville, 1945. (Relation of religion to aspects of culture; consideration of Phillips Brooks, Hawthorne, Emerson, Whitman, Lanier.)

13 ROOT, Robert Walter. "The Religious Ideas of Some Major Early Writers of America." (Syracuse), 1959. *Univ Mic* (1960), no. 60–383. *Diss Abs*, XX (1960), 4378. (Permanently influential ideas, liberal and conservative.)

14 SCHNEIDER, Louis, and Sanford M. DORNBUSCH. "Inspirational Religious Literature: From Latent to Manifest Functions of Religion." *Am J Socio*, LXII (1957), 476–481. (Tendency toward this-world salvation, secularization, making religion "useful.")

15 SCOTT, Nathan A., Jr. *Modern Literature and the Religious Frontier.* New York, 1958. (Incl. remarks on American authors; modern literary intelligence has ventured into spiritual exploration.)

1   SCOTT, Nathan A., Jr., ed. *Adversity and Grace. Studies in Recent American Literature.* Chicago, 1968. (Essays by several critics on religious implications of recent novels and poetry; the first systematic study.)

2   SLATER, John Rothwell. *Recent Literature and Religion.* New York and London, 1938. (Incl. refs. to American literature since 1900; reflects faith in God and man in an age claiming to be skeptical.)

3   SMITHLINE, Arnold. *Natural Religion in American Literature.* New Haven, 1966. (Ethan Allen, Thomas Paine, Thomas Jefferson, Philip Freneau, Theodore Parker, Ralph Waldo Emerson, Walt Whitman; bibliog.)†

4   STEWART, Randall. *American Literature & Christian Doctrine.* Baton Rouge, 1958. (Authors tested by the touchstone of orthodox doctrine; shift from academic agnosticism.)

5   TɛSELLE, Sallie McFague. *Literature and the Christian Life.* New Haven and London, 1966. (Attempts to show relevance to Christian life in some American authors; extensive bibliog.)

6   VOIGT, Gilbert Paul. "The Spiritual Aspect of Recent American Literature." *Luth Q,* XVII (1944), 3–13. (Attitudes of writers toward man's spiritual quest.)

7   WHEELER, B. M. "Research Abstract: Religious Themes in Contemporary Literature, 1959–1962." *J Bib Rel,* (i.e., *J Am Acad Rel.*) XXXII (1964), 50–56, 133–138.

8   WILDER, Amos Niven. *Theology and Modern Literature.* Cambridge, Mass., 1958. (With many illus. from American writers, points to resumption of dialogue between literature and theology.)

9   WINTERS, Yvor. *Maule's Curse; Seven Studies in the History of American Obscurantism.* Norfolk, Conn., 1938. (Considers Hawthorne, Very, Cooper, Melville, Poe, Emerson, Emily Dickinson, Henry James.)

3. Biblical Influence

10   ALLEN, Gay Wilson. *Biblical Echoes in Whitman's Works.* Durham, N.C., 1934. Repr. from *Am Lit,* VI (1934), 301–315. (Use of Bible language and cadence. Bibliog. footnotes.)

11   BAKER, Carlos Heard. "The Place of the Bible in American Fiction." *Theol To,* XVII (1960) 53–76. (See also: essay by same title, in vol. II of *Religion in American Life.* Ed. by James Ward Smith and A. Leland Jamison.)

12   BRADEN, Charles Samuel. "The Bible in Contemporary Drama." *J Bib Rel* (i.e., *J Am Acad Rel*) XIX (1951), 177–182.

13   BURNS, John Robert. "Thoreau's Use of the Bible." (Notre Dame), 1966. *Univ Mic* (1967), no. 67–6092. *Diss Abs,* XXVII (1967), 3864A. (Diversified use to implement style and reinforce interest in doctrine.)

1 FORREST, William Mentzel. *Biblical Allusions in Poe.* New York, 1928. (Reveals astonishing and previously unsuspected knowledge.)

2 JEFFREY, Lloyd N. "A Concordance to the Biblical Allusions in *Moby Dick.*" *Bull Bibl*, XXI (1956), 223–229. (Uncovers broad familiarity with the Bible.)

3 JOSEPH, Oscar Loos. *The Influence of the English Bible upon the English Language and upon English and American Literature.* New York, 1936. (Incl. 14 American poets, Longfellow to James Weldon Johnson. Bibliog.)

4 LONG, Mason, comp. *The Bible and English Literature.* State College, Pa., 1935. (Incl. examples from American literature. Bibliog.)

5 NELSON, Lawrence Emerson. *Our Roving Bible; Tracking Its Influence Through English and American Life.* New York and Nashville, 1945. (Covers very broad sweep of literary and cultural influences; refs. with much bibliog.)†

6 REES, Robert Alvin. "Mark Twain and the Bible: Characters Who Use the Bible and Biblical Characters." (Wis), 1966. *Univ Mic* (1967), no. 66–9960. *Diss Abs*, XXVIII (1967), 692A. (Bible most important factor in his artistic creation, characters used for ridicule or satire.)

7 SPITZ, Leon. *The Bible, Jews and Judaism in American Poetry.* New York, 1923. (Covers 11 poets; chap. on Biblical influences in patriotic songs.)

8 STEVENS, James Stacy. *Whittier's Use of the Bible.* Orono, Me., 1930. (Quotes over 800 passages directly or indirectly derived, comparison with contemporary poets.)

9 STOCK, Ely. "Studies in Hawthorne's Use of the Bible." (Brown), 1966. *Univ Mic* (1967), no. 67–2293. *Diss Abs*, XXVIII (1967), 645A–646A. (Myth of the Fall central to his thought and view of human nature in his best work.)

10 ZINK, Harriet Rodgers. "Emerson's Use of the Bible." *Univ Neb Stud Lang Lit Crit* XIV, Lincoln, 1935. (Appendix of allusions. Bibliog.)

4. The Puritan Strain

11 BOYNTON, P. H. "The Novel of Puritan Decay from Mrs. Stowe to John Marquand." *N Eng Q*, XIII (1940), 626–637. (Apostasy from Puritanism or semi-satire of its decadence.)

12 BROOKS, Charles Burnell. "Puritanism in New England Fiction, 1820–1870." (Princeton), 1943. *Univ Mic* (1952), no. 2921. *Diss Abs*, XII (1952), 296–297. (Analyzes many of Hawthorne's predecessors and contemporaries.)

13 CONDON, Richard A. "The Broken Conduit: A Study of Alienation in American Literature." *Pac Spec*, VIII (1954), 326–332. (Puritan equation between sin and identity in Hawthorne, Melville, Hemingway.)

14 CONGER, Richard Edward. "The Concept of the Puritan in American Literary Criticism, 1890–1932." (N W), 1964. *Univ Mic* (1965), no. 65–3248. *Diss Abs*, XXV (1965), 6618–6619. (The term Puritan transformed from religious to social-conservative symbol.)

1 FAUST, Clarence H. "Decline of Puritanism." In Harry Hayden Clark, *Transitions in American Literary History*. Durham, N.C., 1967. (Literary expressions of changes in New England religious mind.)

2 HOFFMAN, Frederick J. "Philistines and Puritans in the 1920's." *Am Q*, I (1949), 247–263. (Criticizes modern historical distortion of Puritan image.)

3 JONES, Howard Mumford. "The Fictional Attack on 'Puritanism.' " In his *Guide to American Literature and Its Backgrounds Since 1890*. Cambridge, Mass., 1964, p. 113. (Brief bibliog.)

4 JONES, Howard Mumford. "Literature and Orthodoxy in Boston after the Civil War." *Am Q*, I (1949), 149–165. (Deintellectualizing of Puritan creed, revolt from theology.)

5 McELROY, John Harmon. "Images of the Seventeenth-Century Puritan in American Novels, 1823–1860." (Duke), 1966. *Univ Mic*, (1967), no. 67–6108. *Diss Abs*, XVII (1967), 3845A. (Importance of Puritan religiosity in American cultural history; anti-Puritanism.)

6 MILLER, Perry. *The New England Mind; the Seventeenth Century*. Cambridge, Mass., 1954. (Excellent philosophical notes on Puritan literary influence. Bibliog. refs.)†

7 MILLS, Barriss. "Hawthorne and Puritanism." *N Eng Q*, XXI (1948), 78–102. (Reviews copious critical writing; very useful.)

8 MURDOCK, Kenneth Ballard. *Literature & Theology in Colonial New England*. Cambridge, 1949. (Relations between Puritan-Calvinist theology and literary theory and practice. Bibliog. in notes.)†

9 PIERCY, Josephine Ketcham. *Studies in Literary Types of Seventeenth Century America (1607–1710)*. New Haven and London, 1939. (First comprehensive study, with chaps. on religious influences.)

10 STEWART, Randall. "Puritan Literature and the Flowering of New England." *Wm Mar Q*, 3rd ser., III (1946), 319–342. ("Flowering" continued Puritan literature with modifications.)

11 TYLER, Moses Coit. *A History of American Literature During the Colonial Period, 1607–1765*. 2 vols. rev. ed. New York, 1950. (Excellent critical refs. to Puritan literature.)†

12 VITELLI, James Robert. "The Resurrection of the Puritan: A Study of an American Literary Symbol." (Penn), 1955. *Univ Mic* (1955), no. 11,441. *Diss Abs*, XV (1955), 832. (Estimate of the modern critical defense of Puritanism.)

13 WILLSON, Lawrence. "The Puritan Tradition in American Literature." *Ariz Q*, XIII (1957), 33–40. (Puritan considered as originator of realism.)

14 WRIGHT, Mrs. Thomas Goddard. *Literary Culture in Early New England, 1620–1730*. New York, 1966. (On production of literature, largely religious.)

5. *Fiction*

1 BALL, Rachel. "A Study of Some American Religious Problem Novels." M.A. thesis. (S M), 1930. (Special attention to Southern writers.)

2 BRASWELL, William. *Melville's Religious Thought; an Essay in Interpretation.* New York, 1959. (His rejection of the Christian concept of a benevolent deity. Bibliog.)

3 BROWN, Herbert Ross. *The Sentimental Novel in America, 1789–1860.* Durham, N.C., 1940. (A chap., "Stepping Heavenward," is devoted to religious novels. Huge bibliog.)

4 BUNTING, John J., Jr. "Religion Among the Novelists." *Rel Life*, XXIV (1955), 208–218. (Turning from godless emptiness, discovery of basic Christian values.)

5 CHASE, Richard Volney. *The American Novel and Its Tradition.* Garden City, N.Y., 1957. (Covers many aspects of religion. Bibliog.)†

6 DAVIES, Horton. *A Mirror of the Ministry in Modern Novels.* New York, 1959. (Bibliog.)

7 DAVIES, Wallace Evan. "Religious Issues in Late Nineteenth-Century American Novels." *Bull John Ry Lib*, XLI (1959), 328–359. (Reflections of controversies caused by science and problems of urban, industrial society, 1884–1897.)

8 DETWEILER, Robert. *Four Spiritual Crises in Mid-Century American Fiction.* Gainesville, Fla., 1964. *Univ Fla Mono*, Humanities, no. 14. (Reviews religion in American fiction since 1945; Styron, Updike, Roth, Salinger.)

9 DICKINSON, A. T., Jr. *American Historical Fiction.* 2nd ed. New York, 1963. (Refs. to religion. Bibliog.)

10 DRUMMOND, Andrew Landale. *The Churches in English Fiction; a Literary and Historical Study from the Regency to the Present Time of British and American Fiction.* Leicester (Eng.), 1950. (Stresses Social Gospel novels in U.S. Bibliog. footnotes.)

11 EDDY, Henry Howard. "The Utopian Element in American Literature." A. M. thesis, n.d. (Har). (Incl. some with more or less religious inspiration.)

12 FOX, Arnold Benjamin. *Howells as a Religious Critic.* N.p., 1952. Abridged thesis, N.Y.U. Repr. from *N Eng Q*, XXV (1952), 196–206. (Failure of clergy and churches to proclaim the Gospel. Bibliog. footnotes.)

13 GARDINER, Harold Charles. *Fifty Years of the American Novel; a Christian Appraisal.* New York, 1968. (Best general Roman Catholic critique.)

14 GILLEY, Billy Hawkins. "Social Trends as Reflected in American Fiction, 1870–1901." (Georgia), 1966. *Univ Mic* (1966), no. 66–13,599. *Diss Abs,* XXVII (1966), 1754A. (Refs. to Social Gospel theme; group values as primary concern of church.)

1 HACKETT, Alice Payne. *Fifty Years of Best Sellers, 1895–1945.* New York, 1945. (Bibliog. incl. list of religious best sellers.) See also her *Seven Years of Best Sellers, 1945–1951; Sixty Years of Best Sellers, 1895–1955.* New York, 1956; and *Seventy Years of Best Sellers.* New York, 1967.)

2 HART, James David. *The Popular Book: A History of America's Literary Taste.* New York, 1950. (Explores causes of continuing popularity of religiously-oriented fiction. Bibliog. checklist.)†

3 HOCKEY, Dorothy C. "The Good and the Beautiful, a Study of Best-selling Novels in America, 1895–1920." (W Res), 1947. (Incl. comments on the religious best sellers.)

4 KELLER, Arnold. F., Jr. "The Clergyman in Recent Fiction." *Luth Q,* XX (1947), 193–198. (Secularizing of literature has encouraged portrayal of least worthy side.)

5 KOLLER, Katherine. "The Puritan Preacher's Contribution to Fiction." *Hunt Lib Q,* XI (1948), 321–340. (Depiction of New England parsons.)

6 KRUPAT, Arnold. "The Saintly Hero: A Study of the Hero in Some Contemporary American Novels." (Colo), 1967. *Univ Mic* (1967), no. 67–14,064. *Diss Abs,* XXVIII (1967), 2251A. (Portrayal as an American religious folk figure.)

7 MADSON, Arthur Leon. "The Scapegoat Story in the American Novel." (Okla), 1966. *Univ Mic* (1966), no. 66–14,226. *Diss Abs,* XXVII (1966), 1828A. (Nine novels, Cooper to Drury, employing this Biblical religious-moral idea.)

8 MOTT, Frank Luther. *Golden Multitudes; The Story of Best Sellers in the United States.* New York, 1960. (Many refs. to religious best sellers and reasons for popularity.)

9 NICHOLL, Grier. "The Christian Social Novel in America, 1865–1918." (Minn), 1964. *Univ Mic* (1964), no. 64–10,844. *Diss Abs,* XXV (1964), 2516–2517. (Analyzes over 100 vehicles of Social Gospel propaganda; popular religious attitudes.)

10 SCOTT, Nathan A., Jr. *The Tragic Vision and the Christian Faith.* New York, 1957. (Discusses Hawthorne, Melville, and Faulkner. Bibliog.)

11 SHUCK, Emerson Clayton. "Clergymen in Representative American Fiction, 1830–1930; A Study in Attitudes Toward Religion." (Wis), 1943. (Best scholarly study, sociological and philosophical.)

12 SHURTER, Robert L. "The Utopian Novel in America, 1865–1900." (W Res), 1936. (Refs. to some with religious inspiration and purpose.)

13 SMART, George K. *Religious Elements in Faulkner's Early Novels: a Selective Concordance.* Coral Gables, Fla. [1965] (Illus.)

14 THOMPSON, Lawrence Roger. *Melville's Quarrel with God.* Princeton, 1952. (His confused, disillusioned hostility to religion and God. Bibliog. in notes.)†

15 ULBRICH, Armand Henry. "The Trend Toward Religion in the Modern American Novel, 1925 to 1951." (Mich), 1953. *Univ Mic,* (1953), no. 5104. *Diss Abs,* XIII (1953), 395–396. (Tendency away from naturalism and toward broadly religious sympathy. Bibliog.)

1 VOIGT, Gilbert Paul. "Our Evangelist Clergymen-Novelists." *Rel Life*, XXII (1953), 604–615. Eight examples studied, persistent trend in popular literature.)

2 WAGENKNECHT, Edward Charles. *Cavalcade of the American Novel, from the Birth of the Nation to the Middle of the Twentieth Century*. New York, 1952. Section on "purpose novels," sometimes religious. Very valuable bibliog.)

3 WALHOUT, Clarence Peter. "Religion in the Thought and Fiction of Three Ante-Bellum Southerners: Kennedy, Caruthers, and Simms." (N W), 1964. *Univ Mic* (1965), no. 65–3319. *Diss Abs*, XXV (1965), 6604. (All expressed conservative, sectional social ideals; religion a social prop.)

6. Poetry

4 BAILEY, Elmer James. *Religious Thought in the Greater American Poets*. Boston and Chicago, 1922. (Contributions of 19th-century poets.)

5 CONNER, Frederick William. *Cosmic Optimism; a Study of the Interpretation of Evolution by American Poets from Emerson to Robinson*. Gainesville, Fla., 1949. (Evolution reconciled with a benevolent God and spiritual nature of man? Bibliog.)

6 CRAWFORD, Leonidas Wakefield. *Rivers of Water*. New York, 1952. (Search for religious valueš in poetry, until about 1900.)

7 DUNCAN, Joseph Ellis. *The Revival of Metaphysical Poetry; the History of a Style, 1800 to the Present*. Minneapolis, 1959.

8 GREEK, Betty Louise. "Christian Affirmation in Modern Poetry; a Study of the Evidence and Nature of Christian Affirmation in Modern Poetry and Its Values for Christian Education." M. R. E. thesis, Princeton Theol. Sem., 1954. Typ. (With bibliog.)

9 JANTZ, Harold S. "The First Century of New England Verse." *Proc Am Antiq Soc*, LIII (1943), 219–523. (Reviews previous writing, indicates pietist influence. Exhaustive bibliog.)

10 JENNINGS, Elizabeth. *Every Changing Shape*. Philadelphia, 1962. (Incl. essays on mystically religious seeking for meaning and God in Eliot, Stevens, and Hart Crane.)

11 KERR, Hugh Thomson. *The Gospel in Modern Poetry*. New York and Chicago, 1926. (Analyzes American poems to discern religious meaning.)

12 McGILL, Arthur C. *The Celebration of Flesh. Poetry in Christian Life*. New York, 1964. (Essays on Eliot, Frost, and Stevens, pointing out spiritual impoverishment through stressing "pure spirituality." Bibliogs.)†

13 MELAND, Bernard Eugene. "Kinsmen of the Wild: Religious Moods in Modern American Poetry." *Sew Rev*, XLI (1933), 443–453. (Comments on religious quality that is not traditionally "moralizing." Bibliog.)

1 NOON, William T. *Poetry and Prayer.* New Brunswick, N.J., 1967. (Essays on Stevens and Frost; value of non-ecclesiastical approaches to ultimate reality.)

2 O'CONNOR, William Van. *Sense and Sensibility in Modern Poetry.* Chicago, 1963. (Refs. to several American poets, more or less influenced by T. S. Eliot. Bibliog.)

3 OTIS, William Bradley. *American Verse, 1625–1807; a History.* New York, 1966. Reprint of 1909 ed. (Chap. II, "Religious Verse," with critical notes. Bibliog.)

4 POWER, Sister Mary James. *Poets at Prayer.* New York and London, 1938. (Religious attitudes of some contemporary American poets.)

5 STRONG, Augustus Hopkins. *American Poets and Their Theology.* Philadelphia and Boston, 1916. (Discusses nine poets of the 19th century.)

6 VOIGT, Gilbert Paul. "The Religious and Ethical Element in the Major American Poets." Univ of S.C., Graduate School, *Bull,* no. 1, June 1, 1925.

7 WAGGONER, Hyatt Howe. *American Poets, from the Puritans to the Present.* Boston, 1968. (Bibliog.)

8 WAGGONER, Hyatt Howe. *The Heel of Elohim; Science and Values in Modern American Poetry.* Norman, Okla, 1950. (Cosmic and religious issues as treated by six eminent poets.)

9 WELLS, Henry Willis. *The American Way of Poetry.* New York, 1964.

10 WILDER, Amos Niven. *Modern Poetry and the Christian Tradition: A Study in the Relation of Christianity to Culture.* New York, 1952. (Profound religious questions outside traditional poetic structures of church and theology.)

11 WILDER, Amos Niven. *The Spiritual Aspects of the New Poetry.* New York, 1940. (Concentrates on American factors in affirmation or denial of religion. Bibliog.)

12 WINTERS, Yvor. *In Defense of Reason.* New York, 1947. (Discusses theism in several major and many lesser modern American poets.)†

7. Drama

13 ATKINSON, Brooks. "Foreword" in *New Voices in the American Theatre.* New York, 1955. (Growing interest in essentially religious themes.)

14 BASSAGE, Harold Edwin. "The Moral Price of Freedom; Problems of Personal Freedom Reflected in Modern American Drama." (Colum), 1951. *Univ Mic,* (1951), no. 3098. *Diss Abs,* XII (1952), 15–16. (Ethical and spiritual problems since World War I. Bibliog.)

15 BLUESTONE, George. *Novels Into Film.* Baltimore, 1957. (Incl. "religious" films from popular novels. Extensive bibliogs.)†

1   BOYD, Malcolm. *Christ and Celebrity Gods, the Church in Mass Culture.* Greenwich, Conn., 1958. (Discusses American movies and religion from standpoint of Christian ethics.)

2   BRILL, Earl Hubert. "Religion in Modern American Drama: a Theological Analysis of Five Contemporary American Plays." (Princeton Theol. Sem), 1958. (Plays suggest Christian theme of redemption; emergence of realistic religious drama. Bibliog.)

3   BROWNE, E. Martin. "Religion and the Arts, Part III, Religious Drama." *Union Sem Q Rev,* XII (1957), 51–65. (Growing implicit cooperation between drama and religion, rise of interest in churches.)

4   CANFIELD, Alyce. *God in Hollywood.* New York, 1961. (Religious life of actors, religious cults and attitudes of the movie capital.)

5   EASTMAN, Fred. *Christ in the Drama, a Study of the Influence of Christ on the Drama of England and America.* New York, 1947. (Criticizes many American plays, discusses drama in churches. Bibliog.)

6   EASTMAN, Fred. *Religion and Drama: Friends or Enemies?* New York, 1930. (Rise of church dramatic groups, cooperation between religious and theatrical leaders.)

7   EHRENSPERGER, Harold Adam. *Conscience on Stage.* New York and Nashville, 1947. (Important position recently attained by plays in American church life. Bibliog.)

8   GEIER, Woodrow Augustus. "Images of Man in Five American Dramatists: a Theological Critique." (Vanderbilt), 1959. *Univ Mic* (1959), no. 59–4110. *Diss Abs,* XX (1959), 1463–1464. (Bibliog.)

9   KERNODLE, George R. "Patterns of Belief in Contemporary Drama." *Spiritual Problems in Contemporary Literature.* Ed. by Stanley Romaine Hopper. New York, 1957. (Discusses the problem in plays that are not specifically religious.)†

10   LANGLEY, Stephen Gould. "Three Puritanical Stage Figures in the American Drama." (Ill), 1966. *Univ Mic* (1966), no. 66–12,363. *Diss Abs,* XXVII (1967), 2215A. (The reformer, the aristocrat, and the sinner, Royall Tyler to Eugene O'Neill.)

11   MILLER, William Lee. "Hollywood and Religion." *Rel Life,* XXII (1953), 273–279. (Criticizes popular and sentimental "religious" movies as false.)

12   SMITH, Winifred. "Mystics in the Modern Theatre." *Sew Rev,* XLV (1942), 35–48. (Eliot and O'Neill representing a return to Christian faith.)

8. Humor and Satire

13   COLLINS, Beulah, ed. *For Benefit of Clergy; Witty Stories, Quips, and Anecdotes for and About Clergymen and Their Parishioners of all Faiths.* Illus. by Leo Garel. New York, 1966.

14   LARGE, John Ellis. *The Small Needle of Dr. Large.* Englewood Cliffs, N.J., 1962. (Columns by an urban Episcopal rector for parish weekly paper, salted with humor and wisdom.)

1   MARTY, Martin E., and Dean G. PEERMAN. *Penultimates: Comment on the Folk Religions of America.* New York, 1963. (Satirical pieces from *Christian Century*, which will amuse many, but certainly not all church members.)
2   SMITH, Charles Merrill. *How To Become a Bishop Without Being Religious.* Garden City, N.Y., 1965. (Caustic comments on "success" in the church, and popular respectable Protestant piety; shouldn't be taken too literally.)†
3   WAGONER, Walter D., comp. *Bittersweet Grace: a Treasury of Twentieth-century Religious Satire.* Cleveland, 1967. (Selections from numerous writers deflate pompous and absurd aspects of American official religion. Bibliog.)

9. Religious Journalism

4   BAUMGARTNER, Apollinaris William. *Catholic Journalism; a Study of Its Development in the United States, 1789–1930.* New York, 1931. (First comprehensive work on the subject. Bibliog.)
5   BLUEM, A. William, ed. *Religious Television Programs: A Study of Relevance.* New York, 1968. (Programs losing appeal, because tied to structured religion, which has lost much of its relevance; creativity largely lacking.)
6   BOYD, Malcolm. *Crisis in Communication: A Christian Examination of the Mass Media.* Garden City, N.Y., 1957. (Opportunity or dangerous competition? Possibility of honest dialogue between Gospel and American world.)
7   COWAN, Wayne H., ed. *Witness to a Generation: Significant Writings from Christianity and Crisis (1941–1966).* Indianapolis, 1966. (Articles from a liberal journal devoted to exposition of Christian faith in relation to world events.)†
8   FOGEL, H. H. "Colonial Theocracy and a Secular Press." *Jour Q,* XXXVII (1960), 525–532. (Struggle for freedom of press, church press benefits from freedom theocrats sought to restrict.)
9   JENSEN, Howard Eikenberry. "The Rise of Religious Journalism in the United States. . . ." (Chi), 1920. (Bibliog. of journals and abs. Pub. in part in Univ. of Chi, *Abstracts of Theses, Humanities Series,* III, pp. 253–261.)
10 LEE, Alfred McClung. "The Press and Public Relations of Religious Bodies." *Ann Am Acad Pol Soc Sci,* CCLVI (1948), 120–131. (Thorough study. Decline, news agencies, character of approach to society.)
11 McDONALD, Erwin Lawrence. *Across the Editor's Desk; the Story of the State Baptist Papers.* Nashville, 1966. (Bibliog. footnotes.)
12 MARTY, Martin E. *The Improper Opinion: Mass Media and the Christian Faith.* Philadelphia, 1961. (Recent past, presentation of cultural setting, faith should not settle for second best in communication with world. Bibliog.)

1   MARTY, Martin E., et al. *The Religious Press in America.* New York, 1963. (History, influence, handling of public issues, secular uses, need of better relation to social problems.)

2   STOODY, Ralph. *Religious Journalism: Whence and Whither? An Inquiry into the History and Present State of the Christian Press in the United States.* Boston? 1939. (Gordon College of Theology and Missions). Microfilm. (Bibliogs.)

3   THAMAN, Sister Mary Patrice. *Manners and Morals of the 1920's; a Survey of the Religious Press.* New York, 1954. (As related to social life and customs. Bibliogs.)

4   WOLSELEY, Roland E. "The Influence of the Religious Press." *Rel Life,* XXVI (1956–1957), 75–86. (Mainly on editorial policy to mold public opinion.)

NOTES

INDEX OF AUTHORS

INDEX

INDEX

INDEX

INDEX

INDEX

INDEX

INDEX

INDEX

INDEX

INDEX

INDEX

INDEX